POSITIONS OF SHIPS

El Cobre ⊞

⊞ El Viso

SANTIAGO DE CUBA BAY

⊞ Santiago de Cuba

20°

||| PUNTA GORDA BATTERY

San Juan River

Cabañas Bay

SOCAPA BATTERIES ||||

≡ CATALINA BATTERY
/// ESTRELLA BATTERY

PLUTON   FUROR

|||| MORRO BATTERY

CESTER

GLOUCESTER

COLÓN

OQUENDO

TERESA

INDIANA

VISCAYA

NEW YORK

HARVARD

ERICSSON

VIXEN

HIST

ARMY
TRANSPORTS

BROOKLYN   TEXAS   IOWA   OREGON

RESOLUTE (mine

S E A

19°50

A LEAP TO ARMS:

The Cuban Campaign of 1898

★★★★★★★★★★★★★★★★★★

GREAT BATTLES OF HISTORY
Hanson W. Baldwin, *General Editor*

A LEAP
TO ARMS:

The Cuban Campaign of 1898

✶✶✶✶✶✶✶✶✶✶✶✶✶✶✶✶✶✶✶✶✶✶✶✶✶✶✶✶✶

by

JACK CAMERON DIERKS

J. B. Lippincott Company
Philadelphia & New York

The end paper map and the maps on pages 54 and 69 are adapted from three maps in *The Downfall of Spain*, by Herbert W. Wilson (London: Low, Marston and Co., Ltd., 1900). The map on page 100 is adapted from a map in A *History of the Spanish-American War of 1898*, by Richard H. Titherington (New York: D. Appleton and Company, 1900). The map on page 12 is adapted from maps in *The Santiago Campaign*, by Major-General Joseph Wheeler (Boston, New York, and London: Lamson, Wolffe and Company, 1898).

To M. M. D.

For her encouragement

****

Contents

****

MAPS

Introduction

✳✳✳✳✳✳✳✳✳✳✳✳✳✳

They thought it a "splendid little war"—statesman and citizen alike—and if in later years the phrase was to prove somewhat embarrassing to less supernationalistic men, one can't deny the choice of expression fitted the perspective of the day. It certainly wasn't very long or very costly, that fight with Spain in 1898, compared to the Armageddons the next century was to introduce. It lasted only a little over three months, scarcely enough time for the smart Fifth Avenue shops to exhaust their stocks of bunting. Total U.S. battle dead numbered 385, and made hardly more of a gap in the regimental rolls than had the Custer massacre at the Little Big Horn, which had taken place twenty-two years before and was the most recent basis for comparison. Those figures weren't enough to cause the nation much perceptible grief or the administration any noticeable discomfort, particularly in an age which still remembered the casualty lists of Antietam and the Wilderness. Because of this, and because it had been fought with honor against an honorable foe for the avowed purpose of raising America's head to the proud level of the other great powers of the earth and her eyes to a world view, it certainly seemed splendid to the exuberant Yankee of the closing years of the nineteenth century.

The whole thing might have been predestined, in fact, and there were those who chose to look upon the confrontation with Spain as a demonstrable proof of natural law. Just as the young must supplant the aged, so had the United States been ordained by a far-seeing Almighty to don the surcoat and tilting helm and enter the lists against the Old World and what it stood for. On the nation's part it was an easy calling to answer. She'd had enough of being ignored, of chafing under the polite (and all the more in-furiating because they were polite) condescension of the ancient and venerable states. Men of the day were continually conscious of the growth, of the burgeoning farms and factories around them, of the proved success of audacious enterprise. It galled them to think that to many Europeans the great Republic was considered as far removed from the power-roiled inner sanctums of world affairs as Walden forest might have been. Everybody knew Amer-ica was on the move—a force to be reckoned with; it was time for the strapping youth to take his place as a man among men, and a bit of traditional suspender snapping to announce the transition would not be out of order.

In those palmy late Victorian days when the world had, it was widely assumed, seen the last of the great destructive wars of mankind, it was considered healthy in many civilized quarters for a nation and a generation to be blooded just a bit in a limited test of arms. Virile races could grow effete; they needed a stimulant to nourish and drain off the animal spirits. War still retained many of its old glories and rewards, and what young soldier true to his breeding didn't despair along with Winston Churchill and his Sandhurst comrades of ever having the chance to meet white troops in the field again? The expression "shot in the arm" has been overworked, but in this case it does apply. Perhaps "inocula-tion" might be even more appropriate: the injection of antibodies —a controlled dose of the virulent germ of battle to counteract the mounting aggression-fever of a vigorous people. Men-of-war with ensigns flying, the emotional cathartic of a cavalry charge, a few dead eulogized in the dispatches of a Richard Harding Davis and pictured (so as not to offend, of course) in the illustrated pages of *Harper's Weekly* through the wash drawings of a Frederic Remington. It would be enough to bring the temperature down.

The Spanish-American War was an epoch-ending yet logical manifestation of the national temper, direction and purpose in the 1900 era. It was a cause toward which two dominant currents of American Victorianism could unite. The popular assumptions of the time—that the war was shouldered as part of the White Man's Burden purely to relieve the sufferings of a beleaguered Cuba—and the cynical belief of a later day—that the whole thing was plainly and simply a naked attempt at territorial aggrandizement—are equally prejudiced. Humanitarian and imperialistic designs both played their part, contributing in a joint way that only the beliefs of a confident century could have fostered.

If the war shows us what the men of 1898 were willing to fight over, the combined military-naval operation at Santiago de Cuba is the best example of how they went about it. The reader is likely to be as intrigued by the country's self-assurance and self-righteousness as by its peculiar ineptitude in planning and execution, unfamiliar as he is apt to be nowadays with all three qualities. The prides and prejudices that caused the wrangling between Army and Navy, the bitter discord between an admiral and a commodore, the uncomfortable situation of a commanding general failing to hold the respect of his subordinates, the popular press or a critical public will be recognized as less alien to our own controversial time. All these factors mirrored the thinking and customs of the day, and because of some of them and in spite of others the United States emerged from it all a world power. The glory was there to be gleaned and enjoyed, too—the expression of virility through personal combat men had always sought—then and for a few years after. If the world's fever was ultimately to prove uncontrollable and the illness critical if not terminal, if there's hardly more pageantry or grandeur remaining now than can be packed into an intercontinental warhead, it may serve the purposes of perspective as well as nostalgia to recall a campaign and a crusade carried out in the style of the *ancien régime*, at a time when style stood for civilization. A time when flags were kissed in tribute, swords were tendered in surrender and American sailors were admonished not to cheer because the poor devils were dying. We're not likely to see it repeated, any part of it.

J. C. D.

Bugles!
And the Great Nation thrills and leaps to arms!
Prompt, unconstrained, immediate,
Without misgiving and without debate,
Too calm, too strong for fury or alarms,
The people blossoms armies and puts forth
The splendid summer of its noiseless might.

FROM "THE CALL OF THE BUGLES,"
BY RICHARD HOVEY, 1898

CHAPTER I

****

An Idea Whose Time Has Come

When the New York reporter poked his head
into the offices of the Spanish language newspaper *El Porvenir*
on that morning of February 28, 1895, he was taken aback first by
the atmosphere—it was positively galvanic, though he guessed that
was to be expected—then by the fact that he was instantly recognized by some dozen of the swarthiest and most vociferous bravos
present, who were already pushing their way through the hubbub
and the cigar smoke straight for him. The *grito* or shout they let
out as they came up might have been disconcerting to some men,
but he steadied himself by determining that he would be the one
to ask the questions and that he was as prepared as he could be,
under the circumstances.

He had in his hand the dispatch that had come in earlier that
morning—that an insurrection against Spain had broken out on
the island of Cuba—and he had with it the official assurances of
the Spanish minister in Washington that the insurrectionists were
bandidos, already being dispersed and nobody to be alarmed about.
Yet the reporter had come with an open mind. Though he naturally couldn't expect the rabid expatriate group there at *El Porvenir*
to honor any statements coming out of official Havana, the eager-
ness with which he was informed that this was no riot but war in
the most serious sense, launched upon a prearranged schedule and
"prepared with the most minute attention," had the authentic
ring of men who had long waited for "the day." That it was only
the first of many such days to follow would soon become evident,
he was told. The *grito* of freedom, he was to understand, would

soon be in full cry the length and breadth of Cuba, from Santiago in the east to Pinar del Río in the west.

We can hardly blame him if the crowd's fervor was infectious and the facts were laced with his own enthusiasm by the time they reached his paper. Nor can we condemn his editor for giving them the full headline treatment in turn. This would not always have been the case, but since Mr. Hearst's *Journal* and Mr. Pulitzer's *World* would be certain to illuminate the story with a shrieking banner, it was no longer good business to bury such news back among the Sapolio and Pear's Soap ads, the place to which similar foreign copy would once have been consigned. Even if the "yellow press" had not been on hand to goad more responsible publishers, Cuba had become front page. To any shrewd observer of the American scene, an armed rebellion in the largest, nearest and most important of the West Indian islands could point to just one response. It would be only subconsciously felt by the mass, but there would be those to give it voice—and loudly. They were the new believers in power, in progress, in the right and the duty of a maturing nation to abandon the insular life and to assume a hemispheric view of the world (and the right and duty of her forward-thinkers to keep after her until she did). There would be pressure for recognition of the rebels from the more gentle steppers among these elements, scarcely guarded hints for the annexation of Cuba itself from the more jingoistic, and always, supporting both philosophic thought and pragmatic urging, that ever-more-logical justification—"Manifest Destiny." It rolled off the tongue and the big rotary presses with a superbly confident tone and an air that implied there was nothing more that needed to be said, much the way "God's will" might have closed all argument in an earlier age. For many people the phrases could have been one and the same anyway, the word "destiny" suggesting to even the most unimaginative a divine sanction. It had the advantage of being catchy, too, and it looked its best on the editorial page, especially when Mr. Hearst and Mr. Pulitzer themselves took the time to elaborate on it, which they almost always did. "Iron Curtain," "Four Freedoms"—it was one of those sayings that codifies and focuses the thinking of a generation.

Of course the climate has to be congenial for a catch slogan to grow into an instrument of national policy, and in the America of the 1890's it had been able to put down root as it never could have done in a simpler day. Nothing had been seen like the phenomenal post–Civil War flowering of the forty-four states. Their people had conquered a wilderness by sheer pioneer spirit and tenacity, they had brought the laws of civilization to the red man, tamed his wild prairies and introduced them to the McCormick reaper. The nation had become more populous than its old rival Britain way back in the forties and had overtaken her in steel production, the new measuring stick of industrial sophistication, by 1890. Winston Churchill has described the Europe of 1914 as the culmination of an age of accumulation, not merely of material goods, but of the "growing and gathering . . . of all those elements and factors which grow to make up the power of states." Energy— the "vials of wrath" he called it. The comparison to the United States of the nineties is apt. A cruder, less refined distillation of forces; not a vessel boiling with ancient quarrels but a cup that was running over nevertheless, with a restlessness and a frothing vitality of its own that was bound to spill on something or somebody.

If it had taken time to fill, the very process of filling served to sanctify it with the beliefs of the age. "Manifest destiny" itself was not a new slogan, having been coined fifty years before by John Louis O'Sullivan, editor of the *Democratic Review,* and though it caught on immediately and was used by many to explain America's clear duty toward relieving the southwestern territories of the influence of Mexico, it was to suffer when it later came to be associated with extension of the slave system. At first a simple emotional term used to generate pride in America and American institutions, it came as the century progressed to claim a basic *de facto* foundation, which could be explained in no more time than it took to examine the course history seemed to be taking. It was quite evident to anyone who cared to look that the world had always been divided into the rulers and the ruled, and the harnessing of a great continent to a nation's benefit surely entitled its people to a place in the first category.

Those who were unconvinced that the country's future coincided with heaven's purpose might rely upon the sanction of science if they liked. If the Darwinian hypothesis of natural selection had any validity, one could easily adopt the conviction that the same laws—survival of the fittest and the emergence of higher types of life—showed every sign of applying to human society as well. One might not reach exactly the same conclusions as Professor John Burgess of Columbia, but one suspected he was on the right track. Burgess, who had studied in Germany and been much impressed by what he felt were undeniable proofs of the fitness of certain races to rule, echoed the belief of many late Victorians that ability called for responsibility. In regard to "lesser breeds without the law," he considered that the civilized western nations had a duty "not only to answer the call of the unpolitical populations for aid and direction, but also to force organization upon them by any means necessary, in their honest judgment, to accomplish this result." [1]

This of course was the substance of the White Man's Burden. The professor's American readers resented his partiality toward north Europeans, but took it for granted that since the same racial stocks and governing talents were dominant here, his own country would have been included among the favored trustees had he believed her powerful and energetic enough to take on the job. The way was embarrassingly clear, it seemed. If America had yet to be taken seriously, even by her own political theorists, then she had some faults to rectify. Happily, for those who worried about it, they were not to prove very difficult. To a nation with a conscience the ethics of what it does can be worrisome: once a policy has been justified morally, it is often no great task to implement it politically.

It was the kind of revelation that made people particularly receptive to a man whose theories seemed to embody whole new principles of world power politics—new to Americans at any rate. The heritage of empire may have been chiseled in stone, but to Captain Alfred Thayer Mahan of the U.S. Navy its practical implementation was written in water—blue water. He was partial, being a sailor, but he was plain-spoken and he made sense. The most important lesson history held for Mahan was that seapower had been and would continue to be the prime factor in the making and breaking of nations and empires. The past had taught that without it no people, regardless of gifts, vigor or ambition, could gain or hold any worth-while influence in world affairs. The United States was a commercial nation, and as such was going to have to rely on this form of national potency to maintain her trade and relations with the rest of the world. "Seapower," as he defined it, included all that went to make water-borne commerce secure and profitable: an extensive merchant marine to insure that America would not be forced to ship goods in alien bottoms, a powerful Navy to protect the merchantmen and keep water routes open in time of war, and—colonies, to serve the interests of maritime commerce directly and to provide bases and coaling stations for warships.

Those who read *The Influence of Seapower upon History* when it was written in 1890 could sense between the lines Mahan's discontent with the actual state of affairs. Trade had been growing since its post–Civil War slump, but it was carried on largely under foreign flags; the suggestion, but only the suggestion, of a fleet was there: a dozen light cruisers in commission or being built, the keels of two second-class battleships only barely laid—a Navy that just missed being a total embarrassment. As for colonies, they were nonexistent, and without them what ships we did build would be like land birds, hardly daring to let the headlands of the Atlantic coast drop out of sight.

The fact that his postulates were enthusiastically lauded in Europe, especially by the British and in the Germany of young Kaiser Wilhelm, was encouraging only in a disconcerting way, and in lectures and articles he abandoned theory to hammer home principles as they applied to America's current position vis-à-vis the world power structure. It was on the new strategic importance of the West Indies that he concentrated; he took no pains to disguise his hopes that, when the proposed Central American canal was built, the surrounding waters would become an American lake, and scolded his readers for their historical backwardness in the desire for territorial acquisition.

Mahan needn't have worried. His ideas were numbered among those whose time had come, though it took the Venezuelan crisis of 1895 to point up the extent to which the country had become aware of its growing might and the firmness with which it would make others aware, too. There was no mistaking the bellicosity in the Secretary of State's message to Downing Street, which implied this country's right to interfere in what was essentially a boundary claim of the British Empire simply because the United States was "practically sovereign on this continent" and because America's "infinite resources combined with its isolated position render it master of the situation and practically invulnerable against any and all powers." [2] Yankees had surprised even themselves with their spunk.

It did cause sober minds to probe beneath the martial spirit, though, and take a look at how inconvenient our position might be in time of actual war. Senator Henry Cabot Lodge appeared in print to show just how closely the thinking of official Washington went along with Mahan's "Caribbean sphere" urgings: "England has studded the West Indies with strong places which are a standing menace to our Atlantic seaboard. We should have among those islands at least one strong naval station, and when the Nicaragua Canal is built the island of Cuba . . . will become to us a necessity. . . ." It was needed "for future expansion and present defense," [3] and they were mentioned in that order.

With this kind of sponsorship it's really no wonder that the Hearst and Pulitzer editorial pens were kept scratching. If the Cuban situation was never as open and shut as many believed— an oppressed people rising spontaneously to free itself from tyrannical and alien rule—the *Journal*, and *World* and the rest of the reader-hungry press that tagged behind their lead didn't go to any pains to correct misconceptions. If they had, it might have been evident that the United States itself was hardly blameless as far as the island's turmoil was concerned. To begin with, the revolt was structured, timetabled and had its wheels set in motion from within this country. Ever since a previous uprising of several years' duration had petered out in 1878, a group of émigrés—professional agitators banded together into what they called the Cuban Revolutionary Party and led by one José Martí—had been laboring from their place of exile in New York City to involve their nation once more in civil war.

Martí and the others, mostly former leaders of the "troubles" of the seventies, were single-minded and patient men. When in the summer of 1894 Congress passed the Wilson tariff bill which restored the duty on Cuban sugar, it seemed their chance had come, for the measure was bound to deal a crushing blow to the island's economy. Anticipating the advent of a chaos which couldn't help but be congenial to the spirit of mutiny, the revolutionary party loaded three fast steamers with eight hundred rifles, half a million rounds of ammunition and a coterie of the key expatriates to oversee them to their destination. Though U.S. officials learned of the sailing and seized the whole cache on the eve of departure, the countdown had already begun and the *grito*, arms or no, was about to inflict itself in full-throated suddenness upon a primitive Cuban peasantry, an anachronistic Spanish colonial administration, and an unsuspecting but quick-to-be-awakened America.

***

If we consider the views of Henry Cabot Lodge as representative of a growing jingoist element on Capitol Hill, then one can imagine how the possibilities opened up by a revolt in Cuba were viewed. And if consideration for the rights of the imperial power seemed at first to stand in the way of the advocates of expansionism, that nation herself promptly set out to remove all obstacles. Almost from the beginning, the Spain of the Queen Regent was to resemble the Germany of 1914–17 in her relation to neutral America. Both countries seemed bent on justifying, not so much by vicious as by blundering and boorish acts, the preconceived opinions belligerent elements held of them. In both cases the situation led inexorably to war.

On March 12, 1896, the American steamship *Alliancia* arrived panting and flecked with foam, so to speak, in New York with the story that on her way from Colón she had been chased and forced to dodge shells fired at her by a Spanish gunboat. Public opinion came to the support of the flag with an alacrity that seems hardly credible in these days of stoned limousines and incinerated embassies. The New York *Tribune* spoke for many when it claimed the outrage wouldn't have been any more flagrant had the dons entered New York harbor and bombarded City Hall. It called for several American men-of-war to be sent to Cuba without delay. The *Sun* agreed, and advised editorially that the next shot fired by the Spaniards upon the Stars and Stripes be countered by a broadside from an American cruiser.

Anyone who was tempted to write off these sentiments as the bombast of sensational journalism would have found the reactions of Washington more revealing. In the Senate Foreign Relations Committee views were expressed in unprecedentedly frank language. Senator William Frye of Maine could hardly conceal his sense of deflation when it became evident that the *Alliancia* incident was not going to precipitate the country into anything promising. "I had almost hoped," he complained, "that Spain would assume such an arrogant and belligerent tone that it would be necessary for the United States to go over and take possession of Cuba." [4]

The White House must take a large part of the credit for his disappointment, for Grover Cleveland did much to act as a stabilizing influence in those last days of his term of office. The President made no secret of the fact that he was lined up in the opposite corner spiritually as well as politically from the Lodge-ites and the rest of the expansionist element. This is not to say that he failed to recognize the inevitable growing involvement of America in the politics of the entire western hemisphere. Even the most rabid jingoes were satisfied by his obdurate stand during the Venezuelan crisis; he favored building up the Navy and had proved no impediment to plans for an Isthmian canal. But to all proposals for the extension of American sovereignty abroad he was adamantly opposed.

✳✳✳

After the initial surge of *élan* with which it was launched, the Cuban revolution had settled down to the fierce but sporadic guerrilla clashes which so often point up the popular uprising's determined but uneven impetus. Its guiding brain from the beginning was that of Máximo Gómez, a tough, hot-blooded, professional fighter of long experience who had led the first revolt back in the 1870's, knew the land, his people and the Spaniards, and had no illusions about early or easy success this time. He was an unmilitary figure—an American correspondent described him as a "chocolate-covered, withered old man . . . a resurrected Egyptian mummy" [5]—but he was shrewd, dogged, and adept at controlling the roving bands of mounted irregulars whom he sent out to harass the Spanish troops in the traditional cut-and-run manner.

He never had any hopes of winning a military victory over the Spanish Army, but pursued instead the ruthless objective of throttling the economic life of the island through a campaign of calculated terrorism. By brutal means he hoped to force the populace either into his own insurgent ranks or into the garrisoned, Spanish-held towns. He would appear out of nowhere, do his pitiless work and then vanish just as quickly, leaving a burning cane field, slaughtered livestock or a derailed train for his countrymen to remember him by.

His tactics baffled Spanish commander-in-chief Captain General Martínez de Campos, who time after time tried to isolate and contain the guerrilla bands, only to have the cunning Gómez slip through his lines to strike afresh somewhere unexpected. Unrelievedly frustrated, Campos sent in his papers and recommended as his successor General Valeriano Weyler y Nícolau, who was duly dispatched to Cuba with orders to assume a tougher stand and redeem Spanish honor in the New World. Madrid was exasperated with watching the impotent antics of 140,000 regular troops, who apparently found it impossible to neutralize a tatterdemalion, machete-armed peasantry led by one everybody called El Chino Viejo—"The Old Chinaman."

There was no doubt Spain's reputation was hitting new lows every day. What was commonly considered a gallant resistance by the Cuban rebels against great odds was exciting wide sympathy in the United States, where the curious certainly didn't lack for news on the subject. Such a convenient war was a God-sent opportunity for the foreign correspondent, and men of the caliber

of Richard Harding Davis, Stephen Crane and artist Howard
Chandler Christy delayed only long enough to pack tropical kit
and mosquito netting before joining the rush to board anything
that would float and ferry them south to the Antilles.

Before they left they were given to understand that color was
the order of the day. The editors wanted it, the readers wanted it,
and if it was not always immediately available, they soon found
the insurgents themselves more than willing to help out. Almost at
the lift of a newsman's finger—or his pencil—Gómez and his men
were on hand to provide "indisputable" evidence of rebel heroism
and Spanish brutality, much of which was eagerly sent off to American press rooms virtually without blue pencil. It didn't take the
correspondent clique long to learn that Spanish barbarities—the
more frightful the better—were the hottest items back home.
Putting their imaginations to work the writers played up the importance of the atrocity elements, exaggerated by implication and
discovered that solid fact spiced up with the Cuban "eyewitness"
reports made a satisfyingly combustible mixture.

As it happened, this much-relished image of a brutal colossus
whose mailed foot was methodically crushing out the lives and
hopes of freedom-loving subject peoples was not at all accurate.
When General Weyler arrived in the island early in February,
1896, he found a state of affairs which had progressed far beyond
Spanish control. The land was in military and economic chaos, and
mindful as we are of the current expectancies of civil populations
in war, the measures he instigated to combat terrorism—martial
law and summary procedure to be used against those guilty of
dynamiting and incendiarism—do not seem overly harsh. At the
time however, they were taken as just one more example of Spanish
frightfulness, and promptly earned the general the *nom de guerre*
of "Butcher" Weyler. In effect, it was one more hammer blow on
one more nail in the coffin of American neutrality, and now when
Senator Lodge led a Senate debate of February 24 on a resolution
to recognize officially the Cuban belligerents, he could urge that
all vote aye on the "broad ground of common humanity."

All things considered, Lodge spoke for a powerful element of the
Republican party, and though domestic issues were still the prime

bone of political contention, it would have been unrealistic to suppose that the relief of suffering Cuba would not emerge as a vital factor in the campaign of 1896. The spirit of aggressive self-assertion as a vehicle to accomplish it was given plain-spoken prominence in the GOP platform. A "firm, vigorous and dignified foreign policy" was called for, a reaffirmation was made of the right of the United States to support the Monroe Doctrine by answering the appeal of an American State for friendly intervention, and Cuba was named by name as the appealer.

Gómez, the rebels and Weyler were never out of the public view, of course, and in the autumn of 1896 as election time drew near the Butcher blundered again. In an effort to cut off the shipment of foodstuffs and supplies to the rebels from the Cuban countryside, he had ordered the "reconcentration" of a large part of the rural poulation in the towns garrisoned by his own troops. It was really no more than a strong dose of the Máximo Gómez medicine. The rebel leader had scorched the land to stop the sending of that same food from the farms to the loyalist-controlled cities. Now Weyler, up to his epaulets in an exhausting guerrilla war, was determined to draw the line between friend and foe and make sure that peasants were no longer permitted to snipe at his men one day and then appear as placid rustics the next. It was terrible public relations, of course, and all the more ironic because Weyler's campaign held little promise of success in any event. Like Campos's, his attempt to confine the rebellion to areas of his own choosing by means of *trochas* or cordons of troops spread his forces much too thin and completely negated his great advantage in numbers. Weyler sat behind his defenses, letting the insurgents attack him at their pleasure at a time when he should have taken the initiative and hunted his enemy down piecemeal.[6]

It was a type of warfare, too, that tended to be very wearing on the Spanish troops, whose alleged inhumanity—painted in bloody hues in the by-lined dispatches of some of the country's most ambitious journalists—continued to scandalize U.S. breakfast tables. It wouldn't be the first time a reader public would be asked to digest the horrors of war with the morning coffee, and the reaction was just about what it usually is in such cases. We now know there were commanders—Cuban as well as Spanish—who committed acts of barbarity, and without question the loyalist irregular troops recruited on the island were guilty of some excesses. But Spain's top Army leaders perpetrated nothing worse than what has been done by every great colonial or invading power set upon by an enemy seldom respectful of the niceties of civilized conflict, and on the whole the Spanish regular forces behaved with considerable restraint throughout.

✳✳✳

Whatever the attitudes of his party fire-eaters, the new President McKinley shrank from the idea of war. The night before his inauguration he had confided wistfully to departing chief executive Grover Cleveland: "If I can only go out of office at the end of my term with the knowledge that I have done what lay in my power to avert this terrible calamity [a clash with Spain] with the success that has crowned your patience and perseverance, I shall be the happiest man in the world."

Yet it came. When the people of a nation are urged (or urge themselves) a certain distance along the path, it takes no little skill and determination to reverse the emotional momentum which builds up. The President would have liked to stop the accelerating war machine but he didn't have the braking power. The jingoes were winning powerful allies by this time. Stories were coming out of Cuba now that could hardly fail to arouse the sympathy and indignation of the more liberal and humanistic elements of the nation. If anyone was wont to doubt the horrific tales of famine in the island, he had only to look at the front pages of the *Journal* or the *World* where emaciated children, four columns in breadth, stared out in vacant-eyed despair. The sweeping condemnation of the Spanish *reconcentrado* system comfortably ignored the fact that the rebels had been ravaging the land for two years prior to the instigation of Weyler's policy. The suffering was real, however, and if it was not universally attributed to the sadistic tyranny of the colonial presence, it surely seemed to indicate his total incompetence to govern his island.

McKinley, politically sensitive to the plunging barometer of pacifism and feeling the pressure to act, sent off a proposal to

Madrid that Spain grant the martyred Cubans some sort of autonomy by means "honorable to herself and just to her colony."
In fact unless she did reverse her current policy, stopped the
"measures of unparalleled severity" she was using, came up with
some form of settlement and ended the war, America would
intervene.

From then on things happened rather suddenly, but in a way
few would have predicted. Spanish Premier Antonio Cánovas was
felled by an Italian anarchist's bullet and the new Liberal government in Madrid, which had been voicing great dissatisfaction with
things from the opposition side, gave every indication of yielding
to McKinley's demands. Butcher Weyler was relieved of his command and sent home, much to the disappointment of the cartoonists, who had rather enjoyed picturing him in all his bestiality.
It was all too sudden, in fact. Rumors of a pro-Weyler, anti-American conspiracy in Havana sprang up immediately, and the U.S.
Consul there, Fitzhugh Lee, sent off a long, worried outpouring of
sentiments to Washington. Lee saw danger of violence breaking
out among the more militant factions—a reaction against what
they would feel to be undue pressure from the Yankee in Cuban
affairs—and he wasn't prepared to guarantee the safety of American lives and property in the city.

It was a time when the "gunboat calling card" was a traditional
and valued means of international communication, the essence of
showing the flag being that a stitch in time still saved nine, and in
reality more like ninety-nine. What better guarantee to the maintenance of peace and order, by forestalling what could be an embarrassing incident between the two countries, than to send a
United States man-of-war to Havana to be on hand in case of an
anti-American flare-up? True, McKinley thought it might seem
a provocative act, but Lee's urgings seemed to indicate the danger
outweighed the political considerations. Orders were sent to the
battleship *Maine* to take leave of the North Atlantic squadron and
make for Key West, to be ready to sail for Havana if and when she
was needed. For all practical purposes she was placed at the beck
and call of Consul Lee, who might summon her any time he felt a
crisis warranted it.

For a month things seemed to be quieter. Then, on January 12,

1898, a mob led by officers of the Spanish Army stormed the Havana newspaper offices in protest against certain denigrating articles published about the military. Although there had been no real threats to U.S. property, Lee was immediately on the cable with a series of alarming telegrams. Jitters were running high in Washington but it was considered wise to maintain a calm exterior to avoid inciting trouble. When the *Maine* was finally ordered to Havana two weeks later, it was done with the official pronouncement that the ship was paying the Cuban capital city a peaceful courtesy call.

***

The *Maine* entered Havana harbor on January 25, brave with flags and with her crew manning their battle stations. Such was the state of tension aboard and ignorance of conditions within the city that half of them expected to be fired upon. "As we steamed in under the guns of Morro [Castle] we calculated how long it would take to silence it," one sailor was to recall later. The American ship proceeded unchallenged, however, and once she was safely moored, Captain Sigsbee, her commander, sped off in his gig to pay his formal calls on the local Spanish officers. The visits turned out to be diplomatic and cordial. "The Spanish officials on every hand gave us all the official courtesy to which we were entitled," Sigsbee said, "and they gave it with the grace of manner that is characteristic of their nation. I accepted it as genuine." [7]

For this he was greatly relieved, though he wasn't inclined to press his luck further by tempting the combustion point of the fiery Cuban populace. The crew was allowed no liberty, and only officers in civilian clothes and on official business could go ashore. Sigsbee himself went to a bullfight with Consul Lee and four other *Maine* officers and the day passed without incident, except for the intrusion of an unknown man who rushed up and thrust a printed circular into his hand. It was an inflammatory pro-Weyler tract, written in Spanish and ending in the exhortation: "Death to the Americans! Death to Autonomy!"

On board the *Maine* even more than ordinary precautions had been taken. Watch standers were told to keep a particularly sharp lookout, and Sigsbee had ordered a quarter watch at night instead of the usual in-port anchor watch so that one fourth of the crew would be available at a moment's notice to man the ship's rapid-fire guns if necessary. It seemed a lot of extra trouble—not so much as a suspicious skiff was seen—and as the days went by, it appeared as though the "courtesy" implied in the visit was going to be reciprocal.

The day of February 15 turned out to be much like any other. For three weeks the *Maine* had lain at her mooring under a Cuban sun which had a soporific effect, even in winter, on men only recently removed from the North Atlantic. With no liberty the most perplexing problem was the monotony of the shipboard routine and of one's messmates. At least a man could get his fill of sleep, and most of the crew—those who weren't on watch—usually turned in at 9:10, when taps was sounded.

The notes of the bugle that evening were "singularly beautiful in the oppressive stillness of the night," Captain Sigsbee was to remember later. He was below in the admiral's stateroom working on letters. One, to Assistant Secretary of the Navy Theodore Roosevelt, had to do with the installation of torpedo tubes; another was to his wife. He had just finished the message home and was sealing the envelope when he was thrown to the deck by a terrific concussion and deafened by a "bursting, rending, crashing roar of immense volume." On the stern of the steamer *City of Washington* berthed nearby, two passengers turned toward what sounded to them like a "shot" or "report" in time to see the bow of the *Maine* rise a little out of the water and then the center of the vessel erupt in a blinding flash of fire which lighted up the whole harbor. Horrified witnesses saw debris and bodies flung high into the air. "It looked," said an observer on a nearby wharf, "like the entire inside of the ship had blown out."

That in effect was what had happened. The explosion seemed to come from up forward on the port side where most of the crew slept, and whatever had caused it, there could be no doubt that the *Maine*'s magazines had gone up. Some two-thirds of the ship's company were killed outright and many of the luckier ones—those standing watch topside—were hurled into the water by the force of the blast. One seaman just missed being pulverized by a large dark mass which was wrenched up and flung along with him into the harbor. It was the forward 10-inch gun turret. A marine corporal was blown straight up through a deck awning to a height level with the ship's superstructure. When he came down, he struck the awning again, which broke his fall.

Sigsbee himself was unhurt, as were most of the ship's officers. They were quartered aft, and so escaped the full force of the explosion, which had turned the formidable *Maine* into a blazing mass of twisted metal. Only three of the ship's fifteen boats were serviceable but the surrounding water was filled with floating wreckage to which burned, half-drowned crewmen were clinging. Her captain was the last to leave the doomed ship. He and his pet dog stepped into one of the boats as his once proud command gently sank under him into the mud of Havana harbor, rumbling and shuddering all the while with muffled explosions of ammunition deep inside her.

After he had been rowed to the *City of Washington*, Sigsbee, "looking ten years older," scratched off a message in pencil: "Secnav—Washington, D.C. *Maine* blown up in Havana harbor at nine forty tonight and destroyed. Many wounded and doubtless more killed or drowned." And then he added thoughtfully: "Public opinion should be suspended until further report." [8] A brief and laconic note, written almost in a state of shock at the loss, which he suspected would be heavy.

It was. Out of twenty-two officers (four others had been ashore that night) and 328 men there were 252 dead or missing, most of whom never knew what happened. Eight more were to die in Havana hospitals in the next few days.

✶✶✶

Of course once the facts hit newspaper row, one might as well have tried to stopper a volcano with excelsior as suspend public opinion. "THE WAR SHIP MAINE WAS SPLIT IN TWO BY AN ENEMY'S SECRET INFERNAL MACHINE!" shouted a February 17 extra of Hearst's New York *Journal*. No matter that it was gross presumption, coming out as it did only two days after the tragedy

—it moved papers. The Spanish authorities seemed almost as stunned as Washington by what had happened. The cruiser *Alfonso XII* had done great and humane work that night, picking up survivors while exposing herself to considerable risk from the battleship's still exploding magazines, and if General Weyler's caustic comment from Madrid—that the disaster had been due "to the indolence of the vessel's crew"—was not calculated to soothe American feelings other high-placed Spaniards were quick to show grief and shock.

To many Weyler's attitude only added insult to what was clearly a monstrous sample of Spanish treachery. Though the *Army and Navy Journal* printed a reasoned comment on the tendency toward "self-ignition" in modern vessels due to electrical systems, faulty boilers or the spontaneous combustion of stores, the collective public mind had fixed itself on the surety of foul play. Sigsbee's own suspicions are worth recording: "*Maine* was probably destroyed by a mine," he said. "It may have been done by accident. I surmise that her berth was planted previous to her arrival; perhaps long ago." [9]

Whatever speculation might suggest, it was obvious an investigation was called for, and without delay. A court of inquiry was convened almost immediately, its members arriving in Havana on February 21. Captain William T. Sampson, an intellectual and highly respected officer, presided over the four-man body, which met in secrecy—no newspapermen allowed—aboard a revenue cutter anchored in the harbor. Naturally the court's most pressing duty was to settle the question of whether or not there had been sabotage, and Captain Sigsbee and selected crew members were first closely questioned as to the possibility of internal explosion. Asked whether the heat of smoldering coal could have ignited the exposed powder in the magazines, Sigsbee replied no, the temperature-sensitive fire alarms in the bunkers would have given warning beforehand of any danger from this quarter. Failure in the electric plant, or of the ship's boilers was ruled out as well, as was the possibility of carelessness in the magazines themselves, where the men wore special slippers to avoid sparks when working near the ammunition.

This inability to attribute the blast either to mechanical short-comings or human negligence forced the court to assume that the first "shot" or "report" had taken place outside the hull of the ship. At this critical point there was a leak to the press. Walter Scott Meriwether, a former Navy man who had been sent down by the New York *Herald* to get the *Maine* story, was visited in his hotel room one night by an old shipmate who was also in Havana because of his special skills. He was in charge of the divers investigating the wreck, and he told the newsman that very day they had discovered that the *Maine*'s keel had been thrust up so violently that it now lay barely eighteen inches beneath the surface of the water. He didn't have to go into detail; Meriwether realized at once he'd been handed the biggest scoop since the explosion itself. Only a mine, detonated under her bottom, could bend up the battleship's keel plates in this manner.

The way in which he tried to get the information back to James Gordon Bennett at the *Herald* office is an interesting example of the inventiveness the reporter of the day was expected to employ. Knowing that the Spanish censor would never pass anything so damning, he put his faith in a simple code, trusting his paper to ferret out the meaning. With a copy of a popular magazine in hand, he sent off the following wire to New York: "Navy contingent left in Havana interestingly reading Kipling's poem current *Life*, especially last verse." The poem was "The Destroyers" and it read:

> The strength of twice three thousand horse
>   That serve the one command;
> The hand that heaves the headlong force,
>   The hate that backs the hand:
> The doom-bolt in the darkness freed,
>   The mine that splits the main;
> The white-hot wake, the 'wildering speed—
>   The Choosers of the Slain!

Unfortunately the censor caught the rather broad clue and it didn't go through.

The information brought up by the divers was enough for the

court of inquiry. When they discovered too, too, that some of the battleship's plates had been bent *inward*, it was felt no further evidence was needed. On March 21 Sampson and his colleagues ruled that the *Maine* had been destroyed by a submarine mine that had caused the partial explosion of two or more forward magazines. They added that in their view the evidence was insufficient to place blame on any person or persons.

The Spaniards had meanwhile assembled their own investigating body, and though it worked under a handicap (not being allowed to examine the half-submerged wreck) it did manage to come up with some thought-provoking arguments. For one thing no one had seen the geyser which an underwater explosion might be expected to produce. Nobody had noticed any dead fish, either, or had felt the shock which would have been transmitted to nearby ships in the case of a detonation beneath the surface. The *Maine*'s mooring could have been "prepared" only if it were the custom to mine the berths of all foreign warships, for the American vessel had given very short notice of her arrival; it would have been next to impossible to lay a charge afterward, in light of the close watch kept aboard for signs of suspicious doings.

Neither the U.S. nor Spanish investigations were really to prove anything. In 1911 when the *Maine* was raised, towed to sea and sunk in deep water, the mystery went down with her. We are no wiser seven decades after the event. At the time people believed what they wanted to believe. American lives had been lost, American property outraged, and the culprits, which common feeling dictated could be none but the perfidious dons of Spain who struck in the dark instead of fighting in the open like men, must be made to come up with an accounting.

✳✳✳

That terrible night in Havana had given the proponents of war a good deal of moral and emotional ammunition, yet things had still not come to the point where the country was willing to take the final step. A certain legality was lacking. In view of the decision of our own board of inquiry, the destruction of the *Maine* could not officially be made an issue, and as far as the Cuban

situation was concerned, the Liberal government of Práxedes
Sagasta, which had assumed power at the time of Cánovas's as-
sassination, had been guardedly friendly to U.S. interests and had
been doing about all it could to grant Washington's demands of
autonomy for the island. McKinley was still nominally opposed to
war, as were powerful elements in Congress, yet the ferment was
there and the *Maine* had brought it to a boil.

For a certain period in more recent years it was fashionable to
lay the blame for unrelenting warmongering on American industry,
who supposedly saw shimmering beyond a victory over Spain a
Nirvana of foreign trade. As things developed it was there, but
this wasn't wholly recognized at the time. True, American business
could have stood some rejuvenation, having been in the doldrums
since the panic of 1893, but there was a generally accepted feeling,
especially among conservative eastern interests, that armed conflict
would disrupt the signs of prosperity that were just beginning to
appear again. As for territorial gain, many were convinced that
the widespread European enthusiasm for colonies was misplaced.
The Mahans of the world and their followers might theorize all
they liked, but from a profit-and-loss standpoint possessions seemed
likely to be more of a headache than their value warranted. It
would be convenient to attribute the belligerent pressures of 1898
to avaricious capitalism and heartless "munitions makers" rather
than to the culmination of national popular attitudes—fostered
and given voice in the press and representation on the highest
levels in Washington—which was the real moving force. Anger at
Spain, pity for Cuba's plight, awareness of America's power and
her duty toward the imperial concept all combined to make it
irresistible.

Though President McKinley paid obeisance to a peace policy,
it was becoming more evident that he wasn't going to be able to
keep his seat on the simmering kettle. It might have been unfair
to say, as Theodore Roosevelt did say, that he had "no more back-
bone than a chocolate éclair," but he did melt rather quickly in the
face of forces that were obviously spoiling for a fight. Perhaps he
was a little nettled by the revelations of a letter sent by Spanish
minister Depuy de Lôme to a friend in Cuba, describing him as

"weak and a bidder for the admiration of the crowd." It had been one more Spanish indiscretion-turned-blunder and had raised Cain when Hearst got hold of a copy and printed it. How many more insults must the United States take? Congress could hardly have given a more decisive answer when it took the President's bill in hand calling for fifty million dollars for national defense. The measure passed the House 311 to 0 and the Senate 76 to 0.

Reports filtering in of the continuing sufferings of the Cuban people were to give the chief executive no respite either. As he saw it, the humanitarian hue and cry to restore peace on the island had to be silenced as a matter of political expediency, though he still preferred to force Spain into an admission of defeat without resort to bloodshed. Let it be understood by that country and the world, too, that we did not want the troublesome island; what we wanted was peace. He therefore cabled a proposal to the U.S. ambassador in Madrid calling for an immediate six-month armistice, and rather surprisingly was informed in return that (1) Spain was ready to submit the loss of the *Maine* to arbitration, (2) many of the reconcentration degrees would be (in fact already had been) revoked, and (3) the Spanish government would at once grant a truce should the insurgents ask for it.

Of course knowing that the United States was on the brink of positive action, the rebels were not inclined to sue for peace. When this became evident, Madrid bowed to American demands even further. The Sagasta government knew Washington was clamoring for a vote on intervention. If the Spanish queen should proclaim immediate and unconditional suspension of hostilities in Cuba, would McKinley do his best to prevent "hostile action by Congress"? The President, politically conscious of wheels within wheels, promised nothing.

On April 11, 1898, McKinley read out his message on the issue to the House and Senate. He spoke of the devastation caused by the war, deplored the inhumanity of the *reconcentrado* policy as "unprecedented in the history of civilized Christian peoples," recounted the damage suffered by American interests and summed up all the diplomatic negotiations. He asked Congress to authorize and empower him to secure an end to the hostilities in Cuba, to establish a stable government in the island, and "to use the military and naval forces of the United States as may be necessary for these purposes...." [10] Then, almost as an afterthought, he concluded with the revelation that the Queen Regent of Spain had directed her commander in chief to proclaim a suspension of the fighting, "the duration and details of which have not yet been communicated to me."

It is tempting to blame the President for failing to emphasize the fact that Spain had submitted to practically everything asked of her, but in truth it probably wouldn't have made much difference. It was too late for any capitulation on her part, no matter how ignominious. The fever that had the nation in its grip had begun to burn in the brain and imagination of Capitol Hill at last. "A spirit of wild jingoism," the President's secretary noted in his diary of the Senate, "seems to have taken possession of this usually conservative body," [11] and in the House a covey of members gathered in the lobby to sing "Dixie," "The Battle Hymn of the Republic," and in a final fitting parody—"We'll Hang General Weyler to a Sour Apple Tree."

With a single important amendment—"That the United States hereby disclaims any disposition or intention to exercise sovereignty, jurisdiction, or control over said island [Cuba] except for the pacification thereof, and asserts its determination that when that is accomplished to leave the government and control of the island to its people," [12]—the resolution was passed.

The imperialists looked on it as a fainthearted backdown, but comforted themselves by the thought that anything can happen in a war.

For war it was.

★★★

CHAPTER II

****

The Game in Progress:
The Queen's Knight Gambit
Accepted

"It was a war entered without misgivings and in the noblest frame of mind. Seldom can history have recorded a plainer case of military aggression; yet seldom has a war been started in so profound a conviction of its righteousness." [1] With these words the nation's first confrontation with a foreign foe in half a century has been described, and though the stress on American culpability is overly iconoclastic, there is no question about the widespread feeling of propriety and of confidence—well-being, even—with which it faced the adventure. Almost to a man, editors, business, financial and religious leaders all stepped up behind the press lords to be counted in the war effort, and one look at the crowds that mobbed the newspaper bulletin boards to devour fact, rumor and speculation willy-nilly was enough to scotch all doubt as to its popular support as well.

There was no question but that the country was united as it hadn't been for decades. The common enemy provided an excuse to heal the old bitternesses between Yankee and Confederate that thirty-three years of peace since 1865 had been unable to do. North and South alike received McKinley's call for 125,000 volunteers in the spirit of a common cause. All walks of life, humble and distinguished, felt its pull. A complete regiment was formed of Wall Street stockholders and clerks; John Jacob Astor offered to the Army a battery of artillery, purchased and supplied with ammunition from abroad; Assistant Secretary Theodore Roosevelt announced his intention to quit the Navy Department and take the field at the head of his own picked unit of cowboys and college men. If the voice of the Fourth Estate had been loud before, it bellowed like a fighting bull now. The New York *Journal* proposed a special company of shock troops made up of heavy-caliber athletes like champions Bob Fitzsimmons and "Gentleman Jim" Corbett, and the *World*, not to be outdone, ran a feature by Buffalo Bill Cody entitled "How I Could Drive the Spaniards from Cuba with Thirty Thousand Braves!"

Few doubted that thirty thousand of just about anything would be more than enough to dispose of the inept dons, whose fighting capabilities were held in high contempt. Young men were afraid— as young men always are—that the war would be over before they had a chance to show what they could do, and the recruiting offices were choked with volunteers from every section of the country and every state in the union. William Allen White, editor of the Emporia, Kansas, *Gazette*, wrote of the young enlistees from his own great-plains region in proud, almost fatherly terms:

"He may not know how to present arms in May, but he can be turned into a clean-cut, well-oiled cog in the fighting engine before the snow flies. To begin with the American militiaman has the advantage over every recruit on earth; the American knows how to shoot and he knows all about the mechanism of a gun. The average American boy of the inland states has owned an air gun before he is ten. He has been hit in the hand, the foot, the arm or the leg with a 'twenty-two' before he is twelve. He has owned a shotgun before he has grown a mustache. He has learned to hit a squirrel in a tree-crotch with a rifle before he is twenty. . . . When the American recruit shall get the hang of the machinery of the army and see a battalion working, the mechanical poetry of the thing will fill him with joy. . . ." [2]

In fact when one considered the quality of the fighting machine that this example of young manhood was expected to produce, it wasn't thought likely there would be much bloodshed at all. It was a general belief in both the Army and Navy that Spain was not going to offer any physical resistance whatever to Cuba's independence, but would surrender in the presence of superior force. After all, the immense predominance in power, wealth and resources of the United States was common knowledge. It was hoped that with American support the Cuban insurgent armies might be expected to bear a major brunt of the fighting, leaving to U.S. troops the more relaxed duty of an army of occupation. Of course an expeditionary force would be necessary, but if the loyalist regime did the expected and fell in the face of the inevitable like the rotten fruit it was, the troops that were landed might find themselves used merely "to protect from riot and arson," as Secretary of War Long was wont to put it.

✶✶✶

It was hard to overestimate the advantage of fighting a foreign campaign, complete with invasion, a hundred miles or so from one's mainland, yet even the most zealous were willing to admit there were some strategic factors involved. The fact that Cuba itself was engaged in an insurrection against the enemy would obviously make it easier to put men ashore, yet the transportation of troops over a body of water left them vulnerable during the ferrying process to an attack by sea, and regardless of the disdain in which Spain was held, it had to be conceded she did possess a fleet. The gist of the matter then was clear. Before an expeditionary force could be disembarked, the U.S. Navy would have to win and keep command of Cuban waters. Any part which land forces would take in a battle for the island would depend on the outcome of a naval struggle which would almost certainly be waged for this control. If the Spanish were defeated or driven off, the United States could dispatch an army of almost any size with relative ease; if not, the enemy might prevent troops in any number from landing at all.

A pre-eminent task thus fell to a navy which had only just begun to emerge from the bedrock level to which it had been allowed to sink after the Civil War. In 1865 the nation had 626 seaworthy vessels, of which 65 were powerful, up-to-date ironclads. After Appomattox, however, interest in the fleet had declined in direct ratio as energies were channeled into internal industrial development and the exodus west, and for nearly twenty years a country with one of the longest coastlines in the world had no serviceable armored ships. By 1881 the United States ranked somewhere beneath both China and Chile as a power at sea. When the realization struck that there was no longer the wherewithal to protect any interests outside the continental limits, Congress appropriated four small cruisers, and two years later—in 1885—four more. In 1890 further steps were taken to rectify this humiliating weakness when the keels of the battleships *Massachusetts*, *Indiana* and *Oregon* were laid. It was none too soon, either. An army could be recruited, trained and equipped in a matter of months; it took years to complete a first-class capital ship.

It was an appropriate time for the Navy to emerge from the cocoon, not only because it was needed to fulfill a great power's commercial obligations and potential, but because the characteristics of the modern warship itself had begun to solidify out of a long period of technical trial and error. The last forty years of the nineteenth century had seen tremendous changes in the line-of-battle ship and the smaller auxiliary craft. Steam had replaced sail for motive power, iron had done away with the "wooden walls" of Napoleonic days. Shell guns of a wide variety of bores operating from revolving turrets or protected mountings had rendered the broadside obsolete, and steel makers were vying with one another to design plate armor to keep out the shells. Though ships still had and expected to use rams, though gleaming white hulls with buff trim above the weather decks formed a favored color scheme, and bows were emblazoned with escutcheons and coats of arms, the man-of-war would from here on relinquish ostentatious dash and show and the grappling-hook philosophy of close combat, to enter the era of development and perfection that would mold it by technological degrees into an ever more impersonal, long-range and deadly fighting machine.

Because the battleship was an instrument designed to meet other vessels of its class in a decisive action, it had to be a self-contained engine of destruction, able to deliver and take as much punishment as the builders could allow for. And because it was considered such a vital manifestation of national power, its evolution serves as a fascinating example of the state of ultimate military attainment of any given period. The problem of the designers in dealing with the offensive and defensive qualities of warships—the contest between guns and armor—had been acute since the War Between the States, but now, in the nineties, saw striking power win a clear advantage. When naval ordnance had been composed mainly of smoothbores firing round shot, the competition was very nearly equal; however as breech-loading guns firing explosive projectiles became steadily more powerful, subsequent efforts on the part of armorers to protect vessels from them was a losing game. Theoretically, plates could have been developed to withstand the most potent shell, were it not for the tremendous weight involved. In order to be mobile at all a battleship could be loaded down with ponderous armor thicknesses only to a degree; beyond that she might as well be a fortified island. Guns, on the other hand, could be made inimitably bigger with a comparatively minor increase in weight, and generally speaking the larger the gun, the more destructive it would be and the greater penetrating power it would have.

Guns mounted aboard modern United States battleships in 1898 were of 12- and 13-inch diameter. It isn't correct to say they had now "reached" a size of 12 or 13 inches, as if this were an epitome of big-gun construction; 15-inch models had been built and used in the Civil War and some of the European navies had mounted 16-inch guns in the eighties.[3] Because of recent improvements in propellant charges, however, the new types were a good deal more efficient and powerful weapons than earlier ones. Development of slower-burning powders had eliminated the necessity for the bottle-shaped guns in use for so many years, which had been so designed to withstand the tremendous pressures at the breech exerted by older explosives. New propellants now burned more evenly, giving a more uniform "push" to the projectile in its passage through the barrel. Because of this it was found that by increasing the barrel length one increased the power of the gun, as the propellant had a longer time to act on the shell.

The biggest American gun was a 13-inch 30-caliber weapon, the term "caliber" in this instance indicating that the length of the barrel was thirty times the diameter, or nearly forty feet. This monster weighed 60.5 tons, and when it fired—which was roughly once every five minutes with a good crew—it needed 520 pounds of black powder, bundled in a silk bag, to drive its 1,100-pound shell through more than two feet of wrought iron at a distance of a thousand yards.

This penetration power was a standard of measurement only, as wrought iron had not been used to protect warships for some years. In their efforts to keep pace with offensive power, armorers had looked beyond mere thickness and had first come up with a composite armor—a steel face fastened to a wrought-iron plate to break up projectiles as they hit; then, in the 1890's, a 5 percent–95 percent nickel-steel alloy plate which was face hardened by the new Harvey process. A 6-inch plate of Harveysized steel was considered to be more than twice as resistant as the same thickness of iron. In 1895 a still newer Krupp process of toughening armor was developed, which was rated 20 to 30 percent more effective yet than the Harveysized steel, and though it was adopted in the United States Navy in 1898, it did not make its appearance in time for the Spanish-American War. Ships were protected according to their class; the latest American battleships carried eighteen inches of side plating in a "belt" guarding the machinery, and fifteen inches on their main turrets. A cruiser like the New York had only a four-inch belt, but this was supplemented by a steel deck built in the form of an arch, which extended below the waterline and up above the engine and boiler rooms, being three inches thick on the top.

The bigger modern warships had these protective decks of one kind or another, though they were not designed to withstand heavy battering. Vessels in those days were not of course subjected to aerial bombardment or even to the plunging high-arc shellfire which a ship engaging an enemy at extreme range must face. Guns had been built to fire nearly ten miles, but they were not equipped to do so from their normal turret mountings, which in many instances allowed for an elevation of only 13½ degrees from the horizontal. Range finding and sighting techniques were far too primitive to allow for any hope of success at such distances, and it would have been thought insane to try for it. Ranges were calculated by a gunnery officer on a finder called a stadimeter, passed on to sailors who carried the information as fast as their

legs would take them to the turret decks, where it was transmitted in turn to the turret officers. Though European navies
lacked them, telescopic sights were available in American vessels,
but they were low-powered and the cross hairs so coarse they
blocked out a battleship at four thousand yards. The ship's pitch
or roll had to be compensated for by the gunner's own timing (he
fired on the down roll preferably, since close ranges meant flat
shell trajectories, and a short shot might ricochet off the water into
the target), and even at that sights could not be adjusted to correct for wind or the speed of the firing ship, though the newer
ones did have a graduated deflection scale to allow for the enemy's
speed. A gun captain simply let fly when he thought he was "on,"
hoped for the best, and since the sights were not shock mounted,
wasn't even able to keep his eye on the target area while doing so.

Corrections would be made, supposedly, by a spotter stationed
in the tops, who would observe the shell splashes through his
glass, though he was more valuable in a single-ship target practice
than in a fleet action where it was next to impossible to differen-
tiate between the shells from the various ships engaged. Spotting
up to 3,500 yards was considered to be reasonably accurate, up to
6,000 it was thought to be helpful, but beyond that it was considered, and rightly, to be worthless.[4] Few really believed war at
sea would be fought out at much more than a mile at best.[5]

Battleships did not rely wholly on big guns, but were armed
with combinations of the 8-, 6-, 5- and 4-inch secondary weapons
that formed the main batteries of cruisers and lighter warships.
Ideally these smaller weapons would be of the rapid-fire type,
which, in the case of the 4-inch rifles, were capable of spewing out
shells up to five times as fast as the old-fashioned models of the
same caliber. The 4-inchers used fixed ammunition—the shell and
propellant charge was contained in a single cartridge, like a rifle
bullet—and all the newer guns employed quick-working breech-
blocks, improved recoil mechanisms which returned the piece
automatically to firing position, and smaller gun crews.

They were not of course meant for use against battleships, except for sweeping the superstructure or tops at close range, but
were designed to destroy more lightly armored vessels. It was con-

sidered that they would be especially valuable against the futuristic torpedo boats which were themselves armed with the new self-propelled, gyroscopic Whitehead torpedo, a weapon which the battleship navy viewed with trepidation (though they would scarcely admit it). The torpedo boats were light, fast, darting craft whose method of attack would conceivably be an approach under cover of darkness or the smoke and confusion of battle to the 500 or 600 yards considered to be the effective releasing distance for the torpedo. Once launched, this undersea missile would make for the target at speeds up to 30 knots, with what to the recipient's eye must seem like some infernal mind and will of its own, drive a bursting charge of 200 pounds of guncotton against a ship's side and send her to the bottom. In new implements of war and in perfection of the old, technology was clearly making giant strides and was a disquieting intrusion upon a system still governed by the customs, habit and unhurried procedure of a simpler day. For not everything was keeping pace.

To those familiar with the fighting Navy of World War II and the atmosphere of the modern weapons-conscious world, it may be difficult to relate to the attitudes of the Victorian age, when armies and navies of most of the established powers were regarded as much social organizations as military ones by the upper strata, and by the lower as a haven for the idle, the adventurous and the dropouts of that less-affluent time. The services were definitely not the finely and continually sharpened weapons that we know today. In 1898 big land campaigns were considered to be a thing of the past; colonizing or punitive expeditions were all that could be expected, and at sea the mere presence of a "fleet in being" was thought to suffice. After all, if war between civilized states was indeed becoming extinct, it was hardly likely that important fleet actions—on the scale of Trafalgar, for instance—would occur again.

As a result, naval operations were virtually as relaxed as they had been in the days of sail, though the seagoing nations, and especially the newest aspirants to the top competitive level—the United States and Japan—had a hard-core, professional-officer element that was vigilant and a continual prod to the self-satisfactions of their superiors: a "devil's advocate" was often useful. If a ship was required for a specific mission the Navy Department dispatched orders to that effect; otherwise the flag officer of a squadron or an individual ship captain had almost complete freedom over the movements of his command. Schedules were practically non-existent and most operations consisted of pretty casual training, good-will visits to home and foreign ports, and the protection of American interests, as in the case of the *Maine*, for example. European navies in particular were guilty of holding spit and polish and tradition in higher regard than tactical efficiency. The smartness of a ship's company, the gleam of her brightwork, the punctiliousness of her company, the bugles, the boatswain's pipes, the quiet confidence inbred by an unassailable tradition of promotion and precedence found more sympathy in the typical officer's nature than did the tiresome job of "running the guns out and firing at casks," which had often been the customary way of expressing the ship's firepower in his midshipman days. If a captain went "by the book," he might just about forgo target practice altogether. Our own Navy regulations set down in July, 1897, called for each gun of 10-inch or over to be fired once with a full service charge and eight times with reduced charges a *year*. Four- and 5-inch guns were required to be fired twenty-five times a year.

Because of (or, looking at it a different way, in spite of) easygoing attitudes, the Navy didn't offer a bad life for either officer or enlisted man. A newly commissioned ensign would draw $1,200 yearly, and a rear admiral, then the highest rank, $6,000. Promotions were earned according to seniority, which might cause the budding Nelsons in the fleet to chafe a bit (the selection board for line-officer advancement wasn't set up until 1916), but if a man did his job well, he would move up the ladder, and there wasn't likely to be much chance for a budding Nelson to distinguish himself anyway.

The enlisted sailor's life was not a luxurious one, especially by modern standards. Ships were crowded; in the tropics they were virtually floating ovens, and the firerooms where the "black gang" worked were that way under any conditions. Men slept in hammocks and had to shave and wash their clothes in the brackish water that was allotted to them daily—sometimes only a bucket full. Nonetheless, below decks many of the real miseries associated with the Navy of 1800 had been done away with. "Two dozen of the best" was ancient history; commanding officers could be expected to show human qualities, provided a man's shoeshine and neckerchief knot passed muster, and it was usually an easier work day for an apprentice seaman at sixteen dollars a month than farming or ten hours a day in the mills would be. There was a spirit of camaraderie not often found on shore, too, which came from a sense of sharing a colorful and potentially dangerous life with one's messmates, and which showed itself, in the absence of an enemy, in a certain pride of accomplishment. Even the onerous duty of coaling ship, a dirty, all-hands task, had a sense of the occasion about it. The whole crew donned dungarees, while the ship's band took station on the bridge or on top of one of the turrets and the cooks rustled up coffee and sandwiches to be served all day. The men split up into divisions, one shoveling coal into bags in the hold of the collier or barge which had come up alongside, another hoisting the bags aboard ship, another emptying them into the bunker hatches, still others below storing the coal in the bunkers. The band played, the meticulously scrubbed deck turned into a mess, the air was alive with coal dust, and sweat and tears from red-rimmed eyes painted white streaks down the black faces. Everybody joked, sang and went about the job with a holiday good nature.

Ships might still be cramped, smelly and inelegant, but "jacky," as the newspapers called the seaman of the day, was winning quite a few creature comforts for himself. Electric lights had been installed in seven warships by 1890, and electric fans—not too common yet even "on the beach"—were beginning to come into use. Even the salt horse and weevily biscuit had disappeared. In their place a sailor might expect a variety of seven different kinds of preserved meats with all sorts of extras provided. Not that there was a tendency to stint on the basics of solid chow; after all, the government allowed thirty cents a day for feeding a man (compared to ten cents per diem for many merchant seamen). On an armored cruiser like the *Brooklyn*, the crew of thirty-three officers and 447 men did away with 6,000 pounds of bread, 8,000 pounds of fresh beef, 400 bushels of potatoes, 600 gallons of beans and 900 pounds of coffee every month. To supplement this, however, they also put down a ton and a half of sugar, 500 pounds of pigs' feet, 300 pounds of macaroni, 300 pounds of pickles, 480 quarts of catsup, and even 24 pounds of curry powder, as well as butter, ham, bacon, liver, sausages, cheese, rice, cabbage, dried fruit and condensed milk in comparable proportions.[6]

✱✱✱

For the U.S. Navy it seemed a confident and progressive time. If the American people had temporarily forgotten the feats of Decatur and Hull and the "fir-built frigates" of 1812 that had fought yardarm to yardarm with King George's haughty ships, the illustrated magazines now called them to mind. Once again it looked as though it would be the fleet that would personify the nation's strength, fitness and spirit in this test between the old and the new, though to any impartial observer tired, tradition-logged Spain could scarcely be classed as Europe's champion unless one felt, as did many Americans, that fatigue and decadence were the qualities which had come to symbolize civilization across the Atlantic.

On paper our Navy—in units available for combat—would seem to be considerably stronger than Spain's. We had in commission four first-class battleships, embodying all the power and speed which science could build into them—the *Iowa, Indiana, Massachusetts* and *Oregon*—and one of the second class—the *Texas*. The last ship, as well as the sunken *Maine* which had been similarly rated, had not been laid down under the designation, "second class," but such had been the improvement in design since her commissioning that she was now relegated to a lesser category.

The *Indiana, Massachusetts* and *Oregon* were sister ships and their cost—over $3 million apiece—had not been considered a bargain by a parsimonious appropriations committee, in spite of the fact that they represented our sole attempts to put to sea a modern line of battle. The nation had gotten pretty good fighting units for its money, however. They carried four 13-inch guns in two turrets amidships and aft; four smaller turrets along the rails housed two 8-inch guns each, and four 6-inch rapid-fire guns were mounted in sponsons above the side armor. Twenty 6-pounder and six 1-pounder rapid-fire weapons and four Gatling guns were available to handle the light work. The three ships were fitted with an 18-inch steel belt for about three-fifths of their length, 15 inches of armor on the main turrets, 6 inches on the smaller turrets and had a 2¾-inch protective deck. They had been built for coastal defense and thus stressed guns and armor over speed, though they were rated at 15.5 knots, which was not abnormally slow.

The *Iowa*, a newer ship, was bigger and faster, displacing 11,340 tons and being capable of 16.5 knots. She was armed with 12-inch guns, however, again in pairs, eight 8-inch and six 4-inch rapid-fire, and she carried the same number of smaller quick firers as the other three. The *Texas*, the oldest of the vessels, was only a 6,315-ton ship, and was somewhat undergunned by the standards of 1898, mounting only two 12-inch guns and six 6-inch. She could steam 17 knots, however, and was still considered a valuable unit.

Spain had only one battleship, the *Pelayo*, comparable in strength to the second-class American vessels, but she was never to leave home waters and thus would have no bearing on the war. The Spaniards were strong in another area, though, having concentrated on the more lightly gunned, but big, fast and wide-ranging armored cruiser. They possessed six of these, of high quality: the *Emperador Carlos V, Almirante Oquendo, Cristóbal Colón, Viscaya, Infanta María Teresa* and *Princesa de Asturias*. All were 7,000-ton ships except the *Cristóbal Colón*, which was newer and slightly smaller; all were speedy, 20-knot vessels and mounted two 11-inch guns and ten 5.5-inch except the *Colón* again, which was designed to carry a pair of 10-inch. They were powerful, measuring up in displacement and firepower to a second-class battleship, and having in addition three extra knots over a vessel like the *Texas*.

The American armored cruisers *Brooklyn* and *New York* were heftier than the Spanish, displacing 9,200 tons and 8,200 tons respectively, and equally fast, but were more lightly armored and had been given 8-inch main batteries. The *Brooklyn* mounted eight of these guns and the *New York* six. In addition the U.S.

Navy had available for duty fourteen "protected" cruisers—used mainly for scouting—against Spain's five; and six monitors, light-draft vessels of low speed, with thick armor, one or two heavy guns and limited cruising capabilities. Spain had none of these coast- and harbor-defense draft, but she was at this point concentrating some effort on that revolutionary aspect of sea warfare that threatened to take the play away from the battleships and their big guns. She had in commission nineteen torpedo boats, ten torpedo gunboats and six torpedo-boat destroyers, those small, speedy question marks whose potential was as yet untested in combat but whose possibilities had always been recognized by farsighted naval thinkers.

Both powers had a number of smaller, weaker vessels which had no hope of playing a vital part in any engagement. The U.S. Navy had fifteen small cruisers, one large wooden cruiser, thirteen single-turreted monitors, sixteen gunboats, one harbor-defense ram and one dispatch boat. They could be classed with Spain's pair of obsolete iron cruisers, two dispatch boats, twenty-three gunboats and six gun vessels. Most of these were relics and hybrids of the transitory period of naval architecture, and were so slow, thin-skinned, or so outclassed in gunpower or protection as to be all but useless in combat. These, along with certain auxiliary cruisers and a makeshift array of yachts, tugs, colliers, transports and supply ships, constituted the might of the fleets.

On June 30, 1898, the regular Navy of the United States num-bered 1,751 officers, 913 of them line officers, and 13,750 enlisted men. Spain had 1,400 officers and 14,000 other ranks in uniform.[7] In personnel the two forces were thus roughly equal in numbers— the disparity was to arise in the areas of quality and efficiency. In training, discipline, education and seamanship the American sailor —on all levels—was markedly superior. A highly professional officer cadre, which reflected the standards of the academy at Annapolis, had kept the service from ever declining to the state of the Spanish fleet and personnel, which simply were not at home in blue water. American ships spent far more time at sea, generally just keeping the crews in shape, occasionally participating in rather imaginative (for the day) exercises. In the early months of 1897 the North Atlantic Fleet had blockaded the city of Charleston as a great experimental success, and some captains, contrary to the lackadaisical official attitude, ordered work at the targets on a regular basis, including night firing with the use of searchlights. Some even gave out prizes to the best gun crews. Whereas American engineering capability was held in particularly high repute, the Spanish mentality didn't seem any more congenial to mechanical concepts than it did to war games. Spain's officers and men could be and were courageous and self-sacrificing, but they were lacking in adequate training and in efficiency. The almost total absence of general target practice, which had been held only once in the year prior to the war, was a case in point, and when the crucial test came, its need would be sorely felt. Maneuvers were never attempted and drill was badly neglected. Missing, too, was any mutual feeling of respect or trust between officer and enlisted man. The commissioned ranks of the Spanish Navy were filled with socially minded, haughty and often indolent young men of small professional capacity. With bullying words, contemptuous attitudes and with the employment of degrading corporal punishment for minor offenses, they exercised command over crews made up largely of resentful conscripts. Such a system simply didn't encourage warmth or loyalty.

Things were not quite so one-sided as they might appear, however, and any attempt to measure the relative merits of two fleets such as these must explore the principles of naval warfare as they applied in the late nineteenth century and as they would continue to apply up until first the submarine and finally the aircraft carrier changed the system of values. Sea battles in those days resembled as closely as anything can in war a contest over a chessboard—a game of units, purely and simply. There were no terrain, no natural obstacles, no defensive positions, in fact, no "attacker" or "defender" in that sense at all; merely a moving and confrontation of pieces, with the only requisite that one be stronger than an opponent at the place of meeting. Concentration, then, of all the forces at a commander's disposal was paramount, and for this reason it had been the rule ever since the early days of sail for the more powerful, or line-of-battle warships to maneuver and fight in fleets. The smaller vessels would act as scouts, commerce destroyers and auxiliaries, and though they were sometimes combined into fleets themselves to meet enemy ships of similar strength, they seldom played any real part in the contest. The deciding forces were the aggregations of major warships that were built to meet and engage their enemy counterparts in an artillery duel.

Mere numbers, however, had ceased to be an absolute once steam had replaced sail and the development of the big gun had done away with the more or less uniform weight of a sailing ship's broadside. The power of a late-nineteenth-century battleship came to be centered then in the three factors we have been talking about —armament, speed and armor protection—with *distance* a deciding element. The big 13-inch rifles enabled a battleship to slug it out with an enemy, not only with maximum hitting power, but at ranges from which it was impossible for any smaller-gunned adversary to reply at all; armor of course was always needed to protect a ship's crew and vitals from the almost inevitable hits from heavy shell; speed was an absolute necessity to enable a warship or fleet to bring an enemy force to battle, choose and maintain the range it wished to fight at, or withdraw from the action without fear of being overtaken by a foe. More often than not, it was upon this question of speed that effective naval strength at any particular time and place depended. If we assume that the concentration of the greatest gunpower was the first rule of sea warfare, and to achieve this it was necessary to keep the ships together—in other words fight the fleet as a unit—it becomes evident that the mobility of the whole force will be regulated by the speed of its slowest vessel. Any ship having an excess of speed over the most laggard would find those extra knots useless where concerted action was necessary, and it is only by keeping this fact in mind that we can evaluate the respective naval power of the United States and Spain.

In tonnage and firepower the American fleet was plainly superior. What the Spaniards lacked in power, however, they made up in mobility and in the freedom of *choice*. The American battleships were rated at something over 15 knots, and both the American and Spanish armored cruisers were considered capable of 20 knots or so. Spain therefore had six big vessels similar in gunpower and speed which could be fought as a unit, while the United States had only two. Any meeting between the capital ships could well be to the former's advantage, defensively at least. In order to bring his superior weight of metal to bear, an American admiral would have to combine his battleships and armored cruisers into a single fleet, but because of a 4- or 5-knot advantage—a decisive margin in the open sea—this would give the Spanish commander the option of fighting or running, as conditions dictated. If he ran and was chased, he could then turn upon the only ships capable of catching him, the two American armored cruisers, at odds of six to two.

In light of this situation it wouldn't seem unreasonable to expect the admiralty in Madrid to do everything in its power to augment the strength of the West Indian squadron; to see that the ships were kept coaled, armed and mechanically sound, and their crews drilled and ready to play for all it was worth the particular hit-and-run advantage which would be Spain's only ace in an ultimate clash of the opposing navies.

✴✴✴

If the U.S. Navy was only just emerging from the dark ages of the sixties and seventies, the Army, unhappily, was still wearing animal skins and painting its collective face blue. Once the initial enthusiasm of the "WAR! SURE!" headlines had run its course, it began to dawn on people that the "superior force" before which the enemy could be expected to quake and capitulate was as nonexistent as the battleships had been twenty years earlier. Best estimates were placing the number of hostile troops in Cuba at anywhere from 80,000 to 150,000,[8] and if one was handed the manpower of the U.S. Army, kit and caboodle, at the outbreak of war, one would find he had only 28,183 men, many of whom were scattered throughout military posts and garrisons from coast to coast. There were good individual soldiers among them—the Indian wars had kept most of the regulars hard—but nowhere was there even a modicum of experience in anything but the most minor, skirmish type of action. A real plan for mobilization had yet to be devised, there had been no training in combined Army-Navy operations, and no provision for the assembling, equipping or transport of an overseas expedition or for the accommodation of any large body of men whatever. Except for the veterans of the Civil War, now in their fifties at least, there wasn't an officer in uniform who had ever seen anything bigger than a regiment assembled in one spot.

There were in addition to the regular Army about 100,000 members of the National Guard from all states of the union who might be called upon to fill the numbers gap. Though even their most vigorous defenders had to concede the units were woefully weak in every area of proficiency with the exception of close-order drill, it was felt their powerful *esprit de corps* (social, even more than military, affairs filled the calendar of the clublike Guard) would more than make up for the lack of textbook or practical training. Properly armed, properly led, the state troops would pull their weight.

Here, however, the pettiness of politics reared its head. Inherently the individual governors and not the federal administration were in control of the various militia organizations, and these chief executives chose to look upon any suggestion that they should sacrifice their powers of command to President McKinley as an encroachment upon states' rights and as such unacceptable. To Washington, on the other hand, the prospect of signing up forty separate armies which were ill provided for, riddled with rivalries and jealousies and officered by untutored civilians seemed something right out of Gilbert and Sullivan's "Nightmare Song."

Attempts to dispense with existing Guard units and incorporate their members into a newly formed volunteer army met with indignant opposition. The Guard had its own ties, its familial pride and its own traditions, and it wasn't about to deliver itself into the hands of "West Point martinets," Spain, Cuba, and all the rest be damned. Cajoling, appeals to patriotism and old-fashioned, back-room, political infighting had a cumulative effect, however, and Washington finally emerged from it all with a victory of sorts. The militia would be taken into the federal service, but only with the stipulation that units would be ordered

overseas only with the consent of the governors involved, and that
regimental company officers, while appointed by the President,
could be selected only from men recommended by those governors.

In a groping, roundabout way the Army's manpower was being
built up, though at this stage nobody was quite sure exactly what
the troops were expected to do. There were no embarkation camps
for them, but then it was only too plain that embarkation would
have to be some time off, anyway. Most of the men were without
modern rifles, there were no tropical uniforms and there was an
embarrassing lack of horses, mules and every form of transport
vehicle. It goes without saying that the all-important organizational spark was still waiting to be struck. This shuffling-in-the-
wings situation existed within a generally supercharged atmosphere, with the press and public, officially unleashed now along
with the dogs of war, calling for bugles, the unfurling of Old
Glory and the prompt storming of the city where the twisted
and shameful wreckage of the *Maine* still lay rotting and rusting
just offshore.

The "On to Havana!" enthusiasts were hardly cooled at all by
the announcement of the Surgeon General of the Army that Cuba
happened to be one of the world's pestholes in the summer months
and that an invasion launched any sooner than October ran the
risk of a mortality rate from yellow fever of 35 to 50 percent. The
reaction to this seemed to be that, if such were the case, then the
outbreak of war had been ill-timed. Americans were not used
to procrastination once their bile was up, though it was a plain
truth that they would have to contain their demands for a march
on the enemy capital until there were enough cartridges in the
country to carry an Army of 60,000 men through at least one
battle, anyway. As yet there were not. Then there was that nagging
and intrusive undercurrent that somehow everything had to wait
for the Navy. But for how long, they all asked, and what was the
Navy doing, anyway?

✳✳✳

As soon as war had become likely the Navy Department had
picked the island of Key West off the southern tip of Florida as

a major base of operations. Situated only ninety miles from Havana, it was the logical place from which to mount an attack on the Cuban capital or the blockade of the island that would almost surely be called for, and a fleet based there could include the Gulf of Mexico in its patrolling range as well, if it had to.

When hostilities broke out, acting Rear Admiral William T. Sampson, the same Sampson who had presided at the *Maine* inquiry, was placed in command of the fleet at Key West. He had at his disposal the battleships *Iowa* and *Indiana*, the armored cruiser *New York*, four smaller cruisers, three of the big-gunned monitors and a dozen other gunboats, torpedo boats and converted yachts. He would have had a good deal more available to him from the onset were it not felt necessary to provide almost as large a fleet for the nation's own defense. Scarcely had war been declared than the Atlantic coastal cities suddenly realized how exposed they were to an attack by sea from a hostile power. Though one friend of Senator Lodge's sneered that, if the Spanish ever landed in New York, they would be selling oranges before they got to 14th Street, this jocular attitude about invasion was not widely shared. A Newfoundland cable station swore one of the telegraphers had heard the sound of gunfire at sea and the story quickly spread. Before long, strange shapes, assumed to be enemy torpedo boats, were reported off South Carolina; there were rumors of whole squadrons, dimly glimpsed off in the fog by fishermen; and it was said that certain swarthy men were being picked up on the suspicion of signaling to mysterious vessels skulking about somewhere out there.

Reactions were swift. Safe-deposit boxes in Worcester began to fill with securities transferred there by Boston businessmen, Newport society editors warned readers not to open their summer cottages until they "shall know something more of the movements of the Spanish fleet," and in Roosevelt's own Long Island neighborhood, clauses were put into leases specifying that destruction of the property by the Spaniards would result in lapse of the lease. Congress began getting a flood of wires from governors, mayors and influential private citizens demanding naval protection, and the lawmakers reflected their constituents' fears. The belligerent

Senator Frye now asked for a warship to patrol the Maine shore-line, a request that made only slightly more sense than the insistence of a prominent citizen that a cruiser be stationed off Jekyll Island, the posh Georgia winter resort and game preserve. Letters and telegrams pouring into the War Department asking for guns for the coasts and mines for the rivers and harbors were so numerous that even the conscientious Secretary Alger gave up taking them seriously.

The furor was hot enough, however, to assure that a whole second United States fleet be stationed where it could protect the eastern seaboard. Under the flag of Commodore Winfield Scott Schley, it consisted of the battleships *Massachusetts* and *Texas*, the armored cruiser *Brooklyn*, the protected cruisers *Minneapolis* and *Columbia* and the collier *Merrimac*, and was based at Hampton Roads, Virginia, which was considered the best spot from which to counter a possible Spanish raid, and also to check any offensive move further south by an enemy squadron known to be at St. Vincent in the Cape Verde Islands.

And just what was this dread Spanish sea power, whose reputation raised images of bombardments, burnings and sack which had not disturbed the sleep of Americans since the War of 1812? Not counting a squadron of ships based at Manila Bay, in the Philippines, Spain's Navy was divided into two fleets as well. The first, which included the battleship *Pelayo* and the armored cruisers *Emperador Carlos V* and *Princesa de Asturias* along with their auxiliaries, was in home waters when the war broke out. The second fleet—the one at St. Vincent—was commanded by Spain's foremost sailor, a graying, bearded officer of great dignity and well-earned reputation and ability. Admiral Pascual Cervera y Topete, Conde de Jerez, Marqués de Santa Ana, had spent forty-seven of his fifty-nine years in the Navy. As a sublieutenant he had got an introduction to war off the coast of Morocco, and later in the Sulu Islands and the Philippines gained valuable experience in operations involving his sovereign's most remote colony. "Competent" and "steady" was the way he was described from the very beginning, and a reputation for courage was added as a result of his efforts in defending a vital arsenal near Cadiz against the Federalists in 1873. He was no stranger to the Caribbean, having been on the West Indian station during the first Cuban revolt of 1868–78, and was entitled by a grateful government to wear the orders of Military and Naval Merit, Isabella la Católica, and of St. Hermingilde for his service during this and other campaigns. Before the war Premier Sagasta had chosen him to be his Minister of Marine, a post Cervera had resigned when his colleagues placed political expediency ahead of their nation's best interests and refused to support him on naval reforms. Now, ironically, he had been chosen to lead a squadron, which put him in a position to suffer most directly from these deficiencies, but as an old-fashioned patriot with perhaps just a suggestion of the martyr in his nature, he took over his duties without complaint. In March and April of 1898 his force of ships had assembled there at Cape Verde—the fast, 20-knot armored cruisers *María Teresa* and *Cristóbal Colón* sailing from Cadiz to rendezvous with the equally powerful *Viscaya* and *Almirante Oquendo* and the torpedo-boat destroyers *Plutón, Furor* and *Terror.*

It was a far from insignificant command, even for a man of Cervera's distinguished background; nonetheless the admiral couldn't help but be aware of the unpromising strategic picture. Since both the U.S. and Spanish navies had been separated into twin fleets of not unequal fighting power, it was obvious that neither nation could divide its forces and send one across the Atlantic without exposing it to the combined fleets of the other. His own position, then, was disturbingly clear. Since it was hardly a secret that the Caribbean would be a major theater of operations, there was every possibility that anything Spain sent to the West Indies would have to confront overwhelming American strength. It was a situation that might be inevitable, too, for if the United States decided on a blockade of Cuba to choke off supplies and reinforcements to the Spanish Army, she could effectively force Cervera's squadron to come to the aid of the besieged ports sooner or later.

At first Cervera had resisted any plan that might precipitate him into an immediate clash with the Americans. He had proposed to Madrid that he establish a base in the Canaries, where he would be in a position to pick his own time to venture into Cuban waters, and where he could flank the sea route to the mother country in the event the Americans were bold enough to make a transatlantic threat of their own. This recommendation had been signed by Cervera and by all his captains in turn, and within a general tone of dismay, we detect a note of desperation in the admiral's reply when he was nevertheless ordered to the Indies:

> It is impossible for me to give you an idea of the surprise and consternation experienced by all on the receipt of the order to sail. Indeed, that surprise is well justified, for nothing can be expected of this expedition except the total destruction of the fleet or its hasty and demoralized return. . . .[9]

And, two days later:

> I will try to sail tomorrow. . . . With a clear conscience I go to the sacrifice.

If a close look at the chessboard and the position of the pieces wasn't enough to bring about this defeatist attitude, a new reality the admiral had just been confronted with must have seemed to him the proverbial back-breaking straw. He had rendezvoused with the remainder of his squadron only to find the vessels totally unfit for combat! Three of his four cruisers were found to have defective breech mechanisms and no reliable ammunition for their 5.5-inch guns. The *Colón*, newest of the ships, didn't even have her main 10-inch battery mounted, and the bottom of the *Viscaya*, which had been long overdue for a lay-up, was so fouled her speed was cut drastically. He saw his one advantage—mobility—disappear in an undergrowth of barnacles.

True, Cervera had been aware of the *Colón*'s missing guns, and had repeatedly reminded—even begged—Madrid to install them, but nothing had been done, and at this late date nothing would or could be. Now, as if that weren't enough, difficulties with the other ships. The admiral was no faintheart; he was a thoroughly professional seaman, but he knew very well he had only a single high card left in the game. America's Atlantic coastal towns were in many cases as good as defenseless against an attack by sea. Because of this Commodore Schley's fleet, which had been hopefully named the "Flying Squadron," was being kept at or near its Hampton Roads base to protect them against a possible enemy sortie. The initiative therefore was still to a certain extent in the Spaniard's hands. As long as the fear remained that he might make a strike against the mainland of the United States, Schley must remain close by; once it had been determined definitely that Cervera's destination was the West Indies, the American could take his squadron south to join in the blockade of Cuba and to seek him out.

✷✷✷

Of course blockade in itself suggested a policy of attrition, to most Americans an uninspired way of fighting a war, and the troops who had been gathering at the hurriedly set-up concentration camps for training could have done with some inspiration. Chickamauga Park in Georgia, Mobile, Alabama, New Orleans and particularly Tampa, Florida, had been selected as bases for the marshaling and battle indoctrination of the Army, and though the enlistees seemed more than willing to take their places as "cleancut, well-oiled cogs," the concept of the trim fighting engine which would accommodate them thus far applied as little to the expeditionary force as it did to its new commander in chief. Sixtythree years old, a Civil War veteran of the battles of Fair Oaks, Nashville and Malvern Hill where he was cited for "most distinguished gallantry," he boasted thirty years' service in the Indian campaigns, a penchant for hard work, firm discipline, brusqueness, volatility of temper and violence of language. Young, trim and spare he was not, though the pure physical presence of Brigadier General William R. Shafter could hardly be denied. He was built along the lines of a Japanese *sumo* wrestler, a 300-pound colossus whose corpulent aspect might have been provided for the sole purpose of sweetening the careers of the political cartoonists and magazine staff artists.

They were in Tampa and the correspondents too, of course— drawn as much by the brilliant company as by the prospect of a shooting war. The sprawling Tampa Bay Hotel with its airy public rooms, its great verandas broad enough to accommodate a landau and pair, its flowers, comfortable wicker chairs and soft-padding waiters played host to a glittering array of notables who gathered to smoke cigars, swap stories of the last war with speculations on this one and sip gallons of iced tea to the music of regimental bands. It was certainly the place to be. John Jacob Astor, as the new assistant Inspector General, had checked in, complete with valet, and when asked why he had volunteered, told reporters: "I'm looking for adventure and I hope I'm setting an example." Clara Barton was there, representing the Red Cross, as was Captain Lee, the British military attaché, dashing in topee and puttees, Count von Goetzen, the Kaiser's representative, and of course Lieutenant Colonel Roosevelt, all smiles, teeth and enthusiasm, along with the university men and bushwhackers which the press had christened "Rough Riders" or "Teddy's Terrors." The meeting of old friends, the plans, the anticipations, the electricity in the atmosphere gave the whole scene the air of a Brussels ball on the eve of Waterloo.

In the sandy area just beyond the town thousands of men were encamped, with more every day jamming the trains on the single-rail spur that served Tampa. Most of them were regulars—"fine, strapping men" George Kennan of *Outlook* magazine thought them—with the careless, experienced air of long service in the field. They were used to living in the open and in that respect had no complaints about the Florida weather, not those who had just come from the Western plains, anyway. The old timers knew what to do to keep things livable, divvying up the bale of straw that was issued to each four-man tent, spreading their share on a poncho placed rubber side down on the ground and then covering the whole thing with a blanket. Snug and homey, it was. The food wasn't inspiring—sowbelly, hardtack and a few potatoes and peas—but each company had a big "Buzzacot oven," which was a kind of wash boiler set in an iron grill, and when all the comestibles were mixed together and cooked in it, the meal came out edible, at any rate. Of course there were snafus, as in armies everywhere, and even weathered veterans of the Indian Wars weren't above an occasional bellyache—like the time when one regiment found itself with no rations of any kind for three days—but then they agreed that could happen anywhere.

Naturally the people at home were eager for details, and the correspondent faction did its best to supply them. There was no real attempt made at censorship; General Shafter had put the responsibility for discretion on the newsmen themselves, and, odd as it seems, on the Western Union Telegraph Company. Most of the stories were laudatory enough. Richard Harding Davis wrote that the newly arriving volunteers were "as fine a looking body of soldiers as can be seen in any of the continental regiments," and Caspar Whitney of *Harper's Weekly* seconded him: ". . . for alertness—for dash, speed and accuracy in action—these United States troops seem to me to excel any thing I have ever seen . . ."

Some opinions were not so sanguine. Poultney Bigelow of the New York *Herald* and London *Times* had nothing but orchids for the American soldier and nothing but onions for the government planning that had set him down in Tampa. These new volunteers, he said, were not faring so well. "With the thermometer ninety-eight in the shade . . . the U.S. troops sweat night and day in their cowhide boots, thick flannel shirts and winter trousers." He condemned the camp diet with its lack of fresh fruit and vegetables which "brought on dysentery." [10] And in spite of the fact that he felt obliged to attack Bigelow's "un-American" criticisms, Davis' own private view was much the same. In a letter to his brother he admitted, "If I started to tell the truth at all . . . it would open up a hell of an outcry from all the families of the boys who have volunteered." [11]

There was more than one reason to account for the fact that things were not all they should be. The country was still in no real sense prepared for war; the organizational spark was as yet only sputtering, if that. Supply was a problem from the beginning. Men were coming in faster than the food and equipment to sustain them, a situation that war profiteers were quick to recognize and take advantage of. Torn tents, shoes that fell to pieces and barrels filled with the refuse of the Chicago and Kansas City packing houses began arriving by consignment at the Army commissaries. In one instance trainloads of meat had come in sealed in brightly painted tins. The contents, mostly gristle, fat and other throw-away products, had been canned for shipment to Asia during the Sino-Japanese War of 1894, and when hostilities had broken out with

Spain, the lots were retrieved from warehouses, the labels covered over with red barn paint and the whole of it foisted off on Shafter. The stuff had been salted with a powerful preservative to keep it from rotting away before the consumer's eyes, and the resulting "embalmed beef" scandal would drag many a name through the courts before it was done.

In general, inefficient and overcrowded facilities made Tampa a basically poor choice as a concentration area, for there was no provision for keeping a sizable body of men in this current kind of limbo for any period of time at all. The troops, their officers, the home front, the newspapers were all emotionally geared toward invasion with the least possible delay, and like invitees at a party waiting for the guest of honor to arrive, all were fidgeting and milling about until the Navy did what it had to do to insure the whole thing some kind of success.

When news did come from the Navy, it came from an unexpected quarter half a world away. Some had scarcely heard of the Philippine Islands, and many could never have pointed to Manila Bay on a map, even though there was a general awareness that the U.S. Navy had traditionally maintained an Asiatic squadron in the Pacific for protection of American interests and nationals. The Orient, and the possibilities that part of the world offered to an expansion-minded power, had not been overlooked by Washington policy makers, however. When the Asiatic command fell vacant late in 1897, Assistant Secretary of the Navy Theodore Roosevelt saw an opportunity to fill it with a man of his choice whose combative nature and ambition would be in no way a liability in the event of war with Spain, nor a constraint on any designs we might develop on that country's Far Eastern possessions. His nominee was Commodore George Dewey, who not only agreed with Roosevelt that such a showdown with the Spaniards was inevitable, but who harbored strong hopes that his reputation might be made in that part of the world when it did come.

The press, fascinated by the idea of a martial adventure 10,000 miles away, had kept tabs on Dewey during the last hectic weeks of peace, and knew that, just after the *Maine* disaster, he had sailed for Hong Kong with his squadron of four protected cruisers and two gunboats. They knew too that, when war was declared, he had hoisted anchor and disappeared into the vast reaches of the Pacific, and word of his whereabouts had vanished with him. The public was informed the commodore had sailed for Manila, but as for what might happen there—whether he could or would capture the city and/or could or would demolish Spain's own Asiatic squadron which was believed to be nearby—it was anybody's guess.

Finally on May 2 the first legitimate Dewey news had come from Madrid itself via London. It came in fragments and was a little incoherent, but from it the American papers were able to deduce that he had found and engaged the Spanish ships and had won some sort of victory, in all likelihood a decisive one. Without waiting for confirmation or details the nation reacted with an effusive celebration while official Washington sweated out a somewhat anxious waiting period. (The cable from Manila had been cut and no corroboration of anything was forthcoming.)

It was not until May 7, a week after the event had taken place, that the full story finally came over the wire from Hong Kong. What had happened exceeded the most optimistic expectations. Dewey in his flagship *Olympia*, along with the protected cruisers *Baltimore*, *Raleigh* and *Boston*, had sailed for the Philippine capital on April 26, arriving off the coast of Luzon four days later, on the evening of the 30th. It was decided to take advantage of a moonless night and enter Manila Bay immediately, running the forts of Corregidor in the dark and steaming at reduced speed to bring his squadron just off the city at daybreak. All went well—he glided past the dark mass of the island without mishap—and in his first look through the glass, when it was light enough to see, he could make out the hulls of the Spanish vessels—four protected cruisers similar to his own—lying at anchor under the batteries of the Cavite forts where their commander, Admiral Montojo, had elected to do battle.

Closing to an effective range of 5,000 yards, Dewey gave the well-remembered order to the flagship's Captain Gridley to open fire when he was ready; and the *Olympia* passed along the front of the Spanish line, with the rest of his squadron in column astern.

Each ship gave the enemy a broadside as she went by. The fleet came about and passed again, guns thundering steadily, as fast as their crews could load. For two hours and five minutes the exchange continued, with the targets on both sides almost completely obscured by thick clouds of black-powder smoke. When Dewey broke off the action in answer to a report that his ammunition was running low, the pall cleared, and he saw to his astonishment that the Spaniards were conclusively *hors de combat*. Every ship in the enemy squadron was afire or in a sinking condition; the harbor was a scene of wholly unexpected devastation, for the commodore had been largely unaware of the execution his guns had been doing.[12] It was found later that the Spanish had suffered 381 casualties among crews totaling 1,200 men. The American ships had been hit too, and their losses were the most astounding of all—eight men slightly wounded and one dead. Of heatstroke.

The rejoicing had been justified after all, though not everyone was able to participate fully. Back at Hampton Roads, the good-humored and sociable Commodore Schley and his command were on hand only for a few days to join in the latest jingle—"How Did Dewey Do It?"; become convivial on the Dewey Cocktail—Dewar's Scotch whisky, brandy, benedictine, syrup and a dash of bitters; or stay healthy with the laxative that had been named after him ("the salt of salts," the advertisement said). A message arrived for Schley, a confidential wire that sent signal flags running to the mastheads of the Flying Squadron, which had been kept coaled and with part steam up for weeks. It was the one he'd been waiting for, and he lost no time in complying. One day he was there, bantering with friends ashore, charming the belles of Norfolk with his lively conversation at cotillion or barbecue, and the next he and his ships were gone.

*** ✳

Admiral Sampson's blockade of Havana had been levied almost as a matter of course, for it was as yet the only warlike gesture the United States' armed forces were able to make in the Caribbean. Originally he had hoped to force the surrender of the city by a direct attack on its fortifications, but this had been discouraged by the Navy Department, which didn't look with favor on a gun duel with the enemy batteries, and which was all too aware that no occupying troops were available anyway. Sampson had therefore contented himself with maintaining a cordon of warships around the approaches, and seizing any small vessels that came within his reach. These, in the terminology of the Navy, were still classed as "prizes of war"; the booty—ships and cargoes both—were sold and the prize money divided, half going to the U.S. government and the remainder being portioned out between the fleet commander and the officers and men of the vessel responsible for the capture, according to rank or rate. It might have been an anachronism from John Paul Jones' day, but at least it kept blockade duty from becoming too onerous.

Of course it was still mere nit picking, and no one was more relieved than Sampson when the Department got a report on April 29 that Admiral Cervera, with four cruisers and three torpedo-boat destroyers, had sailed from St. Vincent—course: westward; destination: apparently the Greater Antilles. From his probable speed it was estimated he would arrive in West Indian waters on or about May 8. It was also supposed, and correctly, that he would be short of fuel after the 2,700-mile trip and would be forced to seek a port where he could first replenish his bunkers before establishing a base of operations. (It would be a forward stride of great strategic importance as well as convenience when the first capital ships with oil-burning engines began to appear during the first World War. Not only was coaling ship a top-priority task that tied up all hands until was finished, but the rate at which the fireboxes consumed the stuff made it necessary to arrange for a source of supply, either from shore station or collier, within a vessel's operating area. At 16 knots a battleship burned up ten tons an hour, and the Atlantic passage would invariably leave reserves dangerously low.) Cervera would have to drop anchor somewhere, and if one assumed his intelligence was keeping him abreast of American fleet movements, it seemed a safe bet that he would pick the Spanish port of San Juan on the northern coast of Puerto Rico for his purpose.

Such was the Navy Department's and Sampson's guess, at any

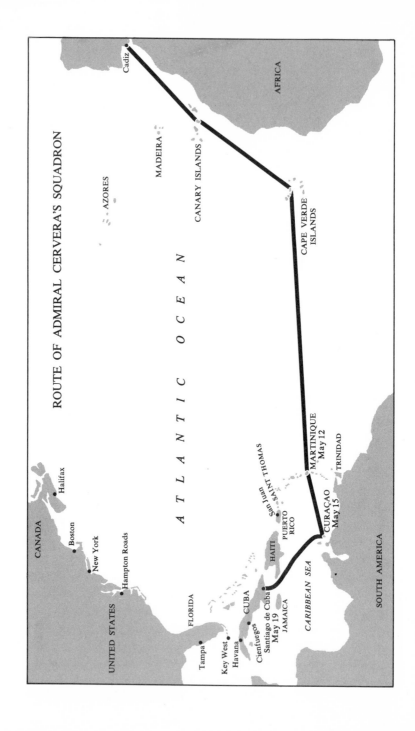

ROUTE OF ADMIRAL CERVERA'S SQUADRON

rate, and it isn't difficult to imagine the latter's crushing disappointment when, after a long and frustrating "surprise dash" from Havana, the morning sun of May 12 revealed an empty harbor to the *New York*'s anxious lookouts. Cervera was not there. Sampson assuaged his disappointment by bombarding the forts for a couple of hours, then broke off the action and headed back to his blockade. He had wasted a lot of time—eight days to make the 1,130-mile trip, towing his cumbersome monitors all the way—and now, nothing.[13] If the Spaniard was not at San Juan, he might be anywhere in the Caribbean, might, in fact, be falling at that moment upon the few weak ships that had been left guarding Havana.

Where, actually, was the *almirante*? Cervera had left St. Vincent under orders to make for the West Indies, but he was given complete freedom of action on what route to take, what port to put into and whether or not he would do battle on the way. He had sent the torpedo boat *Furor* ahead to bring back information on the whereabouts of the American fleet, and in this way he learned first that most of Admiral Sampson's squadron was still patrolling the western part of Cuba from Cárdenas to Cienfuegos; second, that a number of Sampson's big ships, including the admiral's own flagship, were off Puerto Rico, and finally that the port of Santiago was still free from blockade.

Coal was the first and major problem and he must face it without delay. Accordingly he first put into Fort de France, Martinique, and then the Dutch island of Curaçao, but to his dismay the Spanish collier which he had expected to meet at one or the other of these places was nowhere to be seen. Several coal ships had in fact been sent to San Juan and to other Caribbean ports, but bad timing prevented any of them from reaching Cervera's needy squadron. It was a serious disappointment, but he still had several choices as to his next move. Assuming that Sampson had already left San Juan, Cervera still had enough coal to double back there (555 miles), or he might try to make it to Cienfuegos (1,030 miles), a good port on the southern coast of Cuba in direct rail communication with Havana; or he might sail directly for Santiago de Cuba (720 miles), the nearest fortified harbor. The Americans, after all, would have to make allowance for all these possibilities, and with a little luck he might avoid them altogether.

It was something to hope for, but even now the net was starting to tighten. If the Navy Department was still in the dark as to his plans and his straitened condition, Cervera had at least tipped his hand by appearing at Curaçao, and there was no doubt now about his general location. On May 15, as he was returning from San Juan to the Havana blockade, Sampson received official word of the Spaniard's arrival at the Dutch island, and was at the same time notified that Commodore Schley and the Flying Squadron had been ordered to Key West. Sampson was to join him there.

✳✳✳

Had the naval battle of Santiago ended in an American defeat, or, what would be much more likely, the chance had been muffed for an overwhelming triumph, that initial meeting between Sampson and Schley aboard the *New York* would have been endowed with greater significance. "Ah," the observer would say, "enter the two dramatis personae, the man of thought and the man of action, already working at cross-purposes." As it was, the famous Sampson-Schley controversy began with no more dissonance than might be expected from two men of totally contrary temperaments facing a single problem, upon whose solution the future reputation of both would depend.

There were two distinguished careers to safeguard, for both were first-class sailors—hard-working, competent and successful—and noted, too, for reasoning and coming to conclusions in their own particular way. This they demonstrated by immediately disagreeing on where Cervera and the enemy squadron were apt to be found. The admiral thought that all the facts pointed to Santiago, while the commodore went along with the Navy Department view that the Spaniards were more likely to be at Cienfuegos, and as events turned out, Sampson could have avoided much future hard feeling if he'd pressed his arguments more strongly. As it was, he yielded to Washington and to his junior, Schley. That question of their respective ranks was a sensitive one. Another man might have been rather embarrassed about it—Sampson had been elevated to the

command above Schley's and many other heads as well—and
though his own self-esteem kept this from being the case, he may
have felt a bit reluctant to "sit on" Schley so soon.

It mustn't be assumed the two men were strangers—only a year
had separated them at the Naval Academy—but they were worlds
apart in almost every other respect. Sampson had carried with him
to Annapolis a dour and diligent legacy from his Scotch-Irish im-
migrant parents, which took the serious-minded and aloof young
man to the head of his class and kept him there for three years.
Salt water, though, didn't seem to flow in his veins. His was a
scientific bent, his passion the technological problems of naval
warfare—armor, explosives, the precision machinery that may have
seemed so much like the workings of his own mind. By professional-
officer standards of the time he was a consummate scholar. He was
pleased when he was put in charge of the academy's new department of physics and chemistry, and when duty made it necessary
to move on, served just as tirelessly as chief of the Bureau of Ordnance, immersing himself in the questions of smokeless powder,
face-hardened steels, and the other scientific aspects of war at sea
which he felt navies of the future must concentrate upon. Now
age had grayed his beard and given him dignity, and humorless
hard work had turned down the outer corners of his eyes and
mouth so that he looked somewhat like the sad tragedy mask in a
theater playbill.

Perhaps beneath it all he resented the admiration of his colleagues for the record of Winfield Scott Schley, whose life of
action paralleled his outgoing temperament as closely as Sampson's
bookish studiousness mirrored his own career. Unlike Sampson,
the famous general's namesake was no student; in fact young Schley
had just missed bringing up the bottom of his class. The two men
had become well acquainted for the first time during the early
part of the Civil War when they had served together as young
officers aboard the forty-year-old sailing frigate *Potomac*; and back
then Schley, who was graduated with an earlier class, had been
Sampson's superior. From then on their careers diverged. Schley
got his fiery baptism with Farragut in the lower Mississippi, and
even after the war, when action was harder to seek out, managed

to distinguish himself in Korea as a member of the 1871 landing party that stormed the pirate forts there. He continued to make headlines when he led the rescue mission sent to find the Arctic explorer, Lieutenant Greely, and later as captain of the cruiser *Baltimore* in 1891 on the occasion of the famous incident at Valparaiso when the ship's crew was mobbed by the populace. Schley had also grown older in his country's service, but one of his most distinguishing characteristics was the network of crow's-feet laugh wrinkles at his eyes. He seemed to embrace life and sociability, and to all intent nothing he had seen in his long experience dimmed his enthusiasm for either.

As might be expected, the personality and career differences between the commanders—each of whom had proved of great value in his own right to the budding American Navy—were instrumental in fostering two totally dissimilar sets of admirers, who were now watching eagerly to see how the test of war might measure the cerebral preciseness of a Sampson on the one hand, the damn-the-torpedoes-flank-speed methods of a Schley on the other.

Had things taken a different course, the ultimate dispute between the two camps might have had more dramatic import. As it was the whole expectation of a single decisive naval engagement in the Caribbean hung on a very big question mark; an enemy must first be found. Three of the battleships and some auxiliary vessels were to accompany Schley's armored cruiser *Brooklyn* on its search mission to Cienfuegos, while Sampson kept for himself another battleship, a cruiser and his sluggish monitors to watch Key West and Havana. Sampson himself had hopes—perhaps he'd been wrong in his guess that Cervera would choose Santiago to refuel—and though Schley's sortie had to be classed as logically questionable, the memory of Dewey's triumph was fresh in his and a lot of other people's minds. A strong undercurrent of anticipation ran through the fleet. Stephen Crane, sitting on the stern of the New York *World*'s press tugboat, caught the feeling aroused by the commodore's departure and put it into words the people at home could appreciate: "Now in progress is a huge game, with wide and lonely stretches of ocean as the board, and with the great steel ships as counters.... The Spaniard made the first move. He played his fleet plump in the middle of the board, and he watches eagerly to see if our next move is a blunder." [14]

The Flying Squadron made the 570-mile trip in good time and arrived off Cienfuegos at about midnight on May 21–22 with great expectations. Even before it was light enough to distinguish anything, all eyes were searching the harbor but unfortunately, because of the low hills flanking the entrance, it was impossible to get a total view; the men in the tops shouted down that all they could see were a few ships' masts and some mysterious, unidentified columns of smoke. Most of the officers in the squadron were convinced that Cervera was not there. Schley was just as convinced that he was.

As luck would have it, scarcely had the *Brooklyn*'s tops disappeared over the horizon than a messenger brought Sampson a top-secret report telling him the Spaniards had just been seen putting in to Santiago. The whole thing seemed to call for caution— Sampson had got erroneous information in this manner before—but when subsequent cables arrived verifying the first, he knew it might be a grave mistake to wait on the matter. A small fast dispatch boat was sent off immediately to try to catch Schley with the following message:

> Spanish squadron probably at Santiago de Cuba. Four ships and three torpedo boat destroyers. If you are satisfied that they are not at Cienfuegos, proceed with all dispatch, but cautiously to Santiago de Cuba, and, if the enemy is there, blockade him in port.[15]

The wording of this order was a little vague and to Schley's way of thinking it gave him a good deal of latitude, for he was not at all satisfied that he didn't have Cervera bottled up there at Cienfuegos; there were those masts and that smoke. He remained on blockade, steaming slowly back and forth across the harbor entrance, trying to see past a small neck of land that blocked the view inside, while Sampson in Key West began to wonder at first, then grow more and more concerned over getting no word that the squadron had got underway. On the 24th a vessel hailed the *Brooklyn* with another message from Sampson directing Schley in fewer and more cogent terms to make for Santiago with no delay.

The captain of the dispatch boat was surprised that Schley had not been in contact with the Cuban insurgents ashore at Cienfuegos, who had in fact been flashing him signals by light for the past three nights. The Cubans had been trying to tell him that the Spanish weren't there. Upon hearing this, the commodore's frustration and normally volatile temper got the better of him. "He stamped up and down the deck," one of the correspondents writes, "twitching nervously at his little imperial, and grinding his heels savagely down on the deck." He sailed immediately for Santiago, 370 miles distant, and arrived there on May 26.

As he drew within sight of the lofty green hills which rose near the harbor mouth, he met three patrolling American scout ships who told him when questioned that they had no knowledge of a Spanish squadron inside at all. At this point anger, or righteous indignation, or just plain bullheadedness took hold of Schley, for without investigating any further he decided the blockade of Santiago could go to the devil, he was heading for Key West. Not many in his own wardroom would have ventured to guess what their commander was bent on, and the general dismay increased the following day when the squadron—now on course for Florida—met a ship bearing a plea from a plainly baffled and concerned Washington: "All Department's information indicates Spanish division still at Santiago. The Department looks to you to ascertain facts, and that if the enemy is therein, does not leave without a decisive action." [16]

Schley's reply to this was historic, to say the least. His champions have excused it with the explanation that he had become overly obsessed with coal during the weeks that he'd been forced to keep his ships fully fueled and ready to sail at a moment's notice. Even so it shows an inexplicable turn of mind. It is true that the seas were high and his bunkers low and that the disabled collier *Merrimac*, laid up with engine trouble, could not accommodate him, but his determination to home in for Key West seems not only peculiar but peculiarly out of character. "Much to be regretted," he told his anxious superiors, "cannot obey orders of Department. Have striven earnestly; forced to proceed for coal to Key West by way of Yucatan passage. Cannot ascertain anything positive respecting enemy." [17]

Had he faced a different foe, one more able and inclined to take advantage of his uncertainties and procrastinations, Schley's behavior might have been calamitous; as it was, it was merely incomprehensible. Almost frantically, Secretary of the Navy Long sent off a telegram directing him *not* to leave the Santiago area—sent it off "with utmost urgency" written across it.

Fortunately its delivery wasn't necessary. On the 27th the heavy seas outside Santiago began to subside and with them, apparently, Schley's strange and querulous attitude. The collier *Merrimac* reported repairs completed and the ability to begin coaling ships once more, and in the reflection of calm water the commodore's telegram to Washington may have begun to seem petulant even to him, for he came about and put his bows for Santiago again. He arrived on the morning of May 29 and the first thing he saw, moored right across the harbor entrance, was the clear outline of Admiral Cervera's newest cruiser, the *Cristóbal Colón*—serene, new-bright with paint and with her awnings spread, as if in welcome.

***

****

CHAPTER III

Courage and Confusion

Santiago Bay and harbor is shaped like a golf-course fairway some five miles long, with a dog-leg to the right about a third of the way in, and with the city of Santiago, capital of the province of the same name, located on the east side of the head of the inlet, where the green would be. Ships enter through a meandering constricted channel, varying from 350 to 450 feet in width, and flanked on either hand by steep bluffs. In 1898 the right side of the entrance was dominated by Morro Castle, a big, crenellated stone pile dating from the sixteenth century, which looked down from a rocky point 260 feet above sea level. A few yards from the castle, on the very crest of the peak, was a more modern fortification known as the Morro battery, and across the way, occupying the heights on the opposite side, was a similar strong point—the Socapa battery. A ship making its way up the channel had to pass two more redoubts, the Estrella on the south and opposite it the Lower Socapa, and then, about a mile from the Morro, the Punta Gorda battery, which was the final barrier before entering the harbor proper.

Commodore Schley had no real information as to the effectiveness of these defenses; for all he knew they might even have been as strong as those at Havana, which naval intelligence had reported as being both up-to-date and formidable. It seemed wise to assume the Spaniards had mounted additional guns on the outbreak of war, and in fact the past two months had seen gangs of local *trabajadores* preparing new emplacements for two modern 6-inch howitzers, two 3.5-inch Krupp guns, four Hontoria 6.3-inch guns taken from the disabled cruiser *Reina Mercedes* which was lying in the harbor, along with four 1.5-inch quick-firing cannon and a couple of Nordenfeldt machine guns from the same ship.

What might be waiting from him in those green but grim hills bothered Schley, who couldn't make up his mind whether or not to hold off till Sampson and the rest of the big ships came, and two days went by before he decided to risk a shot or two at the beautiful target that lay tied up in plain sight just within the harbor. By then he'd decided it would seem strange if he didn't make some attempt to engage the Spaniard, so he ordered battle stations and made two runs past the mouth of the bay. His flagship *Brooklyn*, followed by the battleships *Texas* and *Iowa* and the cruiser *New Orleans*, steamed by, trying to range in on the anchored *Cristóbal Colón* and on the seaward shore batteries as well from a rather distant 7,000 yards away. The fire was returned briskly, both from the Spanish cruiser and from the shore, but it was all sound and fury, for Schley was too far out and neither side hit anything. It was the only chance he would have. The next morning the *Colón* had disappeared behind the headlands, and later that day Admiral Sampson in the *New York*, with the battleships *Indiana* and *Oregon* with him, arrived from Key West, met with Schley for a short briefing on the situation and took over command of the blockade.

It must have seemed tempting to Sampson, stepping into the picture when he did, to consider the job already well in hand. There appeared to be no real need to force battle with Cervera's trapped squadron; what purpose would it serve to expose his fleet to the unknown strength of the enemy forts, the electrical mines which his spies had told him were sowed in the harbor, or the punishment the hostile cruisers would be able to give his ships as they slowly entered the narrow mouth one by one? Spanish naval power was now, after all, immobilized; it could no longer take the offensive against the United States, nor could it supply or reinforce the Cuban garrison.

Many men would have reasoned thus, yet Sampson was a scientist, well versed in the laws of probability, and had built a long and successful career in thinking like one. This was not Charleston in the blockade of 1897. It was Cuba with the hurricane season waiting somewhere in the rim of dark clouds on the horizon, and if the odds were long that a storm would hit soon—weather severe enough to scatter his squadron and allow Cervera to escape—the possibility still did exist.

To seal the enemy's exit, then, would make doubly sure, and the narrowness of the Santiago channel, if something could be found to obstruct it at its most confined point, made such a plan not only feasible but irresistible. In fact even before the hostile fleet's presence had been definitely confirmed, Sampson had mulled over the idea of using the old collier *Merrimac*, whose unreliability thus far had caused so many headaches, as a blockship in some way. He wasn't sure just how, though. It was then that he called in one of his junior officers, gave him the problem's ingredients—the 350-foot width of the channel, the 333-foot length of the *Merrimac* —and left him to come up with some way by which the two might be matched.

Lieutenant Richmond Pearson Hobson was a thirty-eight-year-old Annapolis graduate who held the now-obsolete rank of assistant navy constructor, and who was officially aboard the *New York* to check the behavior at sea of certain structural alterations in the ship's design. He was bright and reliable. What was most important he had a certain far-reaching imagination that extended beyond his workaday involvement with bulkheads, stanchions and watertight integrity. Hobson's first plan, an audacious one, took shape quickly, inspired as it was by the news that the whole enemy squadron was definitely in the harbor. The *Merrimac* was a collier; very well, she would be a Spanish one. She would disguise herself as one of the coal ships sent out from Spain which had been trying to locate Cervera; she would steam into the entrance of the bay one evening after dark, with American patrol boats pursuing and firing upon her to make it seem as much like the real thing as possible. Running at full speed down the channel, whistle shrieking, and with her searchlight illuminating a false Spanish ensign at her masthead, she might be able to fool the enemy long enough to reach the narrow bottleneck of the passage, where she would then blow herself up and "push in the cork."

It would be a splendid dash. Unfortunately its circusy aspects didn't appeal to Sampson. The way into the harbor was too narrow and treacherous, and an unfamiliar crew would never be able to negotiate it in the dark even if the ruse worked. The admiral favored a stealthier approach which, he hoped, would accomplish something besides piling the *Merrimac* upon the rocks. Hobson then came up with a counter suggestion. The collier would head for the harbor entrance at full speed, yes, but would then stop engines; soon enough so that her momentum would let her glide past and inside the Morro batteries without being noticed. When she had got as far as Estrella Point, where the channel was narrowest, both bow and stern anchors would be let go, her sea valves would be opened, torpedoes below her waterline set off to aid the process, and she would sink, the lieutenant hoped, in something like a minute's time.

Sampson thought this scheme stood a good chance and agreed to give it a try. Hobson would be in command and would take the blockship in. From the hundreds who volunteered, three coxswains, a machinist, a watertender, a gunner's mate, a chief master-at-arms, a boatswain's mate and four seamen from the various ships in the blockade were picked to be his crew; picked quickly and without fanfare, for it was found that the conditions for success—a high tide combined with complete darkness—would be present only on the early morning of June 2 during a 90-minute period between the time the moon set and the sun rose. That left barely twelve hours for preparations, and these proceeded frantically and with almost a suggestion of contrived comedy. First stokers were sent down to unload the coal in the port side of the *Merrimac*'s hull so that the torpedoes which were attached there would have more effect. They misunderstood orders and simply shifted it to the starboard side, heeling the ship over. The torpedoes themselves—ten homemade ones put together from powder charges for 8-inch guns—were supposed to use electric primers, and at the last minute it was found there wasn't a single hand generator in the whole fleet to fire them with. Batteries had to be obtained and hooked up instead. Then as Sampson left the *Merrimac* early the next morning after wishing Hobson luck, the propeller of his launch became fouled in one of her lines and thirty minutes were wasted untangling the mess. Next the lifeboat being towed behind the collier to be used (it was hoped) by her crew after the scuttling parted its line and more time was lost. Finally Sampson ruled it was too near daylight and called the whole thing off, agreeing, when pressed, to let Hobson try again the following night.

The crew boarded the collier once again just before sundown on the evening of June 2, and found to their wholesale exasperation that somehow three of the torpedo firing circuits had become unworkable and would have to be replaced. Hobson had already asked Sampson for permission to reinforce the charges with 200 pounds of guncotton but the admiral, getting testy himself over all the delay, refused, saying it "would blow everything to the devil." Then, unbelievably, Hobson went through his check list and found everything was ready. For the second time he got underway, the *Merrimac's* engines turning over with a throb that seemed to carry for miles in the stillness, the old ship making what speed she could toward the narrow V of slightly lighter sky which was flanked by the masses of black cliff.

It was dark, but not dark enough, and as the steep heights of El Morro loomed larger, the little crew's brief respite from bad luck ended in a flash—or more accurately, three flashes. With still 500 yards to go, the collier's silhouette was spotted by a Spanish picket boat, hailed, and then fired upon once, then twice again. Geysers of water went up a stone's throw behind her. There was no need for stealth now, and Hobson continued at full speed through the "gate" between the hills, hoping that, if he stayed in the middle of the channel, he wouldn't hit the banks. All the batteries seemed to be alert in no time, and as the big guns on shore opened up, one after another, he quickly gave the order to stop engines, praying he'd be able to swing his stern around and sink her in position. As it developed he could not. The *Merrimac* refused to answer her helm, and as she continued straight down the passage, he realized his steering gear must be jammed or carried away. He abandoned all ideas of trying to scuttle the collier broadside; with no control his only chance was to blow her up immediately and hope for the best, before his momentum took him into a wider part of the channel. He let go the bow anchor and ordered the torpedoes exploded, cursing in his quaintly mild way when only two went off. The battery cells of the remaining charges had been knocked out. Frantically he ordered the stern anchor let go but it had been shot away; then the bow anchor parted under the strain and the *Merrimac* drifted onward, taking in water in great gulps through her holed hull and revolving lazily at the whim of the current. A crash at the bow and a crunch of bottom plates brought everything to a stop, and it was with a feeling of genuine relief that Hobson realized he had struck a mine and was aground off Estrella Point.

"It looks," said Captain "Fighting Bob" Evans, watching from the *Iowa*'s bridge, "like hell with the lid off!" and on the spot it might as well have been. Sporadic orange and yellow flashes from the batteries on both sides of the channel outlined the hills as every Spanish gun that would bear concentrated on the helpless American vessel at near point-blank range. Hobson and his crew stretched full length on the deck, listening to the detonations bound from cliff to cliff—the intervals between the rolling booms filled by the sharp pop of the rapid-fire guns and the crack of Mauser bullets over their heads—and waited for the end. It came for the old *Merrimac* in the form of two torpedoes from the *Reina Mercedes* and two more from the destroyer *Plutón*, which lifted her off the rocks and back into the channel and flung Hobson and his crew overboard. In another minute she was on the bottom, right side up, with only her masts and funnel top showing above the surface. True to form she was contrary to the end, picking a spot to go down where the channel had begun to widen and leaving adequate room for the passage of ships.

A small life raft that had been lashed to the deck bobbed up alongside, and soon it was full of men—drenched, deafened, but amazingly alive, and wondering how it was that they possibly could be. If the sun came up, one joked, it would be positive proof that this wasn't Hades, and so they drifted silently on the calm waters of Santiago Bay, long after the guns stopped firing while boats of Spanish sailors with lanterns rowed about looking for them, and until the sky grew light in the east. It was then that a launch drew up, bearing a squad of enemy marines and no less a personage than Admiral Cervera himself, and Lieutenant Hobson, determined to surrender to a "responsible officer," hailed it and delivered himself and all his little crew, one of which had suffered a cut lip and another a scratched leg, as prisoners of the Queen Regent of Spain.

Cervera sent word of their rescue to the *New York*, the newspapers played the story under four-column heads, and America had her first strictly personal heroes.

***

To Washington the news that the "phantom" Spaniards had been run to ground and perhaps trapped had the effect of opening the safety valve on an overheated boiler. The War Department could hardly ignore the fact that Dewey's bloodless triumph at Manila and now Hobson's imaginative feat was giving the whole show to the Navy. If indications were true that enemy seapower in the hemisphere was now neutralized by Sampson's blockade, then it was time for the Army to move. General Shafter's only belligerent act so far had been an attempt to land arms on the coast for the insurgents from an old paddle-wheel river steamer, and that had failed because no Cubans were there to receive them. Now he needed a few successes of his own.

For some time General Commanding the Army Nelson A. Miles had favored an attack on Puerto Rico, which was considered to be the soft underbelly of the Spanish Caribbean empire and a safer introduction to war for the untried American troops than a confrontation with the enemy's main army in Cuba would be. Only after the men were acclimated and learned through mopping-up operations what it meant to be shot at, would he land a big force of cavalry and artillery on the eastern end of Cuba and join hands with the insurgents in a guerrilla-type advance through the length of the island. In so doing he would simultaneously roll up and grind down the opposition while the great mass of American volunteers were put ashore for a direct assault on Havana.

The plan seemed to make sense as long as Cervera's squadron

Tampa

FLORIDA

ATLANTIC OCEAN

GULF OF MEXICO

BAHAMA ISLANDS

Key West

Havana
LA HABANA
Matanzas
Cardenas
MATANZAS
PINAR DEL RIO
Pinar del Río
SANTA
CLARA
Santa Clara
Cienfuegos
Bahama Sea Passage

Yucatan Passage

PUERTO
PRINCIPE
Puerto Principe
Holguín
SANTIAGO
DE CUBA
Manzanillo
SIERRA MAESTRA
MTS.
Baracoa
Santiago de Cuba

Windward Passage

HAITI

JAMAICA

CUBA

MILES
0   200

CARIBBEAN SEA

SANTIAGO   DE   CUBA

San Luís

Guantánamo

El Cobre
SIERRA MAESTRA MTS.
El Caney
Santiago de Cuba
Guaicabón
Las Guasimas
Siboney
Caimanera
Cabañas Bay
Fort Aguadores
Daiquirí
Guantánamo Bay

MILES
0   25

was a worrisome unknown, but now the situation was changed. If the Spanish admiral was at Santiago, what would prevent an invasion force from detouring on its way to Puerto Rico and helping Sampson either to drive the enemy ships to the open sea or to force his way in after them? It was the first time Santiago had been brought up in connection with the Army, but a joint and quick military-naval *coup de main* was an intriguing possibility that appealed both to McKinley and the War Department. Their almost immediate assent to Miles's new suggestion was an example of the precipitate way in which decisions could be made at the time. On May 30, just one day after the arrival of Schley's report that the *Colón* had been sighted, a cipher wire was dashed off to Shafter in Tampa:

> You are directed to take your command on transports, proceed under convoy of the navy to the vicinity of Santiago de Cuba, land your force at such place east or west of that point as your judgment may dictate, under the protection of the navy . . . to capture or destroy the garrison there, and . . . with the aid of the navy capture or destroy the Spanish fleet now reported to be in Santiago harbor. . . . When will you sail? [1]

Even after he had got over his surprise at the suddenness of the directive, it would have been hard for Shafter to venture a guess. Only four days earlier orders had come to get ready to begin loading 25,000 men and their equipment on transports, by which he assumed the War Department must mean the queer assortment of chartered vessels that had been collecting at Tampa ever since April. Shafter had watched their arrival, one by one, and collectively they made an unprepossessing armada at best. The appropriation act of March 9 had stipulated that none of the $50 million allotted for national defense could be used for the purchase or hire of troop transports until war was declared. When it became possible to arrange for them, the best ships had already been taken over by the Navy as auxiliary cruisers, and the Army had to haggle for what was left. Secretary Alger finally obtained the services of thirty-two old one-stacker coastal steamers—some sidewheelers among them—and in order to get even these the government had been forced to promise the owners two to three times normal freight rates. A few had accommodations for passengers, but these had been stripped of all luxuries and comforts, even down to the towels and table and bed linen. Now workmen were refitting them with bunks for troops and stalls for horses and mules, but they still weren't ready to take on supplies.

The peremptory wording of the order reflected official impatience, however, and now as he began to expedite a general embarkation which Washington apparently thought could be accomplished in a day or two, Shafter and his officers found themselves at the center of a frenetic muddle. The troops milled about aimlessly and the ships' cargo nets, which should have been swinging the expedition's supplies aboard, hung idle and empty. There was nothing to fill them with. Most of the Army's stores were still in some three hundred boxcars scattered all over the general Tampa area, invoices were nonexistent, and now small but determined detachments of men with crowbars marched out to the freight yards with orders to smash locks and unload ammunition, sacks of beans, tent poles and mule harness. Soon the single pier at Tampa was piled high with all the paraphernalia 25,000 soldiers might ever need or want for a campaign in the tropics. This was the way it was stowed, too—in the first hold of the first ship to come alongside.

One day went by. Two. Three. And the single track of railroad stretching from the town to the embarkation area was clogged twenty-four hours round the clock with the masses of material and the continued arrival of new volunteer troops. Impatience was coming to a head, both in Washington and on the scene. "When will you leave?" wired the War Department. "Answer at once." And Colonel Roosevelt wrote with some asperity in his diary: "Worst confusion yet...A breakdown of both the railroad and military system of the country."

By Tuesday the 7th the loading was still trying to proceed, spurred on by increasingly goading telegrams from one quarter and another. Admiral Sampson, patrolling off Santiago, grew caustic: "If 10,000 men were here city and fleet would be ours within twenty-four hours. Every consideration demands immediate Army movement"; and at regular intervals from Capitol Hill:

"Time is the essence of the situation," and "Early departure of first importance," and finally "President directs you to sail at once with what force you have ready." [2] It was the exasperated and imperative tone a schoolteacher might take with a pigheaded pupil and Washington was getting resigned to using it. What a war! Schley requiring one entreaty after another to persuade him to stay near the enemy; now Shafter, unable to get the American Army on board ships.

The harried commanders had given up on all ideas of embarking the men by the numbers. When it was discovered the transport fleet would only be able to carry eighteen or twenty thousand troops instead of the planned twenty-five, they simply passed the word to the waiting regiments that the expedition was going to sail at daybreak on the 8th and whoever was on board then would go with it. The eighty-nine correspondents and artists at the Tampa Bay hotel were told to board the headquarters ship *Segurança* at two o'clock in the morning. "For the next few hours," wrote William Dinwiddie of the Washington *Star*, "... a motley assembly scurried through the hotel in canvas hunting suits, in white ducks, in the brown fatigue clothes of the army, and even in immaculate shirt front and patent leathers. Six-shooters, machetes and belts full of ammunition circulated through the halls ... along with canteens, rolls of blankets, binoculars, kodaks and pouches filled with notebooks. ..." [3]

Among the troops there was a wild rush for the gangplanks, with assignments to ships counting less than the ability to establish and hold possession by occupancy. Colonel Roosevelt and the Rough Riders were billeted on the *Yucatan*, and when he found out the same vessel had also been allotted to the Second Infantry and the Seventy-First New York Volunteers, he got down to the dock fast with some of his burlier buckaroos.

"That's our ship," said a captain from the Seventy-First, stepping up with a paper in his hand.

"Do tell," replied Roosevelt, showing all his teeth. "Well, we seem to have it now." His two chargers, Rain-in-the-Face and Little Texas, had just been got safely aboard, and from now to Cuba it was every man for himself.

It was the largest military expedition that had ever left the United States. With Shafter (now a major general) were Brigadier Generals J. F. Kent and H. W. Lawton as infantry commanders, and Major General Joseph P. ("Fighting Joe") Wheeler, a notable veteran of the Army of the Confederacy, to lead the cavalry. A total of 815 other officers and 16,058 enlisted men were accommodated on the ships, along with thirty civilian clerks, 272 teamsters and packers and 107 stevedores. As supercargo were the eighty-nine newspaper and magazine men and eleven foreign naval and military attachés. Altogether 2,295 horses and mules were jammed below decks, as well as 112 six-mule army wagons, eighty-one escort wagons and seven ambulances. Sixteen light field guns had been stowed aboard, with four 7-inch howitzers, four 5-inch siege guns, eight 3.6-inch field mortars, one Hotchkiss rapid-fire cannon, a pneumatic dynamite gun and four Gatling guns.[4]

Hardly had the first of the transports begun to form into line and move out when a wire just received from Secretary Alger was sped out to the *Segurança* via dispatch boat. The previous night the scout ship *Eagle* had sighted what she thought were a Spanish armored cruiser and torpedo boat destroyer in the San Nicolas Channel, and the expeditionary force was directed to wait until it was confirmed and, if so, the enemy disposed of. The ships must come back. For five days the troops slept, played cards and cursed the Spanish fleet and its antecedents while the Florida sun heated the steel hulls of their new quarters to brick kilns and the Navy tried to track down the two ghostly enemy vessels. The men grew depressed and devitalized, a few cases of malaria broke out in the crowded and stifling holds, but typhus, which might have been the quietus of the entire venture, fortunately didn't develop.

The whole Army, from brigadier to lowly militiaman, lined the rail joyfully to watch the garish oriental minarets of Morton Plant's big hotel disappear over the horizon when the flotilla finally got under way again on June 14. Outside the bay the thirty-two antiquated steamers were again nosed clumsily into three long columns, escorted by fourteen warships, which Richard Harding Davis thought "treated us with the most punctilious courtesy and concealed contempt. . . . We could not keep in line and we lost ourselves and each other and the gunboats and torpedo boats were busy rounding us up . . . like swift, keen-eyed intelligent collies rounding up a herd of bungling sheep." [5] Pessimists on board were heard to remark that all the expedition needed to make things continue on their ill-starred course was a tiff with the season's first hurricane en route to Cuba, but in this respect the God Neptune smiled; the armada crept along over a sparkling, sunlit sea as smooth as a pond. "Crept" is no exaggeration, for Shafter was at first determined to keep his flock together and negotiate the trip at the speed of the slowest vessels—a side-wheeler towing a land barge and a schooner loaded down with hogsheads of water—but before long he gave up on that and soon everything was spread out for thirty or forty miles. Speeds rarely exceeded six knots even then.

The convoy proceeded under security that would have seemed suicidal in more recent times. It dawdled for days along the north coast of Cuba at its sightseeing pace, and at night the running lights of the ships looked to correspondent Charles Pepper of the Washington *Star* "like the struggling street of a floating city." The naval attachés in the *Segurança* nervously recalled some recent maneuvers of the French fleet, during which the torpedo squadron had in theory practically destroyed everything afloat in just such a situation, and anxiety grew as the cumbersome columns passed through the Bahama Channel, which for a long stretch was only seven miles wide. Spain's torpedo-boat fleet had never been tested in war, but nobody was anxious that this be the time. The only defense would be the searchlights of the warships, which it was hoped would illuminate the attacking enemy for the crews manning the 1-, 3- and 6-pounder "lead squirts" which would, it was also hoped, drive them off.

Nothing happened, however. Not a single Spaniard was seen; not a single hostile shell was fired from the Cuban shore. The men found nothing to trouble them but the discomforts of shipboard life itself. Bunks four tiers high had been allocated to the first arrivals aboard, but they were too few and late-comers bedded down topside on the bare decks. This had its advantages, as the air down below was so foul that sleep was almost out of the question there anyway. The standard "travel ration" was a far cry from being fresh, too; the canned beef gave off a ripe odor when it was opened, and the cooks had no real facilities for preparing rations. Generally the meat would be dumped into a big wash boiler along with hardtack broken into chunks and the whole lot cooked by steam from an engine-room pipe which was turned on it. "Jamoke" —black and potent—was brewed by the same boiler method. Some men bought officers' food for a dollar a meal (a big bite out of a private's $13 a month and $1.30 extra combat pay) and others were even willing to pay for the leftovers from the officers' plates which the galley crew would slip out to them. The men, sweating in their thick, woolen uniforms, seemed to be perpetually thirsty, and as might have been expected, the water provided was virtually undrinkable. To Richard Harding Davis it smelled like a "frog pond" or a "stable yard" and this was not mere civilian fastidiousness, for it had been sealed in casks lashed to the deck a full six weeks before the ships had sailed—casks that had previously held fish, kerosene and other odoriferous commodities. There was a brisk traffic in water, which was sold by the *Segurança's* stewards out of the fresh supplies provided for the crew at ten cents a glass, a sum that would have bought two brimming schooners of beer back home on Broadway and Forty-Second Street.

The troops longed for the nights, when it was cool. They would sit cross-legged on deck and listen to the ships' bands play, and then later, the instruments put away, everybody would sing, there on the crowded planks under stars made extra bright by a perfectly clear tropical sky. The war of 1898 was not song-minded as that of 1914 was to be; the most popular tune was "Hot Time in the Old Town Tonight," which wasn't really for voices, but the men would do their best with "Sweet Sixteen," "Little Annie Rooney" and, if their spirits happened to be up, the Negro rag tune "I Don't Like No Cheap Man." It was hardly like a war at all then; if you closed your eyes and just let the music sink in, you might have been on an excursion steamer—a sultry summer night on the Hudson, or on Mobile Bay. The days went by slow and easy, and there was plenty of time to reflect on what awaited them all once they reached Cuba.

The Marines could have told them that much. On May 6 Admiral Sampson had made up his mind to establish a coaling station near Santiago and had sent 750 leathernecks ashore to secure the fine harbor at Guantánamo, forty miles to the east. They established a base of sorts—Camp McCalla—without too much difficulty, but then had to fight off repeated nighttime infiltrations by Spanish irregulars nearby. Stephen Crane, who had written *The Red Badge of Courage* without ever having seen men fight, was with them, and his wondering horror over his first experience with the death of a friend stands as one of the few really timeless revealed truths about battle—any battle. "I heard someone dying near me. He was dying hard. It took him a long time to die. He breathed as all noble machinery breathes when it is making its gallant strife against breaking, breaking. But he was going to break. ... Every wave, vibration of his anguish beat upon my senses. He was long past groaning. There was only the bitter strife for air which pulsed out into the night in a clear penetrating whistle with intervals of terrible silence in which I held my own breath in the common aspiration to help. I thought this man would never die. I wanted him to die. Ultimately he died." [6]

Oh, it was war, all right.

✳✳✳

Admiral Sampson had been anticipating Shafter's arrival with growing impatience. Two or three days after Hobson's exploit in the *Merrimac* he had decided to exercise his gun crews, and when he had finished, nearly two thousand rounds of ammunition had been fired off at the Socapa and Morro batteries flanking the entrance and the Punta Gorda battery further in. Damage was virtually nil—one gun out of action at Morro and one at Socapa, a few defenders killed and an inoffensive village on an island in the harbor leveled by shells passing over their targets. Sharpening up the eyes of his turret captains was what Sampson had in mind— they needed it—but though it was a noisy bombardment, the admiral, like Schley, stood too far out to sea for it to be effective. The prevailing theory was that one gun on land was worth approximately three afloat in a contest of strength, sizes being equal. If the shore batteries looked down on the ships, the balance was tipped even more to their favor; on heights from 60 to 100 feet a gun ashore was considered equal to four afloat and on sites from 120 to 200 feet, to five or six.

Sampson—as later events proved—greatly overestimated the strength of the Spanish forts, but his thinking was governed by the cold, yet inescapable fact that while an army might replace casualties, a fleet could not bring forth more men-of-war out of the bosom of the ocean. He had very definite ideas on how his own ships might be used to hasten Cervera's destruction, and by Sunday morning, June 19, when the straggling collection of transports hove into view at last, he was ready to argue his program for the landing of the general's fighting men with the full knowledge that the fate of the vessels and good name of the Navy might be at stake.

Shafter was not idle, either, and had been spending the days in the cluttered operations room of the *Segurança*, forming his own battle plan. He had learned to his concern that in the immediate area of Santiago the coast of Cuba was almost unrelievedly rugged and mountainous. Extending for more than twenty miles to either side of the harbor was a mesalike wall of ridge, from 150 to 200 feet high. In some places it formed the coastline; in others it rose three or four hundred yards back from the shore, and in either case it offered excellent possibilities for defense. The only two logical places where a landing might be made west of the bay entrance were at the small harbor of Cabanas, which lay about two miles from the Socapa battlements, and at the cove of Guaicabón, a little further down the coast. Cabanas was ten miles from the city of Santiago by road and Guaicabón twelve. East of the harbor the only likely spots were at Fort Aguadores, about three miles from Morro Castle, at Siboney, a small railroad town seven more miles to the east, or perhaps at the mining town of Daiquirí, another three miles or so further on.

At none of these locations was there anything like a safe anchorage for big ships, but they were virtually the only open areas; at almost every other point along the shore the ridge threw up a barrier of sheer limestone cliff to an invading army. Then, too, getting men, animals and equipment on the beach would be only the first problem. Santiago was surrounded by vegetation so dense that no large body of troops could reach it except along the trails and narrow roads which were the only means of communication with the surrounding towns, and reports on their fitness to bear the traffic of an army of 16,000 men weren't too encouraging. No railroads connected any of the principal cities of the province.

Shafter's mind was weighted with all these problems as Admiral Sampson boarded the headquarters ship to parley with him. The admiral's own proposal for victory was simple and right to the point. The general would land his troops under the heights of Morro Castle, on the east side of the harbor entrance and attack it directly. Once this strong point was subjugated, he could conceivably flush the enemy from the Socapa battery on the opposite hill with relative ease. The Navy would then sweep up the channel mines, which were fired electrically from these two fortresses, steam into the harbor and blow up Cervera where he lay.

Shafter had learned of the Sampson scheme earlier so he was forearmed, however he still bridled outwardly at the Nelsonian way in which it was wont to toss off the difficulties of what had to be a very harrowing enterprise. Did Sampson realize Morro's battlements were on a steep promontory more than 200 feet above the sea? Launching an infantry assault upon them without the benefit of high-powered artillery was asking for a quick and permanent deliverance from all life's problems, and the whole thing for the purpose of giving a cheap victory to the fleet. His own plan, that of surrounding the city of Santiago itself—though he hadn't yet worked it out fully—would be much less costly in manpower (and give most of the laurels to the Army when the town fell).

That still left the question of where to come ashore. The Marines already at Guantánamo might make a landing there less risky, but it would be a forty-five mile march through virtually trackless bush to Santiago, and Shafter was full of thoughts of an eighteenth-century British expedition he'd been reading about that had taken this route and been virtually wiped out by fever before it could reach the city. Cabanas Bay, west of the entrance, gave access to the objective over easier country, but troops advancing from there would be under direct fire from the Spanish warships in the habor. Daiquirí and Siboney on the east had beaches, and though it was often wavy there, it looked as though one or both of these locations would have to do.

Arranging for a Navy gig to row them in, Shafter and Sampson decided to take the problem to the ally they had yet to meet—Calixto García, current leader of the insurrectionist forces in Santiago province. They were met halfway by a horde of ragged soldiers who ran shouting into the water to beach their boat, and who then escorted them—with Shafter astride a big white mule—up in the cliffs to rebel country, where the Cuban *jefe* had his camp. García, a veteran of the 1878 rebellion, impressed them as a formidable yet peculiarly avuncular figure with his snowy hair and goatee and his loose, white, flapping shirttail. A deep groove in his forehead gave him a perpetual fierce scowl. It had been made by a bullet which had entered beneath his chin, ploughed up through his jaw and gouged his skull when he had tried to kill himself as a captive of the Spaniards in the old days.

Their host spent little time on the amenities, but took one look at the situation and then told his visitors that the Americans should come ashore at Daiquirí. It was defended, according to his own intelligence, by only three hundred Spanish troops. The U.S. Navy would bombard the town and shell two or three other landing places as well to fool the defenders, and he would unleash a thousand Cubans from his side to fall upon the enemy's rear, drive him off and make other feints simultaneously, as a further distraction.

That was all. General García seemed to consider the matter closed, and in truth no one had any arguments to offer; the old soldier knew as much about the country and the enemy as anyone else. His reputation, his logic, and, not the least of it, the frown, were all compelling and his advice was adopted. The maps were folded up, the chiefs—American and Cuban—shook hands and the big white mule was brought up so that Shafter could mount. He'd been described as a stout-hearted animal—*"mucho corazón"* were the exact words of the soldier with the reins. As the general rode him down the rocky path to the beach where the gig was, past clumps of strange-looking trees, with the wild cries of foreign-sounding birds wheeling away at his approach and the sun of an unfamiliar land hot across the back of his shoulders, he could only hope his waiting army had the same.

✳✳✳

CHAPTER IV

★★★★★★★★

The Battle That Fought Itself

Nobody really knew what to expect at Daiquirí.
There was a relatively open roadstead there, very much exposed
to the prevailing winds, and Shafter hoped the surf wouldn't be
too high, but beyond that he and even more so the men who would
make the first landing suspected that this time the American Army
was going to learn by doing; the sort of thing they were walking
into wasn't in the manuals at all. Scuttlebutt—speculation and
rumor—passed and repassed among the tight-faced men who waited
on the decks of the *Cherokee*, the *Iroquois*, the *Concho* and the
other transports, cracking little jokes, nervously fingering knapsacks, breech bolts and ammunition belts. All of it had to do with
the enemy. Some thought they'd be meeting the dons in trenches
and rifle pits on the beach, where there might be some chance for
bayonet play, but the old hands, many of whom had campaigned
against the Nez Percé and Geronimo, scoffed at this kind of ignorance. High ground was always the key, they pointed out, and
it was one rule of war best not forgotten. Why would anybody—
even a Spaniard—make himself conspicuous on the shoreline when
he could dig in along the ridges just behind the beach and sweep
the whole landing area from above? The talk was that there were
blockhouses up there, too, for support—García's Cubans apparently
had reconnoitered them—and that was reason enough to worry;
anybody who thought that knocking out forts with green infantry
would be anything like the mock battles played at summer camp
was going to learn a lot about soldiering. The old Indian hands

wouldn't have said so, but it would all be new to them, too; United States troops hadn't landed on a hostile shore since the Mexican War.

There was an apprehensive hum and quiver all around, then, on that morning of June 22. The commanding officers tried to hide it, the newspapermen tried to capture just enough of it to tone up their dispatches, and it gnawed steadily at the self-assurance of the first wave as the men climbed over the sides of the troopships—with personal effects, photographs and letters to mothers and sweethearts left in the hands of buddies staying aboard—down into the makeshift collection of craft that were to take them in: two light-draft steamers, a tug and a pair of steam lighters to tow the transports' lifeboats and all the launches and pulling boats that Sampson could spare from the warships.

It wasn't soothing to the nerves, either, to have to wait, huddled down on the thwarts while the rest of the loading went on, with one's own boat bobbing about on the swells alongside the bigger ships, although the preliminary naval bombardment helped a good deal once it began. Seeing, listening to and feeling the shock of friendly artillery can be satisfying in a very visceral way and lay some of the jitter-spooks in the belly to rest, and most of the men felt the tight-clutching fist inside let go when the cruiser *New Orleans* hoisted the blue peter and opened up on the beach. Her impressive first salute was followed immediately by the subordinate salvos of the armed yachts *Vixen, Wasp, Hornet* and *Scorpion.* The 6-inchers had a reassuring slam, and several thousand eyes watched with all the intense interest of future involvement to see the shells hit, the muffled crumps coming out over the water as the short shots bored into the deep sand, and the sharper explosions as others smashed higher up into the cliffs, uprooting trees and flinging sticks, palm fronds, chunks of rock and earth up into the sky until a thin curtain of fine yellow dust hung over the green of the ridges back behind the shore. Now the men could pick out the blockhouses—*fuertes*—squat and foreign-looking up there on the heights among the trees, and hoped the Navy gunpowder was doing what it was supposed to do.

After about twenty minutes the barrage ended, and suddenly it was ominously quiet, with only the slapping of the water against the boats' sides as they started in. It wasn't a smooth trip; the swells turned to crested waves which tumbled along with them in slow-rolling breakers as they got closer and some of the less seaworthy boats shipped water, but wet feet weren't anybody's concern, because they would all have to wade the final few yards to shore anyway. There were two places where vessels could dock. The Juragua Iron Company, working the mines in the hills behind the town, had put up a steel pier that could handle small steamers, and there was another forty-foot wooden pier beside it, but if the Spaniards had any sense at all, they could easily blanket these with fire, so nobody was counting on using them for a while.

Yet what was becoming increasingly baffling as the little flotilla came well within range was the complete *lack* of fire. The boats bounced around in the surf and then began beaching, the men clambering over their gunwales, legging-deep in the white water, holding their rifles over their heads with exaggerated care, still without a single hostile shot or sign of an enemy. The fearful-looking forts might have been bandstands in a New England park for all the fight they showed. Nobody could deny the ships had given the immediate area a good pounding, but nobody had looked for a completely unopposed landing, either.

Whatever it had done to the defenders, the show by the Navy was a mixed stimulus to the American side. If it reassured the troops, it had at the same time an unnerving effect on the merchant captains of the transports, who seemed to realize for the first time that they were in a shooting war. Some of the ships wandered out of formation or backpedaled nervously, as if undecided whether to stay or retreat out of range of the shore batteries that were sure to open up with a counter fire. Several skippers refused to come in close enough to unload the men; one steamer with six hundred infantry waiting to get off disappeared altogether, and four launches had to put out to sea and try to find her. The transport captains were civilians "under the direction of the government," and as such subject to the authority of the commanding officer on the spot, but the complete absconding of a vessel and her human cargo at the crucial time was a contingency as unprovided for as it was unexpected, and it took some hours before things had calmed down to where the disembarkation could proceed.

The correspondents and foreign attachés aboard the *Segurança*, on the other hand, were looking forward to a brisk fight for the beach, and the newsmen, kits packed and cameras cocked, fumed at a last-minute order that they remain on board ship until the first wave was ashore. Richard Harding Davis collared Shafter and complained that it was unfair to keep the press out of the first boats; it was their job to go in where the action was. Shafter ignored him until finally Davis protested that he himself was not an ordinary reporter but a "descriptive writer." At this the old soldier's patience gave way. The Army did not, he said, give a damn who he was, everybody would be treated alike. That turned out to be a mistake, for then and there the general made himself an enemy, and Davis could be as good a hater as any Spaniard. He hated in print, too.

If one had to pick the beau ideal of the war correspondent in a day when that profession as a whole was infused with almost unbearable glamor, it would have to be "Richard the Lion-Harding," as he was not always respectfully called. He was good at his trade; he wrote easily and confidently—articles, dispatches, popular fiction—and enjoyed a deserved reputation in a field where the competition was resourceful and ever-present. Colorful as his pen was, he cut a dash physically as well that would have delighted the television and newsreel viewers of a later day. Photographs of Davis show him at all kinds of unlikely locations about the globe: mounted on camels and burros, posed by ancient and ornate pagodas, lounging in deck chairs on Nile River paddle boats; sometimes in slouch hat, immaculate linen and cigar, now and then in pith helmet and puggree, stand-up collar and khaki drill tunic festooned with straps to accommodate binoculars, map case, holster and the other accouterments of campaigning. Always he is serious, yet at ease—collected—the square jaw and blocky features that were to serve as the masculine model for Charles Dana Gibson's pen and ink sketches indicative of a man who has the situation closely under control.

Davis lived his role and for this reason his pique at Shafter unquestionably went deeper than mere petulance over an affront to his professional dignity. The general's corpulence and manner offended his sensibilities and the image of the athletic, steely-spare military type he favored. Davis, like Henry V before Harfleur, always saw his soldiers in terms of "greyhounds straining in the slips," and there was something about the sight of the immobile Shafter (the man even suffered from gout) easing his ponderous bulk among the troops that just missed being obscene. The commander in chief had a special mount, built along the lines of the great European war horses of the Middle Ages, which were bred to carry a man in full plate armor. And when his afflicted foot was too tender or the heat had enervated him, he enhanced the spectacle even more by having himself hauled in a buckboard, all the while gasping and working a palmetto fan, up and down the Cuban *barrancas*. The Davis opinion influenced the other newsmen greatly, and it all made for an unsympathetic press.

That big horse of the general's, as well as the Army's other riding and pack animals, might have posed a landing problem all their own, had not someone thought of the simple expedient of shoving them overboard and making them swim for it. An attempt was made to string them by their halters and tow them in, but some, confused, headed for the open sea and disappeared. Others were turned round and enticed to shore by buglers on the beach blowing "Stables" and "Boots and Saddles" and "Fours Right," and all in all only five or six were drowned. These, along with the fifty or so that had died in the holds of the ships during the trip, were less of a loss than was expected.

Six thousand men disembarked the first day with only two casualties—a pair of Negro troopers who fell overboard and were crushed between their landing boat and the pier, which had been quickly put to use. There had been no fight to wrest the hostile beach from the enemy, no men dying in the bloody surf, or forced to go to ground against the expected rain of bullets from above. When a report came in that the Spaniards had apparently fled after first trying to burn the town of Daiquirí, leaving behind only some empty entrenchments and a pile of Mauser ammunition, it seemed too good to believe. Emotions were let loose in a cacophony of sound. The beach and the dock, both now packed with blue uniforms and with men stripped naked in the hot sun to unload stores from the boats, gave up yells, cheers, patriotic songs and bugle calls which all but drowned out the joyful ships' whistles. The racket continued until the tiny groups of *cubanos*, who were just venturing, confused and shell-stunned from their hiding places, wondered if they had been invaded by lunatics. Major General Wheeler made an appearance and sent a detachment of his dismounted cavalrymen to hoist the American flag over one of the *fuertes*, and the men scaled the menacing ridge in high spirits to have a look at the havoc the naval bombardment had caused. The Stars and Stripes went up, which brought more hurrahs from below, but it was a little sobering to learn that not a single blockhouse had been hit by the shells. Lieutenant General Arsenio Linares' men hadn't scurried like frightened animals from the sound of the American guns at all, but had pulled out at five o'clock that morning, hurriedly but in good order, before the invading fleet had even come into sight.

***

With the problem of establishing a beachhead handily resolved by the Spanish retreat, General Shafter could concentrate on the next big step—getting the Army's ammunition, rations and equipment ashore, the troops marshaled and ready to move as quickly as possible. He had available to him—or would have shortly—two infantry divisions—the First Division under General Kent, composed of Brigadier General Hawkins' Sixth and Sixteenth regular infantry, along with the Seventy-first New York Volunteers, the Second, Tenth and Twenty-first regular infantry under Colonel E. P. Pearson, and the Ninth, Thirteenth and Twenty-fourth regulars under Colonel C. A. Wikoff. General Lawton would lead the Second Infantry Division, aided by brigade commanders Brigadier General A. R. Chaffee, Brigadier General William Ludlow and Colonel Evan Miles. This division included the Eighth and Twenty-second regulars and the Second Massachusetts Volunteers, the First, Fourth and Twenty-fifth regulars, and the Seventh, Twelfth and Seventeenth regulars. General Wheeler's Cavalry

Division consisted of three regular regiments led by Brigadier General S. S. Sumner and two other regular units along with the First Volunteers—the Rough Riders—under Brigadier General S. B. M. Young. These, plus one independent brigade—two regiments of infantry and a squadron of cavalry (the only mounted troops in the campaign)—commanded by Brigadier General J. C. Bates made up the expeditionary force.

There was no confusion about Shafter's objective—everybody knew it was Santiago—and consequently no question of routes, for there was only one. On the maps it was labeled a *camino real* (royal road), U.S. troops called it a wagon road, and sometimes it was that and sometimes nothing more than a path with ruts, hardly wide enough for two caissons to pass abreast. From the open ground just behind the Daiquirí landing it made its way westward for seven miles along the beach to the port of Siboney, then turned inland for another twelve miles, twisting through a gap in the hills to the rolling country beyond, from which point there was relatively easy access to Santiago. Unfortunately the road itself was accessible as well. Once into the undulating ground behind the coast range, it was commanded in many places by low hillocks, blocked at fine ambush spots by clumps of trees and bush, and all too often exposed on the flank to wide savannahs which gave a good field of fire to the defenders.

It seemed logical at this point to query those who had been on the spot—the Cuban insurgents—as to where these defenders might be and in what numbers, and the realization from the reply that local intelligence was several cuts below the professional level sparked a sharp sense of disappointment in our new allies. It was the Americans' first look at the embattled patriots whom many believed they had come to save, and here it was a case of the blind men and the elephant: everything depended on which element you dealt with. Some of the rebels had all the clean-limbed and gentlemanly aspect suggested by the prewar illustrateds, others were just good-natured hooligans, and an all-too-conspicuous few seemed almost to ooze depravity from the pores. Even the best were ragged and unwashed; some went barefoot, some in crude rope sandals, but though sartorially beyond consideration, almost to a man they carried good magazine rifles taken from Spanish dead. There was a highly regulated market for enemy property, the *yanquis* were told. Mauser ammunition was legal tender, and for their services Havana prostitutes were now asking a hundred cartridges from a Spanish private, two hundred from a noncom and a thousand from an officer. Somehow this seemed easier to accept than the stories of rebel football games played with decapitated Spanish heads. This was a little strong even for the frontier soldiers, who preferred to surmise what the rate of exchange in the capital city might be in the new Kräg-Jorgensen caliber-.30 ball ammo, of which they had plenty.

With a foothold in enemy country and the body of the Army to follow it up, Shafter's rightful concern was with the securing of his supply lines. This meant the port of Daiquirí and now especially of Siboney, which had been found to be a better spot for ships and which had been abandoned by the enemy along with Daiquirí on the morning of the landing. Consequently he sent Lawton's Second Infantry Division off down the *camino real* at daybreak on the 23rd with orders to take up a position on the road just beyond the town and to defend it and the beach from attack while the unloading went on. Shafter himself, after ordering Wheeler's dismounted cavalry to bring up the rear on the Daiquirí-Siboney road, decided to remain on board the *Segurança* and oversee what remained of the debarkation. He should have known better, however, than to expect Fighting Joe, whose itch to pull the first lanyard of the first gun of the campaign was the talk of messes from Tampa to Fort Laramie, to hang back as a rear guard. Sure enough, that same afternoon Lawton was annoyed but not really surprised to witness the arrival of Wheeler and his entourage—Colonel Leonard Wood, Colonel Roosevelt, the ubiquitous Richard Harding Davis and the Rough Riders, dust-caked but exhilarated from an all-night forced march.

It was an awkward situation. As long as Shafter was still on board ship, Wheeler was, to Lawton's embarrassment, the senior officer ashore, so there wasn't much the Second Division commander could do but seethe at the old Confederate's contrary interpretation of his orders. Wheeler had learned from the local Cuban commander that about 2,000 Spaniards, supported by a pair of Krupp guns, had been digging in at a strong position two or three miles up the road, and if he could hurry his first brigade up that night, he might steal a march on Lawton, be in a position to attack the enemy before anyone else early the next morning, and thus show the infantry what a few troops of well-led horse—even dismounted —could do, something he always relished.

Wheeler's knowledge of the terrain and the enemy positions was sketchy, and only about half of his cavalry brigade had been able to slip ahead of Lawton's men during the night; nevertheless he'd made up his mind to move out with what he had, and at five o'clock on the morning of the 24th two columns—his regulars under General Young in army blue and Colonel Wood's Rough Riders in mud-colored drill—slung carbines without bugles or commotion and started off on foot in the direction of Santiago. It was found that a trail ran parallel to the road at this point, and according to Cuban General Castillo the two routes turned north together through the broad valley, winding their way in and out of the spotty thickets and jungle, and converging at a grove of guacimo trees, which was just about the place where the Spaniards should be. An army of eight hundred Cubans would await the Americans at the juncture and together they would fall upon the unsuspecting enemy.

Wheeler saw the logic in this, and ordered Young to split his force in two. One column, commanded by Young himself and consisting of the First and Tenth Cavalry, with the latter regiment's two Hotchkiss mountain guns in tow, kept to the main Santiago road. The other, which included the Rough Riders, along with correspondents Davis and Edward Marshall of the New York *Journal* (both of whom had ideas of stealing their own march on their slugabed colleagues back at camp), took the left hand of the fork and proceeded along the trail. Once they split up, both detachments were very much alone; the mile or so of impenetrable bush could as easily have been a continent as far as contact was concerned.

At about 7:30 Young's scouts spotted something through the leaves—stone breastworks sited on a commanding hill which blocked the way about seven or eight hundred yards up the road. They were too far off for Wheeler to tell whether the straw *sombreros* bobbing over the tops of the ramparts belonged to Cubans or Spaniards, and he decided to get an answer by opening fire on them with one of his Hotchkiss 1-pounders. The reply came— from the fort up ahead, from the tall grass, the bushes, the trees, seemingly from everywhere simultaneously; one, and then a second and a third Spanish volley—death-dealing hails of high-velocity bullets that frankly shook Fighting Joe, who remarked that he'd seen no heavier musketry at any time during the Civil War.

That isn't difficult to understand. Thirty-five years before it had taken twenty seconds to load, sight and fire the .58-caliber smooth-bore muskets then in common use. In striking contrast, a good rifleman could squeeze off eight aimed shots in the same amount of time with the 7-mm. Mausers the Spaniards were shooting with. It didn't make as big a hole in a man but there were a good many more holes to make up for it. Slide-rule soldiers had already warned that field commanders were going to have to update their thinking —and quickly; men defending positions with magazine weapons against an infantry advance were presumed to have a six- or eight-to-one advantage, but the lesson had not yet sunk in. Nor would it, for some time to come.

At almost the same moment the Rough Riders had run into the enemy on their own side. Wood had barely got his men down into the dirt when they were met by volley fire from both flanks at almost point-blank range. In the foliage the Spaniards were almost invisible—the smokeless powder they were using didn't give them away, either—and it was an abrupt and frightening first taste of war. The troopers had no idea where Young and the other column was—they could hardly see their own buddies—all they knew was that they were at the vortex of the hottest fire fight any of them had ever imagined. It wasn't comforting to watch men being hit, and it had a sobering effect on the volunteers. Sergeant Hamilton Fish, the grandson of President Grant's Secretary of State, fell without a sound, shot through the heart. Others followed, and everybody who was there remembered that the air was filled with a deadly humming, like the continuous flit of a swarm of powerful insects. To newsman Edward Marshall the *z-z-z-z-z-eu* of the small-caliber enemy slugs was a "nasty, malicious little noise, like the soul of a very petty and mean person turned into sound."

Wood and Roosevelt remained on their feet in the middle of it all, both disdaining to take cover from the enemy fire while any of their men remained exposed. A bullet clipped off Wood's gold cuff links, and another hit a palm tree so close to Roosevelt's head that it spattered chips into his ear. Richard Harding Davis walked around puffing on a cigar and obviously enjoying himself. He had been the first to sight and to point out the Spanish troops, and though a noncombatant, he wouldn't have relinquished for anything the privilege of picking up a carbine and letting go a few rounds when he saw a straw hat move in the leaves.

His friend Ed Marshall had a little different experience, yet maintained his reporter's power of observation throughout it all. "I saw many men shot," he wrote later." Every one went down in a lump without cries, without jumping in the air, without throwing up hands. They went down like clods in the grass. There is much that is awe-inspiring about the death of soldiers on the battlefield . . . the man lives, he is strong, he is vital, every muscle in him is at its fullest tension when, suddenly, 'chug' he is dead. That 'chug' of the bullets striking flesh is nearly always plainly audible. . . . I did not hear the bullet shriek that killed Hamilton Fish. . . . I didn't hear the bullet shriek which hit me. . . . 'Chug' came the bullet and I fell into the long grass, as much like a lump as the other fellows I had seen go down. The tremendous shock so dulled my sensibilities that it didn't occur to me that anything extraordinary had happened." [1]

Marshall was wearing a conspicuous white linen coat and a sniper had hit him in the spine. He was carried back to Siboney where he arrived in a delirium singing bits of "On the Banks of the Wabash." "The surgeon told me I was about to die. The news was not pleasant, but it didn't interest me particularly." He did not die; instead he spent his lucid moments dictating from his stretcher an eyewitness account of the war's first battle.

Roosevelt and Wood decided that there was one way only to get out of the hotbox and that was to charge out, so they did—

straight at the stone ramparts, the men firing and reloading as they crashed through the undergrowth, tripping over creepers and yelling with as much lung as a bunch of New York clubmen and Montana cowpokes could muster. It was bluff on everybody's part, for there was nothing to back the thin line of Teddy's Terrors but the noise; yet the Spaniards chose to believe that the whole American Army was at their heels, and all at once they broke and ran. Wheeler and Young on the other side were in no better position and much to Fighting Joe's embarrassment were forced to bow to necessity and summon aid from Lawton back at Siboney. When the Ninth Cavalry arrived to save the day, however, it was obvious they were no longer needed; Wood's and Young's men had joined forces and already reached the fort on the hilltop. "We've got the damn Yankees on the run!" Wheeler shouted after the fleeing enemy. In the heat of the moment they might have been Billy Sherman's barn burners skedaddling through a Georgia cornfield. He had help from his allies, too, now that the tide of battle had shifted; Castillo's eight hundred Cubans had just come on the scene to share the victory.

Sixteen Americans were dead and fifty-two had been wounded, while the Spaniards lost ten killed and twenty-five wounded. Hardly more than a skirmish, this little brush at Las Guásimas, but it was the first real smell of powder, and Lawton's reinforcements, with blood up and bayonets fixed, swore roundly when they saw they'd come too late and prayed there'd be another day. For the time being there were only the Spanish dead and the first look for most Americans at what steel-jacketed lead does to human flesh, and how the men who have been through it all react. The old soldiers could have told them the reactions, like the men, are different. One wounded trooper ambled back down the trail on a mule, his khaki trouser leg red from belt to knee where he had taken a slug in the thigh. He was white with anger under his tan. "Damn near stepped on the sonofabitch; then he got me—but I got him! Now you go and get yours!" he spat out to nobody in particular. Another kept grinning at his good luck as he held his shirt open. "Got me in the belly," he said with a kind of stunned pride. He pointed to two little blood-rimmed holes about six inches apart, below his navel, linked by a neat purple welt where a bullet had passed just below the skin. "Kinda stings is all, you know what I mean?"

Back at headquarters General Wheeler got a spanking for being rash, but there wasn't much muscle behind it. Though he was accused of headline grabbing in his attempt to circumvent Shafter's plan to make his dismounted cavalry play a rear-guard role, it was a fact that the clash of May 24 did succeed in driving the enemy from a strategic gap in the hills through which the U.S. Army had to pass on its way to Santiago. Important as the little fight was in securing the approaches to the city and removing the danger of interference with the landing beaches, its real value was moral, and beneath official irritation over what could hardly be classed as anything better than an ambush, there was a feeling of pride in the way the Army had got out of a bad job. The untried United States troops—fewer than a thousand of them—had run up against twice their number of Spaniards behind fortifications, and the first meeting had, in the perspective of the day, been momentous. It isn't easy to top the exhilaration of seeing an enemy's back disappearing in the distance, and the men had earned every right to the view; the transposition of catastrophe and triumph had been strictly on the gut level.

One of the Santiago townspeople asked a retreating Spanish soldier if those *yanquis* fought well.

"Well?" he retorted. "They tried to catch us with their hands!"

✳✳✳

Now for six days the Army camped, stretched out in three miles of tents, wagons and pack animals on either side of the Santiago road. Men were still being landed at Siboney, General Shafter himself was not yet ashore, and anyway he wanted to secure the Daiquirí and Siboney beachheads with some newly arrived volunteer regiments before he moved on. The engineers spent ten-hour working stretches trying to improve the road to the point where it could carry the necessary supply traffic, and the rest of the troops, with nothing much to do, took long-needed baths in the nearby Aguadores River and foraged in the woods for mangoes, coconuts, and the pulpy, bananalike *plátanos*, which they found to be edible, but only after one had acquired the taste. To many of the men—farm-bred—it seemed a lush but noticeably inhospitable country. Most of it was too thickly overgrown to be good crop land, and there was no game, either, except a few very timid deer and the packs of wild dogs that hunted them. For a tropic land there didn't appear to be many snakes and none was poisonous, which was a happy surprise, though the particular nemesis of the region —the Cuban land crab—turned out to be even more of a hazard. These repulsive and ever-present crustaceans scuttled about in the dark, rustling leaves exactly as a careless Spanish infiltrator might do, and hardly a night's guard duty went by that one sentry or another didn't unload a few rounds into the bush upon finding his challenge unanswered. The expeditionary force adopted a pact of alliance with the crab hawk that fed on the creatures, though it wasn't so pleased to have the company of the ugly, huge-winged buzzards that glided noiselessly everywhere and could be seen returning heavy-bellied and sated from the bloody field at Guásimas.

On June 7 General Shafter came ashore and spent the next two days inspecting the Army; then, along with his staff he set out on a reconnaissance of the forward area. A mile and a half beyond the furthest American outpost was a lofty vantage point called El Pozo ("The Fountain"), a hill which somewhat ironically had taken its name from a now war-gutted hacienda lying at its foot, and from which a good view might be had of the surrounding country and particularly the valley basin which lay between it and the city of Santiago. To the observer's left, or south, were the bluffs which hid the sea; and on his right he could see the distant peaks of the Sierra Maestra, whose foothills sheltered the village of El Caney, about four miles away and said by García's men to be a Spanish strong point. Directly in front was the road. It led almost straight west to a ford about a thousand yards ahead where the Aguadores River meandered to its left and crossed it, and a few hundred yards further on to another ford where a second stream, the San Juan River, did the same. Just beyond this point and about a mile and a half from the observer on the crest of El Pozo rose a series of high ridges, known collectively as San Juan

Hill, and dominated by the nearest of these—a 150-foot slope capped with a pagoda-shaped blockhouse just to the left of the road. Opposite, on the right, was another rise of land which was promptly named Kettle Hill because of the huge sugar-refining receptacle that could be seen on its summit even at this distance. Behind the San Juan heights and beyond an intervening dip, the whitewashed walls of the barracks and hospital of Santiago itself caught the glare of the sun, with the thirteen Red Cross flags on the roof of the latter plainly visible through General Shafter's field glasses. Between El Pozo, where the scouting party stood, and this prize a sprawl of formidable jungle intervened. It was nourished by the low-lying alluvial soil and the overflow of the two rivers, a dense mass of greenery which included one of the finest mahogany forests in the world. Here there were spreading ceibas and ancient banyans, and trees with exotic and unheard-of names—guayacan, majagua, nogal, ocuje, jocuma; coco, cabbage and corojo palms—and of course Cuba's own majestic royal palm, towering high above the hardwoods to form the top layer in the verdure which hid the ground below the watchers. It is safe to say that General Shafter hardly found it in him to appreciate the flora. He only knew that from here on the trail he must march could barely be followed by the eye through the steaming canopy of green, whose leaves, wet and heavy with the first rains of the season, scarcely moved in the still air. It would not, anyone could see, be easy going for man, beast or buckboard.

Raising his glasses a little he could watch the Spaniards digging entrenchments—4,000 yards of them, two or three lines deep and buttressed with barbed wire—along the San Juan crests and overlooking the route that would take him into the city. According to the Cubans the enemy had about 12,000 men available for its defense, or roughly three-quarters his own strength,* with an additional five-hundred troops holed up at El Caney to the north. Shafter was tactician enough to recognize the threat posed by this latter force; it was well-placed to outflank any American attack on the San Juan positions, and to halt any encircling movement

* Actually, no more than five hundred occupied the San Juan trenches on the day of battle.

toward the northern and western sides of the town. He was anxious to advance in that direction, too, both to block enemy reinforcements known to be fighting their way from Manzanillo and also to cut off the city's water supply, which came through a pipeline from the mountains. He would have to allot some troops to neutralize El Caney, then, but he knew his main force—at least two of his three divisions—must be kept for a direct attack on Santiago. That would mean, first of all, a frontal assault on the San Juan redoubt. If he timed it right and if things went as expected, the enemy at El Caney would be dislodged in perhaps two hours, and the men employed there would be free to join the main battle on the northern flank, it was hoped at the crucial moment.

On paper it looked feasible, though if he'd had his choice, Shafter would have asked for better terrain. While there was some open ground for maneuver in front of Caney, the only access to the San Juan ridge was down the narrow-track, hemmed-in jungle road, which offered no possibility for any kind of deployment until it was under direct fire from the hill. Then from that point on up to the Spanish trenches themselves there was an almost open meadow and no cover at all. It was a lot to ask of untried troops, but nearly a week had passed since Las Guásimas and time was not on Shafter's side. The first cases of fever had already broken out; the showers, which were coming more and more frequently, were beginning to turn the "royal road" into a slimy trench, and he'd just received word that the Spanish reinforcing column was no token battalion but a whole new army of several thousand men—enough to combine with Santiago's defenders and rob him of any advantage in numbers. García's insurgents didn't seem to be having much success holding it up, either.

When he got back to camp, he called his divisional commanders together and told them that a concerted attack would be made the following day. The three brigades of General Lawton's Second Infantry Division, along with one battery of field artillery, would march north just as soon as the present meeting broke up, bivouac that night and be ready to hit El Caney first thing in the morning. The First Infantry Division, the Cavalry Division and a second battery of guns would move forward to El Pozo and camp at the foot of the hill. At first light the cavalry, followed by Kent's three infantry brigades would lead the main advance, crossing the Aguadores ford and deploying along the edge of the jungle on either side of the road and in front of San Juan Hill; the cavalry on the right, the infantry on the left, with the battery being hauled up to the top of El Pozo to support the attack. The troops would remain in skirmish lines until word came that things were under control at Caney. Then they would move forward against the hill, with Lawton coming south to add his weight to the attack when he had finished where he was.

It was four o'clock in the afternoon before the bulk of the Army was ready to start. Lawton had moved off to the north as soon as he could get the mules hitched to the guns, and now, when the order finally came to Kent's and Sumner's men to sling arms, everyone was suddenly jammed onto the little trail simultaneously —the cavalry, still in spurs, attempting to lead the way, then the infantry, complete with the Sixteenth's regimental brass band; then the artillery—one battery of field pieces, Lieutenant John Parker and his Gatling detachment and the Sims–Dudley pneumatic dynamite gun (with a makeshift rig, because no one had thought to have its special harness unloaded), then the supply and ambulance wagons, the pack animals, and somewhere in the crush J. Stuart Blackton of the Vitagraph Motion Picture Company with a 60-pound camera and tripod to record it all. Correspondent Davis thought it looked as though "fifteen regiments were encamped along the sidewalks of Fifth Avenue and were all ordered at the same moment to move into it and march downtown." And that was assuming Fifth Avenue was ten feet wide.

The temperature was in the 90's as it had been every day, and though the gray, wide-brimmed slouch hat which was standard headgear had fought off the sun a lot better than the old Civil War kepi would have done, the woolen uniforms were stifling, and now with the advent of the rains almost continually sodden and smelly. ("Exactly what I would have worn in Montana in the fall," Roosevelt grumbled.) Each man had his 6-shot, bolt-action .30-caliber rifle, along with a hundred rounds of ammunition in cartridge belts slung around his hips; his sheathed bayonet and a canvas-covered tin canteen. He also was supposed to carry half a tent, two tent-pole sticks, a complete change of underwear, socks and an extra pair of laced boots, but many had thrown all these away, to the delight of the Cubans, who followed at a respectful distance and had sharp eyes for Army jetsam. Some of the marchers had the new "Merriam packs"—square boxlike canvas knapsacks—but most sweated along under the old "horse-collar" Civil War blanket roll.

The lucky ones carried their provisions with them, too. In spite of the engineers' efforts the wagon trains were just too much for the tiny road, and the traffic was one long melee of heaving animals, cursing mule skinners and vehicles bogged down in mudholes holding up the whole absurd procession behind them. A trickle of supplies was all that was getting through. The men missed their tobacco; they had been smoking a mixture of dried roots and manure instead of decent plug since God knows when, and because some regimental officers had failed to draw rations, a lot of the Army found itself heading into battle with nothing on its stomach, either. Other men drew a full five days' worth, which consisted of a big chunk of sowbelly wrapped in sacking and hung from the belt or some other convenient place, a can of the Sino-Japanese "embalmed" beef—to be shared by two—an armful of hardtack, which was stuffed into the haversack or the blanket roll, and a double handful of tough, dry navy beans which were dumped into a man's spare socks if he hadn't thrown them away. To supplement this he got two handfuls of unroasted coffee beans, one of sugar, and a few pinches of salt and pepper which he carried mixed in a letter-from-home envelope. A soldier cooked his own meals and ate them out of a portable tin pan with a government-issue knife-and-fork utensil. These rations weren't uniform, but then neither was a lot of the other equipment, from the bottom stratum of the Army to the top. The Seventy-first New York and the Second Massachusetts, the two militia regiments in the field, had to make do with the obsolete, black-powder .45–70 Springfield rifle, model of 1873, and the collection of bowie knives, derringers, "knuckle-dusters," and other improvised weapons of close combat which hung from belts or were stashed away in the tunic pockets or knapsacks all throughout the rank and file of the Army were anything but government issue.

A cold-water-and-hardtack breakfast on top of four hours sleep braced up Lawton and his men for their first view of the ring of entrenchments around El Caney village. These were a bit stronger than expected—four wooden blockhouses, a stone church where Cortez was supposed to have prayed the night before he sailed for Mexico, and which now had been loopholed for rifles, and a solid-looking fort occupying a strategic position on the perimeter about five hundred yards from the town. Nevertheless, at seven in the morning the single battery allotted to him—four 3.2-inch field guns firing unfixed ammunition with black-powder charges— opened the engagement, and the infantry waited while the guns, positioned out of range of the Spanish rifles, knocked chunks out of the *fuertes* and the walls of the church. Lawton's men had ex-pected to move up right away, but every time they tried to follow up the bombardment with a rush they were met by enemy volleys and driven to the ground again there in the high guinea grass. The best they could do was hug what cover was available and try to keep up a respectable exchange with the Mausers in front of them.

The other battery had meanwhile been got into position on El Pozo, and at eight o'clock began directing its own fire at the San Juan crest, 2,500 yards away. One shell after another streaked off to crash against the blockhouses and breastworks, with no reply of any kind from the enemy. "I should think they would tire of receiving these," said the Swedish military attaché after a while. "Have they then no artillery at all?" No sooner had he asked than two explosions in quick succession showered the whole position with shrapnel, the modern Krupp guns having zeroed in easily on the picturesque blossoms of white smoke sent up by the American black powder. The onlookers who had come to watch the show made a quick retreat. "It was thoroughly evident that the Span-iards had the range of everything in the country," recalled artist Frederic Remington, who had been sketching the artillery caissons being hauled up the slope. "Some gallant soldiers and some as

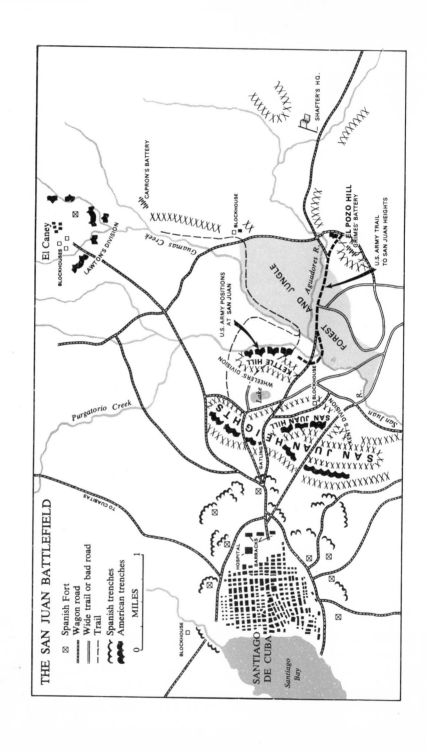

THE SAN JUAN BATTLEFIELD

Spanish Fort ⊠
Wagon road
Wide trail or bad road
Trail
Spanish trenches
American trenches

0   MILES   1

TO CUABITAS

Purgatorio Creek

El Caney
BLOCKHOUSES
LAWTON'S DIVISION

CAPRON'S BATTERY
Guamas Creek
BLOCKHOUSE

SHAFTER'S HQ.

EL POZO HILL
GRIMES' BATTERY
U.S. ARMY TRAIL
TO SAN JUAN HEIGHTS

Aguadores R.
FOREST AND JUNGLE

U.S. ARMY POSITIONS
AT SAN JUAN

KETTLE HILL
WHEELER'S DIVISION

Lake
BLOCKHOUSE

SAN JUAN HEIGHTS
GATLING
SAN JUAN HILL
KENT'S DIVISION
San Juan R.

SANTIAGO
DE CUBA
Santiago Bay

HOSPITAL
BARRACKS

BLOCKHOUSE

daring correspondents as it has been my pleasure to know did their legs proud here. . . . Smoky powder belongs with arbalists and stone axes—in museums." [2]

The artillery duel was providing a colorful spectacle for everybody, but there was one important absentee. General Shafter had suffered a sleepless night—a victim of the heat on top of an attack of gout—and was at this moment in his tent a mile and a half to the rear, too sick to be moved. A relay of couriers from the commanders was keeping him informed, though their dispatches were not yet telling him what he wanted to hear—the news of Lawton's reduction of El Caney. Fearing that the Spaniards might have reinforced their position there, he decided not to wait but to order Kent's division and the cavalry brigades to begin their advance toward the jumping-off area—the open meadow at the foot of San Juan Hill. Circumstances had dictated a shift in command which might or might not be fortuitous. Fighting Joe Wheeler and General Young had both been struck down with fever, and now the leadership of the cavalry fell to General Sumner, with Colonel Wood taking over the second brigade and Colonel Roosevelt the Rough Riders. Sumner's dismounted troopers began to move off down the road, followed by the Sixth and Sixteenth regular infantry and then the Seventy-first New York Volunteers, led by the white-haired General Hawkins. As they pushed ahead, splashing and slipping in the three-inch mud underfoot, they passed a solitary straw-hatted figure on a big horse. It was William Randolph Hearst, who had docked his personal dispatch boat at Siboney and was now on hand to see what the Army was up to. "Good luck, boys," he said solemnly, with a patrician wave of the hat. War might be new to the New York *Journal*'s publisher, but never let it be said he didn't know how to play the role.

There was something new in store for the Spanish, too. Some of his troops may have been hungry or ill-armed, he might be totally bedridden himself, but as far as the application of futuristic innovation to battle was concerned, General Shafter took a back seat to no one. He had with him a "war balloon," a glossy ball laced with guy wires, manned by two officers in a basket aloft and controlled by a ground crew of three or four soldiers hanging on to ropes below. Its purpose was observation, and Lieutenant Colonel Derby did have an unmatched view from his position just under the big gasbag; unfortunately it was seen fit to keep it hovering ditectly over the trail where nearly 10,000 troops were shoving their way in one solid column toward the base of the San Juan heights. The Spaniards knew the Americans had no choice but to use the trail, the balloon might just as well have been a sign pointing out the spot, and now all at once the men heard that metallic insect droning that had been in the air at Las Guásimas, as snippets of leaves and twigs began to filter down on them.

The droning and the leaf shower grew in intensity as the enemy opened up with everything that could be fired out of a gun barrel on the congested masses, who could hardly have returned the fire even had they known where it was coming from. As the column crosed the ford of the San Juan River, it suddenly broke out of the jungle and came into plain sight of the Spaniards on the hills up ahead. The bullets were killing men now—the defenders had had the trail accurately ranged in for days—and Sumner was ordered to halt his division on the edge of the woods and "wait for further instructions" while Kent and his infantry caught up and deployed on the cavalry's left.

Those behind them on the trail were suffering, too. The rifles and the Krupps, firing down through the umbrella of trees over their heads, could hardly help but score on the jam-packed infantry, and not a few cheers went up when the observation balloon was at last perforated by shrapnel and descended, "dying," as Stephen Crane put it, "a gigantic and public death before the two armies." Before it collapsed into the trees, however, Derby had been able to spot a second trail branching off to the left just beyond the Aguadores crossing, which gave another access to the open meadow in front and which led to a knoll from which the Spanish positions might be flanked. The Sixth and Sixteenth Infantry had already spread out in skirmish lines, but the Seventy-first New York was being held in reserve, and it was now decided to reroute that regiment onto the fork of the trail since they were nearest the spot. The Seventy-first was the only volunteer unit with Kent's force; their colonel had reported a month before that a third of his men had never pulled the trigger of a gun, and they carried the old Springfields, which could not be used at all without revealing their position to the enemy. The Second Massachusetts had already been taken out of the line at El Caney because of their outmoded rifles; now no sooner had the Seventy-first detoured off on the new trail than the head of the column was immediately met by a small arms and shrapnel fusillade. When every effort to defend themselves drew an even hotter retaliation from the almost invisible Mausers, it was too much for the raw Guardsmen. Panic broke out in the ranks, the leading troops fell back on those to their rear, and only a cordon of officers stretched across the trail behind them combined with the order to lie down in their tracks saved the regiment from stampede.

Shafter, back in his tent, was really alarmed by now, and this business with the volunteers seemed to be indicative of the way things were going all over. It was already past twelve o'clock, the whole affair should have been done with long ago, yet he could still hear undiminished firing coming from the direction of El Caney. He had already sent off General Bates's independent brigade—his total reserves—to assist Lawton, and to all events this had accomplished nothing either. As it was, the 5,000 men of the Second Infantry [3] were still prone in the high grass outside the town, pinned down by five hundred firmly dug-in defenders. The American artillery was having no success in dislodging them, and the Spaniards were proving a far more tenacious enemy than anyone would have given them credit for. The dynamite gun, which Shafter had counted on to soften up the blockhouse on the hill, had tried one shot and sprung its breech; it would be useless for the rest of the day. Now he was told that the Mausers were killing the men of the supply column a half mile to a mile back on the road, and that sharpshooters were terrorizing the troops from the flanks as well, picking off men crossing the ford, shooting the wounded lying by the roadside and firing into the dressing station which had been set up on the near bank of the Aguadores River.

Six hundred yards up the slope the volleys still came at regular intervals across the intervening meadow and through a six-stranded barbed-wire fence that was strung to living trees directly in front of where the Americans crouched. The Spaniards didn't have a reputation as marksmen, but they didn't have to be; it was almost impossible to miss. As one private of the Sixth Infantry put it: "We didn't have a show, for the hill was clear and the Spaniards pumped over the rifle pits and potted us right along. We were in plain view and they had us at their mercy. The Mauser rifle balls came down that slope, zipping and spitting, while we lay on our bellies giving them shot for shot." [4]

If ever a position was untenable, it was this one. Colonel Wikoff was killed; then Colonels Worth and Liscomb were shot down. It was insanity to hold the men as targets behind that wire; they must give it up or go forward. Lieutenant Miley, Shafter's personal aide at the front, sent word galloping back to headquarters that "The heights must be taken at all hazards. A retreat now would be a disastrous defeat," but it was a mere formality; nobody was going to wait for the commander in chief to decide one way or the other. Lieutenant Jules Ord, a young officer on Hawkins' staff, turned to his superior with a grim expression. "General, if you'll order a charge, I'll lead it." Hawkins made no reply as he watched a bandsman of the Sixteenth drop his cornet, wrench a Kräg from the hands of a dead man and begin firing. "I'd like to volunteer; I only ask you, General, not to refuse permission." "I can't ask for volunteers," said Hawkins. "I won't give permission and I won't refuse it. But," he added, "God bless you and good luck."

"Follow me!" Ord yelled at the men around him. "We can't stay here!" Some jumped up quickly; others weren't quite so sure. "We were in front," wrote one of them later, "and then the Sixteenth, or what was left of it, came up by rushes just as we did and we were ordered to go up the hill. I heard that the Rough Riders were there, too, but I didn't see. All I know is when I looked up that gulch and then up that hill . . . I got cold all over. I could feel the hair stand up on my scalp and my teeth clattered. I tried to pray but I couldn't. I didn't think of my mother or anything like that; I only tried to think of some way to get out of going up that hill." [5]

Ord, with his shirt stripped off, a .45 in one hand and a bayonet in the other, burst ahead of the men who'd hacked away the wire with their machetes and started up the slope, followed by the nearest of the troops. "Good God, how the bullets did come!" one tells. "It was zip-zip-zip faster than you could count. Then right over my head I heard a different kind of bullet singing, and I knew they were going from us to the Spaniards. I heard the roll of the Gatling gun, and pretty soon the zip-zip-zip didn't come quite so fast, and then I heard some kind of an order hallooed; then I yelled because the other fellows yelled . . . and we kept going up shooting from our magazines."

Yes, it was the Gatlings, finally come on the scene. For an hour or more Lieutenant Parker had been struggling to get them along the trail through the confusion of the Seventy-first New York, and his arrival at the critical moment was a bit of personal triumph. Parker had been an artillery, then a machine-gun champion all his career, and had pulled every kind of string he could for official approval to form an independent Gatling gun command and join the expeditionary force. When no boats were available, he'd had to float his battery to the Daiquirí beach on bridge pontoons borrowed from the engineers. Now after heaving the big-wheeled carriages through the mire to within range, he and his crews were spraying 3,600 rounds a minute into the opposing rifle pits, seven or eight hundred yards away. The physical effect of the eight-barreled "coffee grinders" was no less timely than the moral lift it gave the Americans, who could at least now see a reply being made to the galling fire they had been suffering so helplessly. A Spanish officer later paid Parker the compliment he most wanted to hear: "It was terrible when your guns opened—always. They went 'b-r-r-r,' like a lawn mower cutting the grass over our trenches." Almost at once a number of Spaniards fled from the first line of breastworks and disappeared over the hill.

Across the road on the right, in front of Kettle Hill, a bandanna-decorated sombrero and a souvenir revolver in his belt from the sunken *Maine* lent just the proper "gentleman amateur" air to Colonel Roosevelt as he paraded conspicuously back and forth on his mount Little Texas. Contemptuous of personal danger, Roosevelt worried chiefly about his poor eyesight, but he had several extra pairs of glasses fastened to his uniform and one pair sewn inside the hat, and was now ready for anything. The Rough Riders and the Ninth Cavalry were gathered just at the foot of the slope, in an uncomfortably exposed position and with the San Juan River at their backs. This sitting-duck role was bothering Roosevelt; he had no intention of letting his men be picked off where they were, and besides his orders were to support the regulars attacking the San Juan heights. Not wanting to wait any longer, he had the bugler sound the charge, and the Rough Riders, then the Ninth followed him, yelling, with the colonel being as surprised as anyone at the ease with which his cowboys and gentlemen reached the big iron kettle on the summit, and the alacrity with which the enemy took off and made way for them. Roosevelt was the second man to the top, quick enough to down one laggard Spaniard with his revolver before the others disappeared.

Now from the summit they could watch the attack on San Juan over to the left, where the moment of truth was at hand. As soon as the Gatlings had begun their work, General Hawkins had rallied the Sixth and Sixteenth Infantry and started them up through the waist-high guinea grass and chaparral, past the clumps of piñon bush and razorlike Spanish bayonet, and up toward the entrenchments and the tile-roofed fort at the top of the hill. "Come on, come on!" Hawkins shouted, whipping his hat about, white hair and beard flowing in the breeze like some heroic portraiture. It was that famous rush which most people remember as the single most colorful event of the Spanish-American War, and coming as it did, as such a psychological relief to troops able at last to close with the deadly guns to which they had been submitting impotently, it was to grow in the telling into an exhilarating adventure of almost collegiate larkishness. Richard Harding Davis, writing the history of the campaign that same year, took pains to correct the misconceptions that had already formed:

> I have seen many illustrations and pictures of this charge on the San Juan hills, but none of them seem to show it just as I remember it. In the picture papers the men are running up hill swiftly and gallantly, in regular formation, rank after rank, with flags flying, their eyes aflame, and their hair streaming, their bayonets fixed, in long brilliant lines, an invincible overpowering weight of num-

bers. Instead of which I think the thing that impressed one the most, when our men started from cover, was that they were so few. It seemed as if someone had made an awful and terrible mistake. One's instinct was to call them to come back.[6]

The foreign attachés, watching the whole thing, thought so, too. The Americans would never make it, was the general opinion. "Very gallant, but very foolish," one remarked, and probably would have added, *"C'est magnifique, mais ce n'est pas la guerre!"* had it not already been applied to the Light Brigade at Balaclava. Davis continues:

They had no glittering bayonets, they were not massed in regular array. There were a few men in advance, bunched together, and creeping up a steep, sunny hill, the tops of which roared and flashed with flame. The men held their guns pressed across their breasts and stepped heavily as they climbed. Behind these first few, spreading out like a fan, were single lines of men, slipping and scrambling in the smooth grass, moving forward with difficulty as if they were wading waist high through water, moving slowly, carefully, with strenuous effort. It was much more wonderful than any swinging charge could have been.... It was a miracle of self-sacrifice, a triumph of bull-dog courage, which one watched breathless with wonder. The fire of the Spanish riflemen, who still stuck bravely to their posts, doubled and trebled in fierceness, the crests of the hills crackled and burst in amazed roars, and rippled with waves of tiny flame. But the blue line crept steadily up and on, and then, near the top, the broken fragments gathered together with a sudden burst of speed, the Spaniards appeared for a moment outlined against the sky and poised for instant flight, fired a last volley and fled before the swift moving wave that leaped and sprang up after them.

Casualties were almost nonexistent going up the slope, for the Spaniards had been entrenched on the actual crest of the hill rather than the "military crest." (The latter is the rim from which a defender can depress his guns enough to hit an enemy as he comes up, which often cannot be done from the extreme summit.) Yet the American position was still precarious. Shafter had already lost more than a thousand men killed or wounded since daybreak, and now that they had gained the trenches, his troops would have to hang onto them until they could be reinforced by

Lawton's division—still at El Caney. Roosevelt was particularly disgusted with events. He and his men had hurled themselves hell-for-leather from the top of Kettle Hill down into the valley and up again to drive the enemy from the western edge of the San Juan redoubt. He was hot, exhausted, his horse had been wounded twice, and though he emerged from the day with a hero's image from which he was to make the best possible political hay, the whole business had filled him with great professional dissatisfaction. "Not since the campaign of Crassus against the Parthians has there been so criminally incompetent a general as Shafter," he wrote to Senator Lodge a few days later, "and not since the expedition against Walcheren has there been grosser mismanagement than this. The battle simply fought itself." [7]

He might have been thankful, however, for the more fatal short-comings of General Linares, who tried to hold off an army with 1,200 men—less than 10 percent of the large body of troops available to him in the Santiago district. Where he might have called up enough to stop the Americans entirely, he allowed his men at El Caney to be outnumbered twelve to one and those on San Juan Hill sixteen to one. They were simply overwhelmed.

But then things had been handled in an unorthodox way by virtually everybody. The stone church and *fuertes* at Caney had finally been overrun late that afternoon after nine hours of siege by Lawton's encircling infantry. "I have never seen anything," said a captured Spaniard, "to equal the courage and dash of those Americans who . . . offering their naked breasts to our murderous fire, literally threw themselves on our trenches—on the very muzzles of our guns. We . . . mowed them down by the hundreds. . . ." [8] The defenders had run short of ammunition, however; their commander, General Vara del Rey, had been wounded in both legs, and when he was killed in his stretcher while being carried to the rear, his men surrendered. Correspondent Charles Sheldon of *Leslie's Weekly* made a pencil sketch of the main fort with the following caption: "Looking down on the position which we attacked, the wonder is that we were not simply annihilated. There is no doubt that if the Spaniards had held . . . with sharpshooters we would have been defeated with terrible loss." [9]

The British military attaché, Captain Lee, somewhat bewildered by all he'd seen that day, inquired whether it was customary for United States troops to assault blockhouses before they had been successfully "searched by artillery."

"Not always" was the cool but noticeably embarrassed reply.

✱✱✱

****

CHAPTER V

Signal "250"

General Shafter had captured San Juan Hill by storm in a day of fighting that would be remembered as one of the most romantic feats of American arms, yet the glory-that-would-be went unsuspected by the commander in chief, who was wholly occupied by the immediate worry of his still-precarious position. The Army had already suffered nearly 1,500 casualties, including 229 killed—well over twice the 605 Spanish dead and wounded—and it remained under a steady fire from the direction of Santiago. The troops huddled in the trenches on the crest of the hill and behind the walls of the battered pagoda blockhouse, and still the shrapnel seemed to seek them out. Many of them carried a government-issue first-aid packet—containing one small bandage and one big one that could be used as a sling for an arm or shoulder. It even had instructions on it in picture form to show how it was to be applied. Wounded men who couldn't help themselves were tagged with a red, white and blue card at the hill dressing station and sent back down below. The tag was to give doctors back of the lines a fast diagnosis of the victim's injury. The worst cases faced an agonizing journey in makeshift ambulance wagons over the rough, rutted Santiago road to the field hospital which was back behind El Pozo near Army headquarters. Here the hopeless ones were laid out under a tree, and most of these died within a short time. Sometimes a mistake was made. One private had been hit with a slug that made a trim little hole in his left ribs and came out under his shoulder blade. He was taken back to the field hospital and laid out in the shade.

The next day two surgeons passed by, checking for cases worth operating on. One bent over the young soldier, but the other shook his head. "Not a chance." The wounded man was still conscious and heard him. "You're a goddam liar," he said. "I ain't going to die." And he didn't, either.

Field surgeons were to be at the operating tables for twenty-one consecutive hours, yet hundreds of dangerously wounded men remained where they had fallen, unattended. Many downed by sharpshooters back on the jungle paths were not even found until a day or two after the battle, and everywhere those unable to move were alternately drenched by the rain and baked by the sun, going in many instances without food or water for a day and a night.

Men's nerves gave way, too. During a quiet period one soldier suddenly jumped from his trench, threw down his rifle, and ran straight into an officer's arms, his eyes rolling and his jaws chattering crazily. "Captain, I can't go on—I can't stand it—for God's sake send me down to the hospital corps! I'll break, dammit, I'll break!" He was allowed to go back down the hill and his buddies stared after him a moment or two to speculate on whether it took nerve to admit you were about to funk and whether you were worthy of respect if you did admit it.

Everybody was suffering a reaction to the excitement and the expenditure of effort, and the Army as a whole was suddenly a very tired body of men. The infantry who had taken the heights dug in grimly on the ridge, a vantage point from which they could observe the inner defenses of the city. They looked down on banks of barbed wire, entrenchments and gun positions which were as yet completely intact. Reconnaissance had to be brief because of the enemy fire, and when artillery was sent into the front line to try to reply, the clouds of white smoke from the black powder drew the usual retaliatory shells. There were others besides Frederic Remington that day who would have consigned the old ammunition (and its suppliers) to the Smithsonian.

If the troops were experiencing a letdown, so was Shafter. He now faced what looked like a determined foe behind a defense line even stronger than that which he had just overcome, with seemingly no way of getting to him except by yet another frontal assault.[1] He anticipated an ever-growing hospital list from fever as well as the onset of the hurricane season, which was sure to cut his already hopelessly confused communication lines, and he looked with frustrated envy on the task of the Navy, who seemingly had nothing to do but wigwag signals to one another and enjoy the sea breezes under their awnings. On the morning after the battle he asked Sampson for help: "Terrible fight yesterday . . . I urge that you make effort immediately to force the entrance to avoid future losses among my men, which are already very heavy. You can operate now with less loss of life than I can."

Sampson wished the Army every success, but was determined not to let his sympathy with Shafter's position cause him to abandon what he considered proper tactical prudence. He'd said it before and callous it might appear to be, but while men could be replaced, ships, like Rome, were not built in a day, and when they were gone, they were gone for good. He saw no reason to change his original stand on the matter; it was as impossible to force the entrance as it had ever been. Not until he could clear the channel of mines would he go in, and the clearing would take some time after the Morro and La Socapa forts had been occupied by Shafter's troops.

This was not well received by the general. Sick with some kind of fever now himself and with the horrible suspicion that he had thown away 10 percent of his men and gained nothing but a shaky hold on the outer edge of the city's defenses, he answered his colleague with some heat: "I am at a loss to understand why the Navy cannot work under a destructive fire as well as the Army."

Sampson, cooler, no doubt, as a result of his sea breezes, ignored the sarcasm from Army headquarters and took some pains to explain again patiently and paternally that a harbor stocked with explosive would certainly cost him at least one ship if he tried to force it, that the channel would then be blocked against the further entrance, or exit, of any other vessels. The Navy had bombarded the Spanish batteries five times and expended over $2 million worth of ammunition doing it, and in spite of the fact that they had made no effective reply he was still concerned about the strength of the forts. He had been hoping the general would help matters along by at least attacking the enemy gun positions from the rear to create a diversion while he saw about the mine problem.

The admiral had brought up his terror weapon, the *Vesuvius*, to try to make use of her havoc-creating potential, but she didn't seem to be doing the job either. The *Vesuvius* was the U.S. Navy's dynamite ship, the only one in the fleet. She carried no guns in the conventional sense, but instead mounted three 15-inch compressed air tubes capable of firing shells loaded with up to 500 pounds of guncotton each. She was strictly a floating siege weapon, since the tubes were immovable and had to be sighted by aiming the ship itself, much in the manner of a fighter plane with fixed wing guns. The *Vesuvius* crept up near the entrance of the bay every night and lobbed her missiles inside the harbor or up on the high hills. There would be a heavy sigh "like the coughing of a huge animal," and moments later a bright flash and the "rending of earth, timber and stone." She arrived promptly at 11 P.M. to fire three charges, and the Spaniards made a point of not turning in until she'd done her night's work, which was more spectacular than effective, even though one of the blockbusters had thrown up a colossal geyser close to the torpedo boat *Furor* and caused her and the flagship *María Teresa* to change their anchorage.

Aside from this regular nuisance bombardment, Sampson was prepared to play a waiting and watchful game. His order of battle, published on June 1, the day of his arrival at Santiago, had divided his fleet into two squadrons. The first, commanded by himself, was made up of the *New York*, the battleships *Iowa* and *Oregon*, the cruiser *New Orleans* and the torpedo boat *Porter*. The second, under Schley, consisted of the battleships *Massachusetts* and *Texas*, the cruisers *Brooklyn* and *Marblehead* and the yacht *Vixen*. His object was simple but well thought out. The city was to be blockaded tightly, the American ships forming a semicircle keeping about six miles out from the Morro by day. In the event the Spanish squadron tried to come out, the first one to spot them would fire an alarm gun and then run up a special signal hoist consisting of the code flags for "2," "5" and "0," which all ships would acknowledge before going into action. At night the battleships and the *Brooklyn* would move in to four miles. A mile nearer yet would be a picket line composed of the other cruisers and the *Vixen*, and closer still, within four thousand yards or so of the Morro, six steam launches from the warships would maintain patrol. Every night when there was no moon, Sampson had two of the big ships steam up to just a mile off Morro and throw their searchlights on the entrance. The beams were so bright that the flanking hills could be clearly seen, as could the surf breaking on the coral reefs. It was quite impressive. "My God," commented Captain Arthur Paget, the British naval observer with the U.S. fleet, "I never saw such damned impertinence in my life!" Should the trapped squadron attempt to break through these rings of ships any time after dark, the alarm signal would be two red rockets fired by the steam launches on the close sentry duty.

✳✳✳

It was a sharp nocturnal watch, which was a good thing, for a night sortie was what had been in the Spanish mind almost from the beginning. Cervera himself, however, had no real hope of being able either to steal or to force his way out—night or day— and an undeviating mood of impending catastrophe underscores his discussion and correspondence with his own captains, with Captain General Blanco, with General Linares and the Minister of Marine in Madrid.

Cervera's first council of war with his officers was held on June 8, one week after Sampson had arrived to reinforce Schley on the blockade. He threw it open to all opinions on the situation and one by one heard his subordinates' views. Captain Bustamente, his second in command, thought that the squadron should break out immediately, taking advantage of the darkness of the moon. The torpedo-boat destroyers would lead the way, turning south and steaming at top speed to get by the *Texas* and the other three enemy battleships. Then the *Cristóbal Colón*, fastest of the cruisers, would follow on a west-southwesterly course, heading straight for the *Brooklyn*, which usually seemed to occupy that position of the semicircle. With that speedy American ship engaged, the *María Teresa* would make for the east-southeast, followed by the

Viscaya and the *Oquendo*. Out of this scatter-gun formation perhaps half the squadron would get through, which was better than being forced to surrender *in toto* when provisions ran out, as they were certain to, soon.

His was the only optimistic plan. Captain Concas of the *Teresa* hedged by recommending the sortie be made only in the event one of the fast cruisers, *Brooklyn* or *New York*, should leave for any purpose, and the captains of the *Colón*, *Viscaya* and *Oquendo* were not in favor of going out at all. Cervera passed these opinions on to Madrid and to General Linares, along with his own view that he didn't see how he could take the risk of an escape attempt. There was no question of surprise, he told the Santiago commander; how could a nighttime sortie succeed when his every move would be lighted up like a magic-lantern show? Which suggested the obvious: could the general do something about the enemy searchlights? Linares doubted that he could, because of the range involved—the Americans could move out farther and still throw their beams on the entrance—but while favors were being asked, might not the admiral put ashore a portion of his crews to aid in the defense of the city, which was certain to face attack by enemy ground forces before long? They could be of some use for the time being, anyway.

The American landing had already taken place, and Cervera realized too well that, if Santiago fell, it would be all over with him, so he agreed to make available to Linares as many of his sailors as could be armed with the limited stock of rifles on hand. If the Americans succeeded in investing the city, no further supplies or anything else would be incoming, either. In light of this, a blithe and ill-timed message from the commandant of the Havana naval yard arrived to mock Cervera's own material position. It was now possible, he was told, to order ammunition by number, class and caliber if the *almirante* would be good enough to let them know what it was he required. With great restraint the *almirante* let it be known he required practically everything. More than 80 percent of his 5.5-inch secondary battery shells were worthless, his fuses were almost totally unreliable too, and he had virtually no torpedoes. The *Colón*, in case the commandant was unaware of it, had no big guns to fire anything at all with. Would the navy yard like to hear more? Cervera didn't expect an answer from Havana and he didn't get one.

So depressing was the situation that he found the sole responsibility difficult to bear. Accordingly, on June 24, the day of the Las Guásimas skirmish, he again convened a captain's meeting and this time even Bustamente and Concas succumbed. The verdict was unanimous; it was impossible to go out.

All this gloom struck General Linares as unpalatable—there was such a thing as self-respect—and he suggested to Cervera in a rather shocked tone that, if the squadron should haul down its colors without making any kind of show at all, the moral effect would be terrible, both in Spain and abroad. Cervera sat down and wrote a long letter in return, addressed to "My Dear General and Friend," in which he laid bare his thoughts and his whole state of mind. He confessed that he had considered the squadron lost ever since it had left Cape Verde, and for that reason had energetically opposed sailing to the Caribbean at all. He had thought (and undoubtedly hoped) he would be relieved of the command at that time, but such was not the case, and now that he was here, he was attempting to make the best of a bad bargain by putting his men ashore to man the trenches and help keep the enemy out of Santiago. Once an officer in his position had accepted the fact that an escape attempt had no real chance, one had to decide how to sell his ships for the highest price. Should they be scuttled after contributing what they could to the defense of the city, or was he expected to sail out to suicide, "dragging along with me," as he put it, "these two thousand sons of Spain"?

> I, who am a man without ambitions, without mad passions, believe that whatever is most expedient should be done, and I state most emphatically that I shall *never* be the one to decree the horrible and useless hecatomb which will be the only possible result of the sortie from here by main force, for I should consider myself responsible before God and history for the lives sacrificed on the altar of vanity and not in the true defense of the country.[2]

Indeed, such a decree was Cervera's responsibility no longer. The burden was to be placed upon Captain General Blanco, whose shoulders were well able to bear it, not being weighed down by the admiral's humanitarian sensitivities. Putting Cervera under Blanco's orders was not meant as a rebuke; it was considered that the fleet, since it had no immediate destination, was ostensibly there for the protection of the city, and as such should be used to that effect by the commander in chief as he saw fit.

Nobody was really surprised at Blanco's decision that it was preferable "for the integrity of arms to succumb in battle." It was a strong second to Linares' claim that the effect on the world would be ruinous were the ships captured at their moorings; it would be assumed Spain had lost the war. Blanco suspected, too, that Cervera was exaggerating the difficulties, for night battle involved so many imponderables that he didn't think a hostile fleet, no matter how strong, could do that much damage in the dark. (Besides, Blanco would *not* stand for being called vain. By anybody.)

From this point on we see the matter virtually pass out of Cervera's hands. He considered his fate as sealed, and in a sense it hardly mattered anymore. It had been a long time since the blood of the old hidalgo had run hot in his veins. It seemed his honors were behind him now, and only honor—Spain's, if one wanted to put it in those terms—remained. In a letter to Blanco he reflected sorrowfully that it was a pity some sailor more able than himself could not be sent to take over the squadron, but of course it was too late for that now. (Not even Captain Bustamente was available any longer, having met his death a few days before in the Spanish lines ashore.) He then asked for confirmation of the order of sortie, as he would certainly not want to misinterpret Blanco's directive.

It came, and was speedy and to the point. The four cruisers and two torpedo-boat destroyers would remain in harbor and wait for a favorable opportunity to break out in whatever direction Cervera deemed best. If the fall of the city seemed imminent, they would have no choice but to leave immediately. Those among his crews that were ashore would be returned to their ships, and since in the admiral's own estimation it would take him twelve hours to get up steam, his fires ought to be kept going and all six vessels in readiness to make their exit from what was looking to be an increasingly black military predicament. The enemy was at the gates of Santiago and the specter of disaster was in the air.

***

One might have had a different feeling of foreboding from the look of things on the other side of the lines. Colonel Roosevelt, who had been spending the forty-eight hours since the San Juan battle listening to the intermittent but never-ending whine of enemy bullets, seemed to be in a state of agitation—his own form of psychological letdown after the efforts of July 1 had failed to produce a decisive breakthrough. On Sunday the 3rd he dashed off a nervous letter to his friend Senator Lodge:

> Tell the president for Heaven's sake to send us every regiment and above all every battery possible. We have won so far at a heavy cost; but the Spaniards fight very hard and charging these entrenchments against modern rifles is terrible. We are in measurable distance of a terrible military disaster.... Our General is poor; he is too unwieldy to get to the front....[3]

For two days now Washington had been anxiously hoping for some news that would counterbalance the dismal hints of serious losses, the illness of the commander in chief and the rumor of a yellow-fever outbreak among the troops. It could hardly have been comforting when the War Department finally got General Shafter's dispatch that morning, informing Alger that the Santiago defenses were too strong to be overrun by the men and equipment he had with him and that he was "seriously considering withdrawing about five miles and taking up a new position." In one of his less pessimistic moments, however, Shafter let himself be persuaded by an officer on his staff to make a demand on the city to surrender, and accordingly a message went off to the enemy lines, employing what the sender hoped was a properly intransigent tone in calling for a capitulation, with the threat of a bombardment to put some teeth in it. It couldn't hurt to try, particularly since it might be he was about to get some cooperation from Sampson at last. The admiral, weary of the Army-Navy bickering over how best to get at the Spaniards and feeling some obligation toward the sister service that had thus far incurred the whole of the war's casualties, had agreed the evening before to come to Army headquarters and once again go over the problem of ways and means.

***

Resigned as he was to his belief that the last bow of a long and conscientious career would be little more than a vainglorious gesture, Admiral Cervera was listening with some detachment to reports of the American investment of the city. He suspected it wouldn't be long now, and so it wasn't with any surprise that he awoke early on Saturday morning, July 2, to find one of Captain General Blanco's short and pointed notes, marked "very urgent," waiting for him. It said: "In view of the exhausted and serious condition of Santiago, as stated by General Toral, your excellency will reembark troops of squadron as fast as possible, and go out immediately." [4]

That was it then. He called for his aide and gave his orders calmly—there was no cause to alarm the men any more than necessary—though of course there were preparations to make and things to be decided. Quartermasters on the *María Teresa* turned to with both signal flags and searchlights; all ships' companies in the city would return to their vessels at once, the ships themselves were to have full steam up by two o'clock that afternoon, pilots should come aboard immediately and all captains were to assemble without delay in the wardroom of the flagship for a council of war.

Though they had been prepared for them too, some of the officers flared up hotly at Blanco's arbitrary orders, and angry suggestions that they should not be obeyed at all went round the meeting table. Cervera himself had fought against making the sortie as long as he could, but now they must do what had to be done, and when the mutinous talk subsided and the others realized it too, he turned the meeting to the problem of whether the escape should be tried that night or the following morning. The two previous nights had been moonless, and a cloudy sky seemed to indicate this would be the case again, but then it was remembered that two lines of mines had first to be swept from the channel, so the attempt would have to wait till the next day. It had been noted, too, that the Americans always held religious services on the decks of their ships, and when in church formation would hardly be ready for battle. Perhaps they could be surprised. The Spanish vessels would get underway at nine o'clock, come out the harbor entrance as fast as safety permitted, shooting as they came, ram the United States ships if they were near enough, and if they were not, head west around Diamond Shoals and make with all speed in the direction of Cienfuegos. The meeting broke up with reluctance. Every officer present knew it might be his last visit with the white-bearded figure who presided with his customary dignity at the head of the table there in the ornately paneled wardroom. It seemed the occasion demanded that something be offered—a bit of inspiration or even of irony—but there was nothing to say. The boatswain's pipe said it all instead, with mournful finality, as one by one the captains went over the side and were rowed back to their ships. Boats were hoisted in, anchor cables shortened, and that afternoon the gunboat *Alvarado* crept out to the channel mouth to take up the mines.

✳✳✳

There had been an early reveille, and from about 5:45 to 7:30 the big ships of the American fleet had tried another lambasting of the batteries, with the same negligible effect, except for knocking down the corner of one of the towers of El Morro, and with it the big red and yellow Spanish flag. Then normal shipboard routine got something of a stir when officers on the *Brooklyn* noticed a little enemy one-stacker chugging about the harbor entrance, and a definite jolt later on at about two in the afternoon when lookouts shouted down that columns of smoke were rising from back behind the bluffs. This brought everybody out on deck for a look. George Graham, Associated Press correspondent aboard the cruiser, claims in his account of the battle that among the *Brooklyn*'s crew "there was no possible doubt but that the Spanish squadron was firing up," and that Schley assumed the enemy was either readying to come out or else was moving to a better spot in the harbor in order to enfilade the American positions on the hills with gunfire and hold up an attack on the city. At any rate the commodore sent the yacht *Vixen* along the semicircle of the blockading fleet to notify each ship in turn to stay in as close as possible during the night and to make sure that Sampson in the *New York* at the far end of the line was aware that there were peculiar goings on in the bay.

Sunday morning, July 3, dawned gray and overcast, as it so often did now in the early days of the rainy season, and to Graham, looking shoreward with a poet's eye, Cuba was "like a huge fog bank—a surging, rolling wave of tinted mist, in which the huge shapeless mass of the island had sunk, and seemed drowned." As the sun rose higher, early watchers could discern first the white line of the breakers beating on the beach, and then a changing pattern of color as the mist took on a warmer hue and the green of the lower hills began to show through. A breeze came up and the bank of haze vanished, revealing the outlines of the battery on the left, then El Morro on the right, and then the blue water between them. The sky became blue, too—bright and clear—and the sun began to get hot and drove the watchers beneath the shade of the awning that stretched over the *Brooklyn's* quarter-deck.

The blockade line was a little broken that morning. The cruisers *New Orleans* and *Newark* and the converted tender *Suwanee* had all made the forty-mile trip to Guantánamo the previous day to coal, and observers noticed that the *Massachusetts* had also gone; surprising, in light of the fact that for the first time since the fleet had arrived there was noticeable activity within the harbor. When Schley asked, the officer of the deck told him the battleship had left her station at dawn to refuel at Guantánamo also.

At about a quarter to nine he was even more surprised to see the *New York* hoist the signal "Disregard the movements of the commander in chief" and begin to get underway quickly to the east as well. Schley was of course aware of Sampson's plan to meet with Shafter, but thought it was strange, in light of the suspicious smoke, that the admiral would remove the *New York*—the only ship on hand, other than the *Brooklyn*, with speed to match that of the Spaniards—when there were any number of small craft which could take him to Siboney. That, and the departure of the

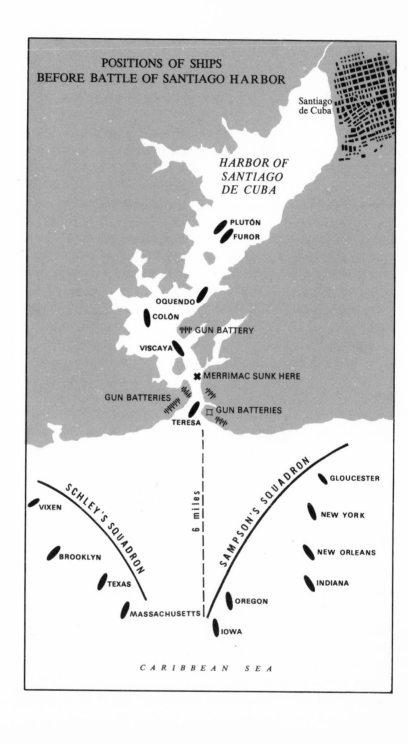

POSITIONS OF SHIPS
BEFORE BATTLE OF SANTIAGO HARBOR

Santiago
de Cuba

HARBOR OF
SANTIAGO
DE CUBA

PLUTÓN
FUROR

OQUENDO
COLÓN
GUN BATTERY
VISCAYA

✖ MERRIMAC SUNK HERE

GUN BATTERIES

GUN BATTERIES

TERESA

SCHLEY'S SQUADRON

SAMPSON'S SQUADRON

6 miles

GLOUCESTER

VIXEN

NEW YORK

BROOKLYN

NEW ORLEANS

TEXAS

INDIANA

MASSACHUSETTS

OREGON

IOWA

CARIBBEAN SEA

Massachusetts, which represented one-third of the fleet's heaviest fire power, were both ill-timed, he thought.

With two big ships missing there was now a noticeable gap in the half-circle, and that was bothersome. The *Brooklyn*, *Texas* and *Vixen* grouped together a little less than five miles to the west of the harbor, the *Vixen* nearer shore, the *Texas* southwest of the entrance and the *Brooklyn* in between—all three out of their usual positions. Farther out to sea and looking straight into the harbor mouth was the *Iowa*. Next to her to the east lay the *Oregon*, and between her and where the *New York* had been was the *Indiana*, with the little yacht *Gloucester* well in toward the Morro.

The orders of the day called for the ships to muster all hands at 9:30. It being the first Sunday of the month, the Articles of War would be read to the crews as was customary before divine service, and the long lines of men in dress whites were forming on the decks already, squaring away hats, straightening collars and neckerchiefs. Commodore Schley, dressed for comfort in a pair of white-duck trousers and a worn blue coat, lounged in a deck chair with George Graham, watching the ceremony. He leaned back, propped his feet up, stroked his imperial as he often did when relaxing and listened to the men count off. "This is pretty slow," Graham remembered him saying.

On the forward bridge Navigator Hodgson had relieved the officer of the deck while the quartermaster was keeping the long glass trained on the suspicious black smudge that hovered just behind the steep heights at the harbor entrance. But was it only hovering? He'd been idly watching one smoke plume in particular because it lined up with a hilltop in a way suggestive of a volcano. Now as he kept his eye on it, he could see the column was moving. The navigator grabbed the glass and took a long look himself. One was enough. In two quick strides he was at the rail with his megaphone: "After bridge, there! Report to the commodore and the captain that the enemy's ships are coming out!"

Schley jumped to his feet and snatched his own binoculars. He seemed elated and stamped his foot, his fingers digging into Graham's arm. "We'll give it to them now! We'll give it to them now!" Captain Cook dived down the ladder to his cabin, stripping off his uniform coat and collar on the way, donned an old black alpaca jacket and was back on deck by the time his executive officer, Commander Mason, had ordered the crew to quarters. Schley headed for the bridge and on the way called to Ensign McCauley to signal, "The enemy is escaping." McCauley already had done so. "Signal the fleet to clear for action, then!"

The commodore pulled out his watch as he and Graham reached the conning tower. It was just 9:35. Where was the *New York?* he asked Quartermaster Anderson, who still had his telescope. Could he see the flagship? Schley took the glass himself and searched the horizon, but Sampson and the *New York* were nowhere in sight, and he smiled a little and let his breath out slowly; it was going to be all his fight. "Signal, 'Close in' and 'Follow the flag,'" he ordered.

Just then a 6-pounder cracked out on the *Iowa.* Steaming from the signal mast was a yellow flag with a blue ball in the center, beneath it a half-yellow and half-red flag, and last of all, a yellow swallowtail pennant with a blue cross—"2," "5" and "o." Fighting Bob Evans had been having breakfast with his son, a naval cadet from the *Massachusetts,* when the sound of an alarm gun from the *Oregon* brought them to their feet. Bells suddenly began to ring all over the ship and Evans was already on his way to the bridge. There he looked on what he would always remember as one of the most momentous sights of his life. Heading straight for him out of the harbor was the enemy fleet, the leading ship "with a bone in her teeth," twin waves of white water parting from the trim dark hull, oily black smoke pouring from her funnels, the sun catching the gilt escutcheon on her prow and playing on the huge red-and-gold battle ensign of Spain at her masthead.

The *Oregon's* bugler had just blown first call for muster when the 6-pounder which had been kept ready and loaded as an alarm gun broke the Sunday morning stillness. In his excitement Captain Clark's marine orderly broke into the skipper's quarters unannounced. "The old man jumped up a-standing!" he afterward told his messmates. By the time Clark reached the conning tower, the *Oregon* was underway. The boilers of the rest of the American ships had been kept fired up for a speed of five knots, but Chief

Engineer Milligan demanded and got much from his sweating black gang, and the *Oregon* was ready for 10 knots on short notice. Ever since her dash around the Horn, his men and his engines had been almost one; she'd steam, he'd see to that.

On the *Texas* the last notes of church call had only just died away, and Captain Philip was making his way up on deck for services when the electric gong sounded and he was nearly bowled over in the companionway in the rush. "They're coming out!" someone yelled at him, and a moment later he, too, was on the bridge, where his executive officer, Commander Harper, reported every man at his post in three minutes time. Philip was pleased, but something was bothering his navigator, Lieutenant Heilner. Apparently the *Texas* was flying only one small ensign; couldn't they hoist the battle flag? Philip pointed to the signal yard where "250" flapped in the morning breeze. "I guess," he said, "there won't be any doubts about our being ready for action." Nevertheless it was the kind of spirit the captain liked and he told Heilner he might fly it if he wanted to. The flag locker was secured and the quartermaster's key unavailable, but there was an ax close by, and in a few moments the *Texas* was off, decked out now to everyone's satisfaction.

Three minutes was good time in clearing for action; in fact anything less than five was considered fast, for there was a lot packed into those 180 seconds. To the uninitiated it always seemed like the wildest chaos. More than two hundred watertight doors had to be secured, sealing the ship into compartments that would keep her afloat even if some of them were flooded; heavy steel battle plates were put down over hatches, hoses were hooked up to fire plugs, small boats were swathed in wet canvas to keep them from catching fire, and protective nets of rope were hung around the pilothouse, gun sponsons and other exposed places to ward off splinters. Davits, hand rails and anchor hoists were taken down and laid out flat on the deck to give free swing to the big guns, objects that might fly about were stowed below, and gangplanks, paint buckets and other deck gear were simply jettisoned. Division tubs throughout the ship were filled with fresh water and doors were left ajar so that blast wouldn't blow them open. Topside, officers in charge of the turrets put on working clothes—canvas jumpers, old trousers, battered caps—the Japanese messboys were sent to the powder division, and half a dozen apprentice boys reported to the bridge to act as runners. There signal men, range finders and searchlight crews were already at work. In the pilothouse or conning tower were men at the wheel—alternates standing by—with others at the speaking tubes which controlled the ship by internal signal. In the fighting tops of the military mast, their crews had hauled up ammunition for the 1-pounder lead squirts and were standing ready at the guns like their shipmates in the turrets below. Down in the depths of the vessel firemen labored to get up steam in the boilers and, in some cases, couple the engines. Dynamos were started up to work battle circuits, hydraulic turret-turning machinery tested, ammunition-hoist mechanisms, steering engines, fire pumps and ventilating blowers made ready. Magazines were opened for the rush delivery of shells to each of the ship's big 12- or 13-inch guns via the hoists and ammo "cars." In the torpedo rooms gratings were removed and pneumatic pressure turned on to charge compressed-air flasks, the torpedoes rolled in and the tubes prepared. In the sick bay the surgeons and their ratings laid out cases of instruments, rolls of lint, splints, bandages and antiseptics and covered the operating tables with rubber. Unless a ship were very fortunate, they would be as important as the shells, the signal flags and the fire hoses.

At nine o'clock, as the bells of Santiago's churches began to ring out for morning Mass, the Spanish flotilla had slowly and silently got underway. The cruisers fell into column 800 yards apart behind the flagship *María Teresa* as she moved off toward El Morro. The *Cristóbal Colón*, then the *Almirante Oquendo*, next the *Viscaya*, and finally the torpedo boats *Furor* and *Plutón* disappeared one by one from view around Ratones Cay, drew a salute from the Punta Gorda battery as they passed, and moved carefully into the narrow channel where their bow waves lapped at the exposed funnel top and mastheads of the sunken collier *Merrimac*.

In Havana the arrival of Cervera's message announcing his departure made General Blanco's thick breakfast chocolate taste even better than usual. This sortie was surely the thing to do and would come out right in the end. He ordered the following cable sent to the military commander at Cienfuegos: "Make preparations for the reception of the squadron commanded by Admiral Cervera and which may arrive any moment at Cienfuegos. Facilitate the admiral with whatever he may need. Congratulate him for me on the distinguished victory over the enemy." [5]

It was with a certain fatalistic humor that Cervera viewed the great columns of smoke spewing from the funnels of his squadron. There would hardly be any surprise to this morning's adventure, enemy church services or no; even pious men lost in their devotions couldn't fail to notice those heaven-sent signals. However Captain Concas of the Teresa had reported in a last-minute reconnaissance from El Morro that one of the blockading ships had disappeared about daybreak, leaving somewhat bigger spaces than usual between the remainder, so the original plan would be adhered to, and the admiral gave himself a chance—a slim one but only just a chance—of carrying it off. The New York and the Brooklyn were the only Americans that could match his speed, and if he turned to the west as planned, the latter ship alone would be in a position to keep pace with him. He had even considered steaming straight at the Brooklyn to try to ram and cripple her, thus giving the rest of his ships better odds, and he would determine when the time came if that were feasible.

Headlong flight was about the only hope, and it depended upon his coming about to the west as soon as possible, yet the hands clasped behind his back showed only the least tremor as he asked Pilot Miguel Lopez when the helm might be shifted. Not until they passed El Diamante—Diamond Shoals—he was told. Then, when the lighter blue of the shallow water, roiled with foam from the flagship's propellers, disappeared astern, he accompanied Lopez to the ladder that would drop him into the boat towed alongside. "See that they pay you," he told the pilot. "You've done well."

"Full speed ahead" was the admiral's next order, and as Captain Concas came up, saluted and asked permission to open fire he nodded without looking at him. Concas stepped to the rail, gave the command and was countersigned by the *Teresa*'s bugler, whose notes were answered in turn by the ships behind, a picturesque and fateful overture. "The sound of my bugles was the last echo of those which history tells us were sounded at the capture of Granada. It was the signal that the history of four centuries of grandeur was at an end and that Spain was becoming a nation of the fourth class." [6]

The crash of number two gun of the main-deck battery and the broadside that followed shook the captain back to the business at hand, and he could only murmur, "*Pobre España!*" as the *Teresa* trembled under the concussion. Admiral Cervera answered him with a hopeless shrug that said more than words ever could.

***

Schley had just stepped up on the small raised platform which he'd ordered built around the base of the *Brooklyn*'s forward 8-inch turret in time to see the first hostile shot land short of the *Iowa*, then the geysers thrown up by the *Teresa*'s salvo, which also was short. The Spanish guns gave off a lot of smoke—black powder—which surprised him a little. Then a gust of wind blew it away momentarily and gave the American watchers a better look at the enemy. Lieutenant Sears, his glasses fixed on the harbor mouth, had been counting the emerging cruisers silently; now he reported they were all out and slowing down to drop their pilots one by one, the torpedo boats with them. Schley warned Cook to have his rapid-fire guns ready for the latter; he knew everybody would be laying for the fast *Brooklyn*.

He'd opened fire himself now, and an eager gunnery lieutenant, having just got off his first shot at an enemy, stuck his head up out of the 8-inch turret and waved at the commodore: "Did that one hit, sir?" "I couldn't see, Simpson," Schley answered, "but keep at them." He smiled. "Tell your bullies to give them hell." [7]

Somebody was sure to get it, for the Spanish ships were heading straight toward the *Brooklyn*'s bows, and when Navigator Hodgson called his attention to the fact, the commodore only told Hodgson to continue to head right for *them*. Almost as he spoke, though, he saw the leading enemy ship turn west, and he knew he would have to change course now. Sampson's only battle plan, which Schley was carrying out, had been to rush and close with the Spaniards as they came out of the harbor, but this was not going to work in the present circumstances; if the enemy squadron tried beating its way along the coast toward Cienfuegos, it would wind up as a running fight and to Schley's way of thinking this put the *Brooklyn* in an awkward position. Being on the extreme left, she was closest to the enemy and a lot depended on her. She couldn't very well keep in toward shore or she'd be outdistanced; yet if she turned west with the Spanish column, she would expose herself to the raking fire of every ship, not to say a ramming and torpedo attack.

Schley had to make up his mind in a hurry, and the maneuver he decided on was a peculiar one. He would come completely about to the east, describing a great loop *away* from the enemy, then continue his turn and place the *Brooklyn* on a parallel course with the Spanish line, hoping by that time some of the other American ships would have caught up and they could all concentrate their fire more effectively. As he ordered the helm put over, the *Viscaya*, following aft of the *María Teresa*, headed out of line as if to ram him, but fortunately the American cruiser had already begun to swing to starboard and the two vessels passed with only some thousand yards separating them, close enough for Schley to see daylight between the legs of Spanish sailors running from turret to superstructure deck. Hodgson suggested backing the *Brooklyn*'s starboard engine to get her around faster, but Schley told him no; he didn't want to lose headway.

Unfortunately the commodore's 360-degree turn was as unexpected as it was precipitate. The battleship *Texas*, which had been the *Brooklyn*'s blockade mate on the right and was now the next American ship in line, was pounding along to the west at full speed, firing all the while and assuming the *Brooklyn* was doing the same up ahead. As Captain Philip put it: "The smoke from our guns began to hang so heavily and densely over the ship that for a few minutes we could see nothing. We might as well have had a blanket tied over our heads. Suddenly a whiff of breeze and a lull in the firing lifted the pall, and there, bearing toward us and across our bows, turning on her port helm, with big waves curling over her bows and great clouds of black smoke pouring from her funnels was the *Brooklyn*. She looked as big as half a dozen *Great Easterns* and seemed so near that it took our breath away." [8]

Hodgson caught his superior's arm as he saw the big prow come out of the smoke at them. "Look out for the *Texas*, sir!" he yelled, the niceties of naval etiquette lost for the moment. "Damn the *Texas!* Let her look out for herself!" snapped Schley, and the old battleship just managed to, backing both engines and frantically racing against herself in a collision near-miss. [9]

The *Brooklyn* kept blasting away as she made her turn, her port side "a perfect mass of flame and smoke" as the eight 8-inch, six 5-inch and even the little 6-pounders all let go furiously. Schley ordered the men at the guns to aim deliberately and make every shot tell, something the Spaniards obviously were not doing, for his own ship was practically untouched even though she had been under a deluge of enemy fire all the while. The Spanish fleet, while presenting what Fighting Bob Evans of the *Iowa* called "the finest spectacle that has probably ever been seen on the water," was way off target. "Their broadsides came with mechanical rapidity," Evans recalled, "and in striking contrast to the deliberate fire of the American ships. A torrent of projectiles was sailing over us, harmlessly exploding in the water beyond." [10]

The *Iowa*, third in the chase behind the *Brooklyn* and *Texas*, wanted to try to ram either the *Teresa* or *Viscaya*, the first and second in the Spanish line, and Evans was dismayed to learn that his ship's best speed was only about 10 knots, while the enemy seemed to be making about 13. As they pulled ahead, Evans swung off to port and gave the *Teresa* his whole broadside at about 2,500 yards and then turned back, keeping the *Viscaya* on his starboard bow. His port battery kept firing on the *Teresa* and his starboard guns at the *Viscaya* and *Oquendo*. The latter ship was being zeroed in on, and was now getting hit for the first time by the *Indiana*, which had moved up on her quarter, and by the *Oregon*, too, which was keeping in position off her port bow.

The gun duel had been stepped up on both sides. The *Indiana*, like the *Iowa* slower and bound to fall behind, was still in range and firing with good effect, one of her heavy shells having hit the *Teresa* almost immediately and doing, it was later found, massive damage. Another was seen to explode just abaft the *Viscaya's* funnels, and for a moment the after part of that vessel was swallowed up in a flash of flame. The Spanish salvos were coming at brief intervals, though enemy marksmanship was still poor. Captain Taylor of the *Indiana* gave the Spanish gunners credit for their energy if not their skill, admitting his own men had a great advantage over them in range finding. "It had been our daily, hourly habit for many weeks to estimate our distance from the Morro by the eye and verify it with our sextants and stadimeters; and in emerging from the narrow entrance the Spanish ships almost touched the Morro, so that in the first few minutes . . . we had their range absolutely." [11]

He, too, recalled that the enemy aimed high, being impressed by the "screech and hum" of shells of all sizes passing over his head, and was surprised that it took them so long to correct the mistake. The *Texas*, for example, was working her guns slowly and deliberately, and only when a good target presented itself, which was not very often, due to the thick banks of funnel and gun smoke which masked every hostile ship but the lead one. Captain Philip later remembered a couple of Spanish shells that were on target, however, one of which exploded with a terrific crash over the forward superstructure and "lifted the bridge contingent off their feet." He recalled "pitching up in the air, with my coattails flying out behind me, as if I had been thrown by one of Roosevelt's broncos." No one was hurt except a cadet whose eardrums were split. Another Spanish 6-inch shell exploded in a locker below and set fire to the hammocks which were stored there, causing such a billow of smoke some of the men thought the ship had blown up. [12]

✷✷✷

Seven miles down the coast Admiral Sampson and his flag lieutenant, Staunton, stood by the gangway waiting to go ashore. Brown-canvas leggings and clanking spurs contrasted oddly with their trim, high-collared white uniforms, and neither man was exactly looking forward to the hot, cross-country ride to General

Shafter's headquarters. The *New York* was at Sunday morning inspection, her crew drawn up by divisions on her broad, holystoned weather deck, three or four officers and a yeoman with a clipboard to record defaulters' names, leisurely checking the front of each rigid rank, and then the back. The ship's ladder was down, the admiral's launch idling in the water below, and the officer of the deck getting ready to pipe the two men over the side, when suddenly there was a hail from the lookout in the foretop. Sampson, the O.D., the sideboys and the inspecting party froze for a long moment; then somebody gave the commander in chief a pair of binoculars which he trained in the direction of Santiago harbor.

At first he couldn't see any movement at all—just smoke—then, as he watched, a tiny silhouette, a black sliver against the white cloud bank on the horizon, emerged from the contour of the shore. Even at that distance her size and her lines told him she was one of Cervera's cruisers. It wasn't in Sampson's character to show excitement, and those present could only guess at the admiral's feelings as he watched the "250" signal hoisted, and how the import of what was happening must have struck him. What timing! The few brief hours when he was forced to be absent from the scene! Even his dour nature rose to the occasion to hotly curse this Spanish caprice, along with the whole meeting at Siboney and the general whose unknowledgeable demands had made it necessary. He allowed himself the luxury of one moment in which he asked: Why this of all days? Then he was brought back to the realm of duty and decision by the general-quarters gongs and the white-clad lines dissolving in a rush of legs on the deck below him as the helm was put over and the big cruiser swung round toward the enemy.

The suspense at this point would have tried anyone's nerves. One following the other, the black hulls slipped out of the harbor, at intervals of about four minutes, at which time each was immediately enveloped in a dirty haze penetrated by minuscule intermittent flashes. What happened now would decide everything, for if the slivers turned east, it would be to the commander in chief and the *New York* that the job of heading off the whole Spanish squadron would fall. In the fireroom the open mouths of the furnaces gave off a hot-bright orange glow as the black gang worked furiously to get full steam in the boilers. Up on the flying bridge Sampson kept the long glass on the scene being played out just up the coast—little lightning flashes and the distant rumble of a summer storm—so near and yet so out of reach. He counted the enemy as they came out and was surprised to see the torpedo boats bring up the rear, all alone. Risking these little vessels in broad daylight would have been understandable were they protected in the lee of one of the bigger ships, and it made no sense at all to expose them nakedly to a fleet action.

His view was almost wholly obscured by the spreading gray smudge, but the tiny bursts of orange from within, which could have been either guns firing or explosions, told him that things were happening nevertheless. The brief white spurts against the black funnel smoke were shell splashes, no doubt about that. He watched Cervera's ships turn end on as they reached the open sea, and for a while he told himself there was still a good chance. He could feel the hum under him as the New York's engines labored, gaining speed little by little. Were the dots larger now, the summer-thunder rumble closer? Erect and silent, he continued to search the horizon. In a few minutes Captain Chadwick came up and told him that the flagship was now making twelve knots, but Sampson showed, again, no visible enthusiasm. He had reason this time. There could be no doubt now that the Spaniards had turned west and the battle, with all it represented, was moving irrevocably away from him.

★★★

CHAPTER VI

****

"Tell Your Bullies They're Doing Great Work!"

The torpedo boats *Furor* and *Plutón* had every right to feel bare as they came out from behind the dark bluff of the Morro at a following distance of about 1,200 yards from the *Almirante Oquendo*. Supposedly faster than anything afloat, they could send a battleship to the bottom with a single well-placed hit from one of the two 14-inch Whitehead tubes they carried, but speed and torpedoes were their only weapons against a capital ship, as they had no protection and carried only minor armament —two 14-pounders, two 6-pounders and two 1-pounder quick-firing guns each.

Only one American ship stood in their immediate way, however, and she was no lumbering dreadnought, but only the little armed yacht *Gloucester*—862 tons at fighting weight and boasting all of four 6-pounders in her own main battery. The *Gloucester* was nothing more than a peaceful gentleman pressed into uniform for the duration, and the more socially astute among the fleet's officers might have recognized her as J. P. Morgan's pleasure boat *Corsair*, which he had sold to the government for $250,000 when the war began, and which up to now had known nothing more threatening than a surprise squall on Long Island Sound.

Her skipper, Lieutenant Commander Richard Wainwright, was a little more experienced, anyway. In a navy where relatively few officers had, till that morning, seen war at first hand, he enjoyed the distinction of already having had a ship go down under him— in Havana harbor the February before, while serving as Captain Sigsbee's executive officer. With more reason to "remember the *Maine*" than most, and with a fine contempt for the fact that either of the Spanish boats was a match and then some for his *Gloucester*, Wainwright put his bows across their course and attempted to cut them off. The *Indiana* had just warned him by signal flag, "Torpedo boats coming out," but in the smoke he had interpreted it as "Gunboats move in," so he quickly complied. He had been lying in wait outside the harbor and had zeroed in his quick firers on the entrance, so as the *Plutón* appeared, she was met by a hail of American 6-pounder shells which were on target right from the beginning. To this welcome was added another from the secondary batteries of the *Iowa* and *Indiana*, both of which used the torpedo boats for target practice as they went past. The *Gloucester* and her foes were at such close quarters, though, that all three ships were equally threatened by the battleships' guns.

Wainwright graciously gave the Spaniards all credit for the geysers frothing up around him. "The Maxim automatic one-pounders from the *Plutón* and *Furor* appeared likely to be our most dangerous enemies. When we came to within three thousand yards of the destroyers these guns began to play rapidly in our direction. Their fire could be traced by the splashes of the projectiles coming closer and closer to us.... I can remember my astonishment at not seeing any wounded or sign of blood when I looked about the decks.... Had these guns secured our range the execution on board would have been terrible...." [1] But perhaps some of the house of Morgan wizardry had rubbed off on the little yacht, for she remained unhurt.

The Spaniards had no such luck, even though they hugged the coast to try to escape notice by the big American ships. The battered *Plutón*, suffering a serious hit, met her end quickly, as Lieutenant Caballero, her second in command, later recounted: "As we were making a great deal of water we continued close to the shore to Punta Cabrera, and when we were close to the headland we received a 32-centimeter [13-inch] projectile, which exploded the forward group of boilers, blowing up the whole deck. The ship veered to starboard and struck on the headland, tearing off a great part of her bow.... I jumped into the water and reached the shore." [2]

She'd run up on a coral reef, with only a delicate column of boiler steam and coal dust pluming 150 feet into the air to mark her place. The *Gloucester* now faced only the *Furor*, which was steaming in lazy, aimless circles as the result of a freakish and grisly accident. "A shell," recalled Lieutenant Bustamente, who was on her deck at the time, "struck boatswain Dueñas, cutting him in two; one part fell between the tiller ropes and it was necessary to take it out in pieces." The second destroyer's end wasn't far off, either. "Another shell destroyed the engine and the servo-motor, so that the ship could neither proceed nor maneuver." [3] Wainwright had closed to within 600 yards of the helpless vessel and was pouring a furious fire into her when the Spaniard was struck again in the engine room by a 6-inch projectile from the *Oregon* and blew herself to fragments. One moment she was there and the next she was gone. Bustamente and a few others had abandoned ship just moments earlier.

The two threatening torpedo boats destroyed, and within a matter of minutes! Yet hardly anybody even knew about it. The *Brooklyn* had completed her sweeping turn and was back on a pursuit course, and the rest of the big ships were beginning to string out according to their available speed, which was not in every case their maximum. In spite of the time she had lost in her unorthodox maneuver, the *Brooklyn* was still in the lead, with the burden of chase still upon her, and in that respect it was a somewhat embarrassing situation. Both she and the *New York* were twin-screw cruisers, having two sets of triple expansion engines coupled to each shaft in such a manner that either the forward or after pair could be disengaged and the ship run by the other as a fuel-saving measure. When the alarm guns had sounded, Schley's flagship had her forward set of engines uncoupled and there had never been time to hook them up again. It was a job which took fifteen minutes, and which would cost her at least four miles now in the chase. As it was she was able to make seventeen knots, a good bit less than her rated twenty, but still more than any of the battleships had been designed for, so she must stay in the van as best she could.

Cervera's idea of ramming the commodore's ship with the *María Teresa* had been foiled by Schley's turn, and by the arrival of the *Iowa* and the *Indiana*, which had pulled up almost between the two of them. If Cervera cut across the battleships' bows, he would face the danger of being rammed himself, so instead he was now heading straight down the coast with every knot he could force out of his boilers. Schley was racing abeam of him, exchanging shots through the smoke, feeling very much alone and a little concerned, too, because the Spanish ship, along with the *Viscaya* and *Oquendo* behind her, was beginning to pull ahead of him perceptibly, and the *Iowa* and *Indiana* were losing ground. "Cook," he shouted through the noise to the officer beside him, "we're going to have to stick with this crowd."

Just then he saw a bright flash in the midst of the smoke directly aft, which was followed immediately by a blast and the rolling clatter of a railroad car on a trestle just overhead. Only a 13-inch shell made that kind of commotion. The wind threw the smoke aside and revealed first a bow wave, then the bright, starred-and-striped shield on a ship's prow. It was the *Oregon*, which had racked her men, boilers and machinery from the Pacific around Cape Horn in order to be there at all, and now was leaving one ship after another in her wake as she thundered on under forced draft. A welcome surpise just behind her was the *Texas*, the unlucky "hoodoo" ship of the Navy—old, outclassed and not a little shaken by her near-collision with the *Brooklyn*, but nevertheless keeping her place in line.

The two fleets were trading heavy broadsides now, the Spaniards firing very rapidly; and aboard each of Schley's ships there was a feeling of wonder at their good fortune so far and a sense of apprehension over the pasting the others must be taking. The American gunners were replying at a little slower rate, and it was hard to tell whether they were on target, either; all anyone could see was that the water between the parallel columns heaved and tossed up continual geysers from the projectiles. The gunfire was incessant and deafening; it was the heaviest cannonade anyone in the U.S. Navy had ever experienced, and the "hardware" in the air was both audible and terrifying. Reporter Graham jumped at the screech of a particularly close miss, and Schley offered him the traditional comfort that the one you heard wouldn't hit you. It isn't recorded whether Graham was comforted. A few moments later, when he saw the newsman gamely trying to aim his camera through the smoke, he sent him back to the quarter-deck where there was a clearer view and less exposure.

A virtual swarm of shells of all calibers was passing over the *Brooklyn*, and to Schley at any rate it was obvious the Spaniards had not corrected their earlier fault; they were still aiming high. The ship's signal halyards were shot away and a heavy speed cone crashed to the deck, missing the commodore's head by inches. Another shot carried away the big battle flag at the main peak, and a man was sent up to the tops to lash in fast again. A shell struck the side armor and two more perforated the tall funnels, but considering what was being thrown at her, the cruiser might have led a charmed existence.

Things were much different in the Spanish line, where unknowingly the American gunners were hitting with telling effect. An 8-inch shell passed through the protective shield of one of the *María Teresa's* 5.5-inch guns and exploded within, and another penetrated the after barbette and blew up on the gun deck, scattering the crew like so many bundles of rags. Two big 12-inchers from one of the battleships struck in quick succession beneath the berth deck, making a bloody mess of the ship's after torpedo compartment, and a shell from the *Brooklyn* tore into Cervera's quarters, splintering the ornate paneling and woodwork. "One of the first projectiles burst an auxiliary steam pipe," the admiral wrote later, "making us lose the speed on which we had counted. . . . In this critical situation a fire broke out in my cabin where some of the 2.24-inch projectiles stored there must have exploded. At the same time I was informed that the after deck and deck house were burning . . . the fire that had commenced in my cabin was spreading with great rapidity to the center of the ship. . . ." [4]

When the crew tried to fight the flames, they discovered their hoses were dry; one of the explosions had cut the *Teresa's* water mains. It was now all too evident how shockingly unready the battered flagship had been for a fight at all. Unaccountably she hadn't fired a shot from her 5.5-inch secondaries until they were loosed off against the American fleet in battle, and now it was found at the most critical moment that shells didn't fit the guns for which they were intended, electric primers didn't work, breech-blocks became overheated and wouldn't close, and in several cases guns blew out their firing pins and wounded men in their crews.

One of the first American hits had struck down Captain Concas on the conning tower, and when his second in command could not be reached, Admiral Cervera, alone and untouched in the shambles of the bridge, was forced to take over direct control of the ship. He could only wonder at the way she seemed to draw the enemy shells to her. The entire after part of the vessel was a gutted wreck, blazing furiously, and ammunition was beginning to explode there. The live steam from the severed pipe was everywhere aft of the funnels and had forced the gun crew from one of the ship's two main turrets. "The fire was gaining ground with great rapidity and voracity," writes the admiral. "I therefore sent one of my aides to flood the after magazines, but it was impossible to penetrate into the passages owing to the dense clouds of smoke... and the steam escaping from the engine hatch... or to breathe in that suffocating atmosphere." [5] Realizing it was hopeless to go on and that the decision was his only to make, Cervera ordered the wheel put over and the *Teresa* headed for the beach.

Colors still flying, she went up on the rocks with a nerve-rending shock in the shallows near Cabrera Point, six miles west of Santiago. It was 10:31, less than an hour after her bugles had led the sortie proudly out of the harbor. The admiral hurriedly assembled what officers remained and asked them whether they thought the battle could be continued with the ship aground. He knew there was no question of it. With the *Teresa*'s motion stopped, the flames, which had trailed out behind her torchlike and left the forward part of the vessel untouched, were now being blown toward the bow by the offshore wind, and at this rate her magazines would be in danger of going up. The hopelessness of things was obvious to all, and the answer to Cervera's question was a hasty and decided no.

Lieutenant Sears, studying the beached enemy through the glass, called Schley's attention to her condition. It looked as though the *Teresa* had surrendered, but couldn't get at her flag to haul it

down because of the flames. Schley ordered the *Brooklyn* to stop
firing; even if the Spaniard hadn't yet struck, the others behind
could take of her. "Tell the boys below," he said. "They can't see
what's going on and the news will cheer them up."

If they could have seen, they might have watched all the Spanish
crew who were left and who were able to dive, jump or lower
themselves by rope from the *Teresa's* blood-slippery deck into the
surf. The very last of them, having stripped off his admiral's uniform with its gold lace and sword belt, crossed himself, bid *adiós*
to his shattered command and struck out, stark naked and with
quite a capable stroke for the beach.

***

As the *Teresa* stopped engines and turned for the Cabrera shore,
she was passed by the other Spanish cruisers, still heading west.
The *Viscaya, Colón* and *Oquendo* had kept on in that order; however the three ships were no longer in line but now formed a tri-
angle, with the *Oquendo* following in the *Viscaya's* wake and the
Colón, a half mile further in toward land, being masked by the
other two from the American fire. It seemed the Spaniards were
trying to protect her, as the fastest of their number, and give her
the best chance of getting away. She just might be able to do it,
too, for while the *Brooklyn* was steaming abreast of the *Viscaya*
about a mile and a half to seaward of that ship, the enemy cruiser
was still pulling away slightly and the American battleships were
further behind than ever.

The "big boys" were giving all their attention to the vessel
closest at hand. Almost from the beginning the *Oquendo*, as the
last big ship out of Santiago harbor, had been taking concentrated
punishment from the whole of the U.S. fleet, and had been hit
several times by the slower *Iowa* and *Indiana* before she could
bring her speed into play and outrun them. She wasn't making the
time she'd hoped to, either, and from her unlucky rear-guard position was now continuing blindly on under one of the heaviest
showers of shells ever to be let loose on a ship in the history of
naval warfare.

The very first American hit had been an 8-inch projectile from the *Brooklyn* that struck the hood over her forward barbette and passed through, exploding with terrific effect in the confined space to jam the turret and spatter fragments of the gun crew against the inner bulkheads. One mast fell to the American salvos, then the other, and the big guns punctured her hull again and again above her 11-inch side plating, some of the armor-piercing shells going right through and coming out the other side without exploding. One particularly disastrous shell crashed into her torpedo compartment, where a 14-inch Whitehead lay armed and in the tube ready for launching, and the powerful warhead went off, tearing a huge chunk out of the deck and killing everyone in the surrounding compartments. At long range the plodding but straight-shooting *Indiana* sent one big-caliber projectile into the gun deck below the conning tower and another through the superstructure in front of the forward stack.

The hail of fire from all quarters had been pummeling the *Oquendo* continually all above the waterline, and now half of her crew—probably 250 men in all—lay dead or wounded at their stations. As in the case of the beached *Teresa*, the piping system had been wrecked, and there were few men and fewer means left to try to control the fires that had begun to rage. Like the *Teresa* and the other Spanish cruisers, her planking had been laid directly on the supporting stanchions with no armored deck interposed, and when the wood caught fire the flames, with no sheet of steel to seal them off from the working spaces below, spread with alarming speed. Lieutenant Calandría, the ship's paymaster, watched in horror as they consumed the officers' mess, their cabins, and the galley pantries. "The fire spread to the after deck as a result of burning wood from the mess falling through the ammunition hoist. This would have caused the explosion of the 5.5 ammunition if third gunner German Montero and sailor Luís Diaz had not stopped up the hatches, first with wooden gratings and then with wet bedding...." [6]

All this time the American rapid-fire guns had done appalling destruction to the upper works, and there was virtually nobody left to give orders. A sudden and fearful judgment had been delivered on her officers; the *Oquendo* hadn't been out of harbor fifteen minutes before every man unlucky enough to be in her superstructure was a casualty. Captain Lazaga was struck down almost immediately, and his executive officer had scarcely taken his place when a shell from the very next American salvo cut him in two. The third officer then took the conn, but an explosion of some ammunition, set off by another enemy hit, blew him to pieces. Within ten minutes the next three officers in rank were cut down, one after another by the lead squirts of the *Oregon*, which were sweeping the *Oquendo's* conning tower from the stone's-throw range of 900 yards. Now the bodies of 130 dead crewmen strewed the deck, the ladders and the bridges.

The *Oquendo's* own big guns were replying sporadically or not at all. The forward 11-inch turret had got off only three shots, and the messenger sent to find out the reason for the gun's silence climbed now to a bizarre and macabre scene. In the turret lay six corpses without a visible wound on them, while up in the little cupola where the gun was sighted was the headless torso of an officer. All had been victims of an 8-inch shell which struck just at the gunport. Fired at long range, presumably by the *Brooklyn*, it had lacked the force to penetrate the ten inches of turret armor, but had nevertheless exploded against the face. The flash had come through the port into the turret, where the crew had been in the process of loading the gun, and where the 350-pound powder charge which was required for the firing of the big 11-inch rifle was just being placed in the breech. The silk bag flared up instantly and violently, killing all the gunners present, and the force of the blast was directed through the opening of the little tower where the officer was sitting, tearing off his head.[7]

Captain Lazaga, wounded but forced by the terrible attrition of his officers to exercise command still, looked about him at the floating shambles and decided that he had no choice but to beach what was left. There was no question of continuing to fight his vessel, either. He directed that all the remaining torpedoes be discharged—they might hit one of the pursuing Americans by chance—and that oil be poured on the decks to make sure they would burn against the possibility of any salvage on the part of the enemy. As Calandría, the senior officer left alive after the action, explained: "The men . . . were determined above all that the enemy should not set foot on the ship." It was Lazaga's last order. At first it was assumed that he had been killed during the heat of the battle, but it appears he was on hand till the end. His fate remains a mystery. According to some, he disappeared, either by choice or by accident in the pilothouse, where he was incinerated. Spanish survivors say he drowned trying to swim to the beach.

In any event the *Oquendo* ran aground about half past ten, the hull so cut up by the American shells that she broke in two when she hit. A good part of what was left of the ship's company got to shore, and many more stayed in the water, stunned, clinging desperately to chains at the stricken vessel's head, waiting for help of some kind. Captain Clark of the *Oregon* watched the death of the Spanish cruiser from the top of a 13-inch gun turret. "We've settled another!" he shouted to the seaman who was stationed at a hatch to relay news to the working spaces below. "Look out for the rest!" This was answered by a loud cheer, begun by the gun crews and the men on deck, which traveled through the ammunition passages and magazines down to the heroes of the boiler and engine rooms where it came out again on the bridge through the speaking tubes.[8] That run around the Horn had been worth every ounce of sweat and every hour at the scorching fireboxes; the *Oregon* was Johnny-on-the-spot now because of it all and she wasn't about to secure for the day yet—not by a *long shot.* And with two of the enemy ships now where all good Spaniards must eventually go, there was even time to laugh at the play on words.

✷✷✷

Impatience and impotence, not elation, were the predominant moods aboard Admiral Sampson's flagship, still miles to the rear. The commander in chief had been watching what he could make out of the fight, which was running tantalizingly before him, with all the frustration of a distance runner who has picked himself up after a fall and who knows, infuriatingly, that only an accident has put him so far behind the field. While he could see he was overtaking the slower battleships, he knew at this rate he would never play any kind of part at all unless the leading combatants slackened speed through maneuver or became disabled. His current inefficacy was brought home to him when it struck him that he had already done the only thing he could under the circumstances—send word to Guantánamo for the *Massachusetts* to break off coaling and join the fleet.

By now he was passing the Santiago harbor mouth, and flashes from the tops of the hills on either side showed that the guns of Morro and Socapa were firing on him. Chadwick asked if they should give them an answer, but Sampson had no time for forts and never for a moment took his eyes from the glass and from what looked like a hopeless embroilment up ahead, with all formation gone. The illusion of disorder was the result of his own mental fidgeting, for on the brief occasions when the smoke was blown away he could see that the two squadrons of ships were in lines after all, running on parallel courses.

Only once was the formation broken. A smoke-shrouded shape headed out from the seaward, or American column, and at first Sampson thought one of the Spanish cruisers had forced her way through Schley's line and was trying to escape to the south. Then he picked out the three pipestem funnels of the *Brooklyn* silhouetted against the lighter sky. She had been making her full-circle turn, but from the *New York* it looked as though she were hurt and out of control, which would have meant that his own ship—seven miles astern—would be the only one remaining with the necessary pursuit speed. He was relieved when the *Brooklyn* turned back into line and headed west once more.

His attention was drawn from the scene ahead when someone sighted the wreck of the *Plutón*, about four miles to the west of the Morro. Following Captain Chadwick's pointing finger, he could see the little *Gloucester* and two of the hindermost battleships engaging a small enemy which must be the other torpedo-boat destroyer, and the *New York* fired three shots from one of her 4-inch guns—more as a gesture than anything else. As the flagship thundered by, Captain Chadwick led his crew in a round of cheers for the *Gloucester*, but she had no time to wait for details, for on the western horizon an orange glow blossomed out from the midst of the black and white funnel and powder smoke—things were being resolved one way or another up ahead. "She's on fire!" the shout went up—excitedly, for the victim was on the Spanish side of the fight—and as the crippled cruiser slowly turned to the north, Sampson almost hoped she was coming about to face the *New York* in an effort to break past him back to Santiago. He was denied any such satisfaction. The flame-trailing hull kept on shoreward and then was seen no more, with only an oily black pall to mark the place where it disappeared behind a point of land.

The *New York* was now doing about sixteen knots and was passing through the scene of the earlier fighting. Her bow surged into the refuse and flotsam of battle; bits of boats, woodwork and canvas, ammunition boxes and the bodies of men sped by on either side to gather again, swirling and bobbing in her wake. Here and there the struggles of the living could be seen—Spanish sailors clinging to planks, tables, anything afloat, some paddling or kicking for the shore, others too exhausted to do anything but try to keep their heads above water. Ahead a second bright orange ball took shape and flared from within the smoke hugging the Spanish line. Another ship was afire! The *New York's* crew watched in fascination as the drama was played out again—the turn, the broadside view of the flaming mass, rocked by smaller flashes of shells and exploding ammunition, heading for the shoals.

The men grew exhilarated, threw up their hats, pounded each other, for the burning torches, far away as they were, could mean only one thing: they were winning—unequivocally, spectacularly. Up till now all they had seen of the enemy were the few inhuman figures thrashing helplessly in the water to avoid the *New York's* propellers; one sped by these creatures remote and godlike, dispensing life jackets. Was this all there was to war? W. A. Goode, Associated Press correspondent with the ship, describes that enemy: "He was a black-headed, fine, swarthy Spaniard, and as he swam his great broad shoulders stuck out of the water like the sides of a boat. The *New York's* course was changed so as not to run him down, and as we flew past him he threw up one arm and cried despairingly, 'Amerigo! Amerigo! Auxilio! Auxilio!' Some of the crew standing near me laughed at this 'lingo.' 'Damn you, shut up!' came in strident tones from an officer that overheard the jeers, and there was silence." There being nothing else at hand just then, the ship's pulpit, which had been set up for Sunday service, was tossed overboard as a life-buoy, "and we left him struggling in our wake to take his fortunes of war." [9]

✳✳✳

At this point neither Sampson nor Schley was appreciative of the great victory that was already won: Sampson because he couldn't see what was happening to the American ships; Schley because he was afraid his casualties were going to be considerable— after all, you couldn't get hit as often as everybody must be without losing men—and because he was still too occupied with the chase to take it all in. It was now past 10:30, and of the six Spanish ships that had rounded the shoals at El Diamante barely an hour before only two were still afloat. Because of her superior speed the *Cristóbal Colón* had drawn abreast of the *Viscaya*, which up till now had been leading her. The *Colón* was still about a mile closer in toward shore, however, far enough from the hostile fire to permit Captain Moreu to make unhampered use of his extra knots, so it was on the hapless *Viscaya*, sister ship to the wrecked *Teresa* and *Oquendo*, that the full retribution of Schley's squadron was now directed.

On the American side it was essentially a three-ship race by now. The *Brooklyn* was doing her best to keep up with the *Viscaya*, and the *Oregon*, practically captained now by the indefatigable engineer Milligan, was doing at least as well, while the *Texas* was beginning to lag behind, though she was still in range. The *Iowa* was further back yet and the *Indiana* brought up the rear; she was having engine trouble and was hopelessly out of the fight. It was still very much the *Brooklyn's* battle, though had she really fought it out alone with the *Viscaya*, it could have been hard on her. Under most conditions the *Brooklyn's* eight 8-inch guns would have been rated a match for the *Viscaya's* two 11-inch were it not for the Spaniard's 12-inch armor belt, which gave her double the broadside protection of Schley's ship. She was ably commanded, too; Captain Juan Antonio Eulate was one of the most accomplished and courageous seamen to wear the Queen Regent's uniform, a man whom many American officers knew personally, for the *Viscaya* had been sent by the Sagasta government to New York on one of those good-will visits at the same time that the *Maine* had been in Havana. While she was there, the American press had maliciously declared that she held a clear edge in fighting qualities to cruisers like the *New York* and *Brooklyn*. Not the least of Schley's satisfactions would be a chance to prove them wrong.

"Get in close, Cook," he ordered now, though the enemy was so near already that only three seconds separated the flashes and the reports from her guns. "Nine hundred and fifty yards!" Commander Mason shouted to the turret decks, and a rolling 8-inch broadside was followed by the even more ear-punching crack of the 5-inch secondaries and the pop of the 6- and 1-pounders to fill the interval while the bigger guns loaded again. Everything—even the marines' rifles—would hit at that range. The Spanish ship was completely obscured by smoke, but even the flame from her quick firers could be seen from here. 'Way off toward shore the *Colón* was belching out regular salvos, too—unfamiliar brown billows rather than white—she was the only vessel in action using smokeless powder. Between the two of them Schley was surprised that the *Brooklyn* was not being blanketed by shells, though one look at the geyser-torn water between his ship and the little yacht *Vixen*, a mile and a half to seaward, told him the Spaniards once again had their sights high. They must be trying to bring down his topgallants, was the thought that ran through his mind.

His own marksmanship was a lot more satisfying. A marine aloft called down that "every shot was telling," and the rate of fire was stepped up, with the shell hoists, loaders and rammers working easily into the swing of things now, and with a 2,000-pound salvo crashing out against the Spanish cruiser every three minutes. The fire of the *Brooklyn*'s lead squirts was especially lethal, and time and again the men working the guns in the *Viscaya*'s tops were driven from their stations. Once, as a shell hit her superstructure and wiped out two gun crews which were working side by side,

Schley shook his head. "My God, but she's getting a terrible baptism of fire," and he turned to Captain Cook. "Tell your bullies they're doing great work."

The excitement that had raced through the American fleet with the general-quarters gongs had expended itself, and as a result many men were enjoying the pleasant discovery that they could be cool, steady, even jocund in their first action. Correspondent Graham, passing near the starboard 8-inch turret, heard one of the gunners say that he couldn't see the shots fall, a complaint that struck Turret-captain Doyle as the remark of an ignoramus. "You damn fool, when you don't see them drop in the water, you know you're hitting," chided Doyle, who'd never fired at a ship before that day himself. In the after main turret Lieutenant Rush, a bandanna round his sweat-sodden hair, stuck his head out of the top and called to the officer with the stadimeter: "Which of them do you want us to aim for?" And Commander Mason told him the *Viscaya*, with the reminder that the New York swells thought her a better bet in a fight than the *Brooklyn*. His two 8-inch rifles went off with a roar and the head popped up again with a wide grin for Graham. "How about that, did you see me soak them?"

All told the flagship's crew was bearing the strain of battle buoyantly. A big shell that hit the upper works and flailed the decks with a shower of metal fragments drew only hoots and disparaging remarks about Spanish gunnery, and Graham had plenty of time to snap pictures of a row of white hats on a turret top within easy reach of everything the enemy had, leading "locomotive" cheers for Commodore Schley like sophomores at a Dartmouth pep rally.

Even the more than three hundred engineers, firemen and ammunition handlers imprisoned below the protective decks were enjoying the fight—as much as men can, anyway, who aren't able to see what's going on. Every so often someone would holler down some good news from topside and the black gang would answer with a lusty whoop and bang their shovels. Once a shell ripped through the gun deck and Graham went below with his camera for a "blood and guts" shot, only to find the men in the compartment on their hands and knees digging souvenir pieces of still-smoking steel out of the decks and bulkheads.

Schley was as cool as anybody—trying to to keep the enemy in his bouncing field glasses—though his heart jumped with apprehension once when he felt a grinding smash that jolted the deck beneath his feet. "They've landed something in us," he said and sent an apprentice boy down to see how many men were gone. In a moment the messenger returned with the news that a big shell had hit below and apparently missed everybody. Annoyed, he ordered the boy down again for a casualty report, telling him to keep his wits about him this time, and he could hardly believe it when the same answer came back—two seamen slightly wounded.

Luck not only smiled but could take the time to chuckle, it seemed, and when there was a mishap, it was prankish in nature. There was the case of the 6-pounder being manned by marines that was put out of action when one of its shells got stuck in the barrel. Embarrassment at having such a thing happen with the regular ship's jackies looking on can only be imagined. One of them, a Corporal Gray, straddled the barrel and inched himself out with a rammer to try to work the lethal impediment loose from the muzzle, but the gun was too hot and he had to let go and drop to the sea ladder below, just missing a sousing in the Caribbean. A second noncom tried with the same result, and it finally took a private to knock the stubborn shell to the deck—just as the jokes were reaching the point of insult—and publicly redeem the honor of the Corps.

Though the *Viscaya* had been absorbing a good deal of punishment, she was still making good speed. Schley noticed the *Brooklyn's* shots beginning to fall short and asked for a reading from Yeoman George Ellis, who was acting in the place of Navigator Hodgson as range finder from a spot just in front of the conning tower. Ellis stepped out with his stadimeter and called a figure of 1,200 yards to Commander Mason, who repeated it in turn to the messengers relaying corrections to the individual turrets. They were the yeoman's last words, and characteristically a correspondent was on hand to take them down and to describe, in the conventional, spiced-with-sensation journalese of the period, the United States Navy's only battle death of the entire action. "Plainly distinguishable from the hum and buzz of the Spanish shells which were flying over us, there came a dull sickening thud, the warm blood and brains spattering in our faces and on our clothes gave warning of a fatality even before the smoke cleared. When we could see, there lay Ellis' body curled in an inanimate heap on the deck, the head having gone overboard, carried away by the impact of a large shell. Luckily for us the shell had not exploded or a very many more of us might have been injured or killed." The doctor and a nearby ensign picked the corpse up to drop it over the side (it having been decided to dispose of mutilated dead quickly so that the sight of them would not unnerve the men) but Schley stopped them. The body would not be jettisoned, he said, but would go below where it would later be given a Christian burial.[10]

When the commodore looked at the *Viscaya* again, he noticed she was closer. The Spanish cruiser had pulled out of line and was sheering to the south on a collision course with the *Brooklyn*. It was obvious Eulate was going to attempt what Cervera had been unable to do—drive his ship's gilt-topped ram into the American's relatively thin side plating forward of her armor belt. Apparently, though, this was no time for luck to desert the American cause. Almost as Schley realized what was happening there was a terrific explosion aboard the Spaniard and large pieces of her prow flew a hundred feet into the air, as a fortunate 8-inch shot from Lieutenant Doyle's starboard turret struck her dead on and set off a torpedo seated in one of her forward tubes, ready for launching. The *Viscaya*, with a gaping maw now where her beatuiful escutcheon had once been, veered away again. A critical moment had passed, and Lieutenant Eberle, captain of the *Oregon's* forward main turret, thought his own ship had saved the *Brooklyn*:

> Our [the *Oregon's*] speed steadily increased, and when we were about three thousand yards from the *Viscaya* she swung offshore and headed across our bow, firing her forward guns at the *Brooklyn* and her port ones at us. By this maneuver the *Viscaya* exposed her broadside to us, and a big shell from one of our turret guns seemed

to strike her in the port bow, and she immediately resumed her former course. A few minutes later, at about a quarter to eleven, the man in the fighting top reported that a 13-inch shell had struck her amidships, heeling her to starboard and sending up a volume of steam and smoke. Cheer after cheer rang through the ship, and our gunfire increased in intensity. . . . Captain Clark, who had been moving about the decks commending officers and men for their good work, and telling his "children" not to expose themselves needlessly, was at this instant standing on top of the after 13-inch turret. The turret officer was deploring the fact that his guns would not bear on the enemy's remaining ships, when suddenly the burning *Viscaya* was seen off our starboard bow . . . and the captain exclaimed: "There's your chance! There's your chance!" and in another moment the after turret was thundering away with awful effect.[11]

Now it could be seen that the Spaniard had been hit severely above the waterline. Her morale, too, had been shattered along with her decks and superstructure. The loss of life on the *Viscaya* was not as great as it had been on the *Oquendo*, but she was through as a fighting unit. A shell had wrecked Captain Eulate's cabin and, as in the case of the *Teresa* and *Oquendo*, had set fire to the decks, a blaze which spread quickly through the working spaces and engulfed the sick bay, which was packed with wounded. Another well-placed hit obliterated a deck gun and its barbette, the six-man crew and shell-handling party that was trying to do the work of the ship's faulty ammunition hoists. She was taking in water through her mangled forepeak, her pumps were out of order, every man in her fighting tops had been killed, and those of her crew who were still on their feet would fight no longer. Officers screamed frantic orders at unheeding men as the ship's guns stopped firing.

Eulate was himself wounded in the head and shoulder but still exercised command; only a few minutes before he had stood at the ladder to drive a number of engineers and firemen back to their stations below when they attempted to mutiny. A hysterical officer, who raced through the holocaust that was the quarter-deck with the idea of reaching the flag at the stern, was brought down by a revolver shot. At this point, though, the Spanish captain realized that determination no longer had a part in the matter. He might play out his own piece with courage and tenacity to the end, but it would be a brief gesture, for he now captained little but a floating bonfire which was in the process of barbecuing his crew, alive and dead. It was only a question of time before her magazines went up and finished what the flames had started.

As the captain himself recounted: "Almost faint from the loss of blood I resigned my command to the executive officer with clear and positive instructions not to surrender the ship but rather to beach and burn her. In the sick bay [a temporary one, which had just been set up] I met Ensign Luís Fajardo, who was having a serious wound dressed. When I asked him what was the matter with him he answered that they had wounded him in one arm but he still had one left for his country." [12] This show of spirit did something to counteract the disgraceful scenes topside, and after receiving first aid Eulate insisted on going back on deck. "I immediately convened the officers who were nearest . . . and asked them whether there was anyone among them who thought we could do anything more in the defense of our country and our honor, and the unanimous reply was that nothing more could be done."

Back on the *Texas* Captain Philip watched the *Viscaya* put her helm over and make for the shore. He saw the *Brooklyn* had stopped firing on her as he had himself a moment before, and now he brought the *Texas* in as close as he dared to see if anything could be done about survivors. To Philip the scene was terrible and unforgettable. Flames leaped from the enemy's decks as high as her funnel tops—the Spanish ship was going up there on the rocks like a Viking funeral pyre—and from where he was he could hear the helplessly wounded shrieking like damned souls in a Doré illustration of hell. Panic-stricken seamen, some with their clothing ablaze, were throwing themselves into the shallow water or just crawling to the side and rolling overboard, but many others were simply being consumed. The crew of the *Texas* sent up a yell, as much of nervous relief as of victory, but Philip stopped it immediately. "Don't cheer, boys! Those poor devils are dying!" It was a reprimand that would immortalize the captain as much as anything else he did that day, though at least one minister of the gospel back home suggested that a man of faith like Philip must surely have said "fellows" and not "devils."

By the time the *Viscaya* had turned for the beach she had slowed down enough to allow the *Iowa*, following four miles astern, to catch up. Lying to just offshore, the battleship's crew saw the survivors in the surf face a new threat. "The Cuban insurgents had opened fire on them from the shore," said Evans, "and with a glass I could plainly see the bullets snipping up the water among them. The sharks, made ravenous by the blood of the wounded, were attacking them from the outside." Evans quickly sent in a boat, warning the rebels to belay or be fired on themselves by the battleship's guns. The *Iowa*, too slow to be of any use in the case anyway, remained on the spot and managed to bring away two hundred of the *Viscaya*'s crew, among them her commanding officer. All were glad to see the brave and personable Eulate alive. He and his ship hadn't fulfilled the expectations of the New York press, but he'd fought the good fight till the decks were red-hot beneath him, and a Spaniard at sea that day could not have asked anything more.

✳✳✳

The only enemy ship left now was the *Cristóbal Colón*. All the while her sisters had been taking the punishment of the American men-of-war, she had been pouring on the coal; she now held a six-mile lead over the *Brooklyn* and *Oregon*, the nearest of her pursuers, and she had an accredited speed of 20 knots, which was about 4 more than the *Oregon* could do, and a couple of knots faster than the *Brooklyn*, too, with her uncoupled engines. She was a highly regarded vessel, though of unusual design. She was not Spanish-built at all, but had been laid down at Sestri Ponente, just outside Genoa, and she carried two squat, widely spaced funnels, with a single mast rising between them, which gave her a blocky, fortlike appearance. The *Colón*, even more than the other three Spanish cruisers, might have been ranked equal to the *Texas*, in strength—defensively, at least. She carried a complete stem-to-stern, nickel-steel armor belt, boasted an improved welded hull construction and should, of course, have mounted two 10-inch guns of a modern powerful design.

All she had now was her speed, and though on paper that should have been enough, Schley was unwilling to concede anything at this point. "We may be able to wing that fellow," he told Graham, "slow him up and let Clark and Philip get a show at him, even if he sinks us for it." Schley based his hopes on the fact that the Spaniard seemed to be making a serious navigational—and in this sense tactical—error, and if his own observations were correct, it might put the Brooklyn in the right spot to decide the issue. He made a signal to the Oregon to cease firing and continued to study the position of the Colón through the long glass. Lieutenant Hodgson came down from the chartroom with a map of the coast, and the commodore, spreading it out on the forecastle where the view was clear, scrutinized first the map and then the fleeing cloud of smoke up ahead.

Then he smiled, and his fist cracked into the other palm explosively. He was right. The Colón had been running in close to shore and before long would be forced to make a detour to the south—toward him—in order to clear Cape Cruz, sixty miles west. The Brooklyn was two miles further out to sea than the Spaniard—she had the angle on him, like a tackler heading off a ball carrier—and if Schley ran a straight course to Cape Cruz, he saw he had a good chance of putting the crusher on, speed or no speed. The Oregon, meanwhile, would have to stay closer in to shore, in order to get a range on the Colón's broadside if she turned and tried to run straight south, across the Brooklyn's bows. It was a neat bit of figuring that Sampson, with his calculating mind, would have reveled in—reveled in it even more so, some who knew him might venture, than the fight at the end of the whole thing. It was probably as cruel to deny him the one as the other.

Now that Schley saw he had a profitable course of action, there was nothing to do but keep the stokers at the fireboxes and hope he didn't foul a propeller. He folded up his map and told Mason to get all his men out for some air, and in a moment or two the top of every gun casement and turret was thick with grimy, sweating white hats in every form of undress. Even the "monkeys" from the powder magazines below the steel protective deck came up and gulped the twenty-mile-an-hour headwind, cool as a spring morning compared to the suffocation below. After the commotion of battle the silence—for the *Brooklyn* had broken off firing completely—was almost other-worldly. The ship plowed along under a brilliant tropical sky, quivering and humming under forced draft, half of her engines doing double work, and but for her battle flags, the smoke-blackened faces and the decks that crunched with saltpeter underfoot she might have been on a peacetime shakedown cruise.

It was the first time Schley himself had been able to relax, and the sudden lift of tension brought out his puckish side. He called Ensign McCauley over. "Wigwag to the *Oregon* that the ship ahead looks like an Italian." McCauley did so and got the answer from Captain Clark: "Maybe so, but she'll end up on the coast of Cuba!" Then the *Oregon* hoisted a flag string of her own: "Remember the *Maine*," and the *Brooklyn* answered promptly: "We have." A huzza went up for Commodore Schley from the crew, and then another one for the *Oregon*.

It was an oversight that nobody offered up any accolades for the two black gangs, for it anybody deserved "three times three," they did. Deep down in the subterranean innards of the big ships, with the clang of iron to keep rhythm by and the open furnaces to hold temperatures at a searing 170 degrees, they worked, naked bodies sweat-glistening and iridescent in the white-hot glare: the coal passers hauling bags from the bunkers to be emptied in piles on the fireroom deck; the firemen shoveling it in, raking ashes, breaking up clinkers with the slice and pricker bars to keep the blaze bright; pausing only to step back and give their heads a quick douse in the tubs of water that were there to provide some relief, or snatch a gulp of coffee or hunk of bread and corned "willy" which had been toasted on a shovel over the fires.

One stoker describes what it was like when a warship was in action and cruising at top speed: "The battle hatches were all battened down and we were shut in.... It was so hot our hair was singed. There were several leaks in the steam pipes and the hissing hot steam made things worse. The clatter of the engines and the roaring of the furnaces made such a din it seemed one's head would burst.... We could tell when our guns opened fire by the way the ship shook; we could scarcely stand up on our feet, the vibration was so great.... The ship shook so fearfully that the soot and cinders poured down on us in clouds. Now and then a big drop of scalding water would fall on our heads...." [13]

Every so often a man would collapse from the heat, but after having been in the open air for a few minutes he was usually ready to go back to the coal piles. The respite on deck was like a whiff from an oxygen tank. One stoker was carried up topside and opened his eyes to see four of his mates watching him anxiously. What were they lollygagging around for, he growled, and as they left him and went down the ladder again, he winked at the medic who was with them. "Hey, Doc, are we catching the dago?"

Those who were where they could see made it a point to keep the gang shut up below informed. As one seaman noted in his diary: "The poor men in the firerooms was working like horses, and to cheer them up we passed the word down the ventilators how things was going on, and they passed the word back if we would cut them down they would get us to where we could do it. So we ... settled down for a good chase for the *Colón*. I thought she was going to run away from us. But she had to make a curv [*sic*] and we headed for a point that she had to come out at." [14]

Of course there was no guarantee that the *Colón* would not be able to increase her speed and beat them to the cape up ahead, and Captain Cook thought now might be the time to couple up the other two engines. The *Brooklyn*'s after engines could only use just so much steam, and that point had been reached; in other words she was making her best two-engine speed right now. Schley shook his head. "If she does get around the Cape first, we'll stop and couple, and then, by God, I'll chase her to Spain but I'll get her!" He stepped to the speaking tube and called down below, "Bullies, we've only got one more to get, and it all depends on you now," and from beneath, as out of the depths of the Pit, came the dull, metallic-echoing roar of a cheer. Up above he noticed the sun was high in the sky; they'd been steaming west for an hour and a half and it was now past noon. He climbed down the conning tower ladder, sat down on the edge of the forward turret, dangling his legs over like a schoolboy on a fence, and took the plate of bacon and mug of coffee that the mess boy had been holding patiently for him. The breeze from the *Brooklyn*'s headway was fresh and the meal was already cold.

Just behind, the *Oregon* was doing heroic work, with Engineer Milligan below at the fireboxes himself to keep the hands at their shovels, and even the *New York*, nearly out of sight as the chase began, was coming on; Sampson may have missed the start but he was determined not to be out of it at the finish. W. A. M. Goode, on the bridge at the admiral's elbow all the while, describes the pursuit:

> The decks of the flagship trembled with the screws' vibrations. The *Colón* was supposed to have a speed of twenty knots. We knew the *Oregon* and the *Texas* and the *Vixen* could not make that, and we doubted if the *Brooklyn* could, with her foul bottom. We were making our level best, and it was more than we had dared to hope after our long wait in the warm waters of the South. Knot after knot we covered, and the outline of the *Colón* grew plainer. At first we thought this was imagination; it seemed impossible. But there was no mistake; we were surely gaining, both on our own ships and on the enemy.[15]

As he passed the *Indiana*, Sampson signaled to her to abandon the chase and head back to Santiago. He was afraid the enemy gunboat *Alvarado* or even the disabled *Reina Mercedes* might try to slip out in his absence and raid the transports at Siboney. Then he sped by the *Iowa*, which was standing by at the point where the wrecked *Viscaya* was sending up a greasy black tower of smoke into the bright sky. "Join the blockade after you've picked up survivors," signaled the *New York*.

The admiral was trying to join the game, like a new boy on the playground, but there were only two American ships that would determine anything now. The scene on the *Oregon* was much the same as on the *Brooklyn*, with one exception. While they were still in the Pacific, the battleship's crew had got hold of several big spools of red ribbon which they cut up and had made into hat bands with "Remember the Maine" printed on them. Now, somehow, the blue winter flat hats with the ribbons on them had appeared out of seabags, and some of the men were wearing them, though summer whites were the uniform of the day. Nobody cared, though, as officers and men alike packed the tops of the forward turrets or climbed aloft to get a better look. Sometimes it seemed as though the enemy cruiser was nearer, then sometimes a little farther away again. One old boatswain's mate, stationed up in the fighting top, couldn't stand it any longer and yelled through his megaphone: "Captain, can't you give her a 13-inch shell, for God's sake!"

Then at about 12:30 the last bit of Spanish bad luck—a calamity under the circumstances—struck the Colón. All that day she had been feeding on her original supply of Cadiz coal, and now the stokers were beginning to shovel in fuel she had taken on at Santiago. It was different stuff entirely. Her steam gauges began to fall and with them her speed. Schley, seeing the range closing, signaled to the Oregon: "Try one of your big ones on her," and a moment later there was the sound of the boxcar going over the bridge as the battleship sent a pair of 1,100-pound projectiles on their way. Two splashes wide of the mark showed where they had missed, and Lieutenant Simpson in the Brooklyn's forward turret asked if he could try. "I don't think you can reach," the commodore answered, "but if you want to, go ahead."

The Oregon followed shot with shot very carefully, and her sixth attempt dropped just ahead of the target. Then another struck under the Spanish cruiser's stern. Somebody thought they saw a white flag fluttering at the masthead, and a whoop went up around the decks of the Brooklyn. "That's not a flag," Schley said, studying the enemy through his binoculars, "it's steam." Graham thought the commodore looked tired but triumphant in those final moments of what certainly must be the day of his life. "His lips were cracked, and little flacks of blood showed where the saltpeter from the gunsmoke had affected him. His eyelids were red from staring through his glasses so continuously, his eyes were bloodshot and there were dark lines down his face. But his hands were steady, his voice was even, though somewhat hoarse...." [16]

Commander Mason, who had been watching the Colón through

the telescope, lowered it and grinned. "She's hauled down her colors and fired a lee gun."

"What does that mean?" Schley asked.

Mason's face showed surprise. "Why, that means she's struck."

"I'm damned glad I didn't have to surrender," Schley laughed wryly. "I wouldn't have known how."

He could be puckish again.

***

In a way it was anticlimactic. They'd chased the Genoese the farthest of all only to have her give up virtually without a fight (it wasn't known she had virtually nothing to fight with). Yet it might be just as well; of the four beaten enemy cruisers, she was at least intact; now it looked as though the U.S. Navy would wind up the day in possession of a handsome prize of war. She was on the rocks like the others, jammed up firmly, for she had gone in at high speed, and there she sat, listing sharply, still panting out smoke like some exhausted animal. It took about twenty minutes to get one of the *Brooklyn's* boats lowered and ashore, as they had all been filled with water and covered with wet canvas as a fireproofing measure, but the crew of the *Colón* seemed content to wait. When Captain Cook finally boarded the enemy prize, he was greeted with tentative cries of *"Bravo Americanos!"* from some of them who may have suspected they would be treated harshly. On the other hand it might have been merely bonhomie, for nearly everyone he saw seemed to be the worse for liquor. Cook learned they had been given a double rum ration, and this went into stomachs that had held no food since the men had left the trenches at Santiago the day before.

The ship herself had been almost untouched. There were the scars of two 5-inch shell hits from the *Brooklyn*, but aside from this the only evidence of battle were the bodies of six black gang on the deck near the superstructure. They had been shot by their officers for refusing to go back to the fires below. Cervera's second in command, Commodore José de Paredes y Chacón, and Captain Emiliano Díaz y Moreu were down in the wardroom with a tureen of soup in front of them. After congratulating Cook on

his victory, they accepted his terms of unconditional surrender
without argument and invited him to have a bowl also. It was
good soup, made from the milk of one of the five cows which were
still tied up on the forecastle.

Meanwhile the steady approach of a three-plumed smoke cloud
to the east told watchers on the *Brooklyn* that Sampson and the
New York were coming on the scene. She was by herself, as all the
other American ships had hove to near one or other of the blazing
wrecks to attempt rescue operations, but the flagship didn't slacken
speed in the least as she went by them. The *Texas* was flying the
signal "the enemy has surrendered," to let him know what had
happened up ahead, but Sampson made no acknowledgment that
he had seen it.

All the way in his furious race up the coast, he had been hoping
that the battle might not yet be beyond him. Any semblance of
maneuver, any disablement of the Spanish squadron that would
slow the pell-mell dash would allow the *New York* to catch up
and take her part with the fleet, and Sampson his role as its rightful commander. As he passed the bonfires on the shoreline, one
by one, he realized that the unthinkable was happening: he was
to remain a spectator only, and a distant one at that. It was a
crushing thing for Sampson to have to accept. The admiral was
of not only a taciturn, but an unbending nature. Not volatile and
sanguine like Schley, who was quick to anger and quick to forgive,
Sampson was meticulous and unsparing of himself, the type of
man who would feel most keenly the frustrations that can come
from being victimized by a situation not of one's own making. He
could only think now of how terribly unfair it all was.

The *Colón* had run on the beach at 1:15 and now, after forty-
five minutes, Schley considered the *New York* to be within signal
distance. He had news he scarcely dared to believe; the only
casualties of the action given him so far—one dead and two
slightly wounded—had been from his own ship, and he ordered a
joyful salutation hoisted: "A glorious victory has been achieved.
Details later." The men of the fleet watched the flagship eagerly,
wondering what words of praise or congratulation the commander
in chief would bestow. None was forthcoming. Physically Samp-

son was as stolid as ever, but just now his mind wasn't equipped to deal with the amenities the moment demanded. Instead it brooded over a grotesque circumstance which had been shaped by some Fate with a diabolic sense of irony. It featured a sailor, lying in wait with a battle fleet outside a hostile port, all with the prime purpose, after limitless planning and patience, of luring the enemy within to sea and destroying him. The weeks of waiting are justified, the escape is tried, the fleet is ready and the foe is smashed utterly, just as it has been conceived; and at that crucial moment—the moment for which he has trained professionally all his life and once past will never come again—the victors' leader and guiding brain is somewhere else. It didn't even have the dignity of classical tragedy; it was more like the plot of a nickel-thriller pulp magazine.

The *Brooklyn* tried another string of flags: "This is a great day for our country." It was, but not for the silent and solitary figure on the bridge of the *New York*. A terse answer ran up Sampson's halyards: "Report your casualties."

Schley repeated it to himself in a pained and disgusted manner, turned on his heel and strode to the opposite rail. His blood had been up from the excitement, and what fatigue he felt was the happy weariness of triumph. The arrival, and now the perverse reaction, of the man who had been advanced over him to command was an added deflation coming on top of his normal cooling off. As if to compensate for the hurt of the snub, the commodore sent his own congratulations to the other ships. To the *Oregon* he wigwagged: "Thanks for your splendid assistance. If it had not been for you we might not be here." Then to the *Texas*: "You did glorious work; thank you for being with us"; and finally to the little yacht *Vixen*, which had done what she could to stay close to the fight: "Thank you for trying to keep near us." In each case these met with cheers from the ship in question, but the crew of the *New York* remained chillingly silent throughout it all. To Schley it was an infuriating manifestation of icy inhumanity. How could the man be such an unfeeling automaton?

To make things worse, the *New York* now nosed her way between the *Brooklyn* and the *Colón* and ordered Cook, who was on his way back to Schley's ship with the Spanish commodore and captain, to report to Sampson with his prisoners instead. Seeing what was happening, Schley picked up a megaphone and hailed the flagship: "I request the honor of receiving the surrender of the *Cristóbal Colón!*" His call was met with a half-insolent "What?" from a midshipman, and Schley repeated it. This time there was no reply at all.[17] Captain Cook duly appeared on the *New York's* quarter-deck with his Spaniards and told the admiral that the *Colón*, though virtually undamaged by gunfire, was in a sinking condition; it seems her crew had opened her torpedo tubes and knocked the heads off her sea valves in an effort to prevent capture.

When Cook returned to the *Brooklyn*, Schley took the gig and was rowed over to the flagship to meet with Sampson in person. As his boat passed the *Oregon* and then the *Texas* and *Vixen*, bluejackets lined the rails and yelled and waved their hats with the gusto that might have greeted a Caesar's triumphal parade, but there was still not a peep from the *New York*. Schley was piped aboard with stiff formality; Sampson was ill at ease, overly conscious of the new relationship between the two of them; his own starched dress whites, complete with the leggings and spurs which he had neglected to remove, contrasting painfully with the powder-blackened and bloodstained battle dress of his victorious subordinate. Both were too self-disciplined to let any strong emotion show, but there was a notable absence of cordiality there at the gangway; no one remembers seeing any handshaking or even smiles exchanged.

In the midst of this awkward moment the scout ship *Resolute* came alongside with some startling news. Incredible as it seemed in the glow of victory, the *Resolute's* captain had just seen what was unmistakably a first-class battleship flying the colors of Spain bearing down on the American fleet from the east. If true, she could only be the *Pelayo*, flagship of Spain's home squadron, which everyone had supposed was still in the Mediterranean. Sampson didn't look as if he believed the report, but nevertheless turned to Captain Clark, who was standing by, and told him to take the *Oregon* and have a look. "You go, too," he added to Schley.

The commodore was even more taken aback at this, though he was getting accustomed to these strange reactions from Sampson and didn't let on. After all, he and his men had just come through a major engagement. The *Brooklyn's* stokers had been in front of the fires for four scorching hours, and both they and the gunners were completely ragged. The only American fatality had been one of his crew, and the only wounded were from the *Brooklyn's* company also, yet here was the *New York*, with plenty of coal and her magazines full of ammunition—she had fired only two or three shots all day, at a sinking torpedo boat—and her crew aching for a smell of powder. Schley shot a quizzical look at the man who was content to sit tight rather than seize an opportunity to participate personally in what might be the climactic capping of his fleet's victory. Sampson didn't meet his eye and there was nothing for the commodore to do but follow Clark over the side.

But the *Oregon* was not to accompany him after all. Back on his own bridge Clark got a message from the *New York* to wait where he was for further orders, leaving Schley and the *Brooklyn* to go it alone. At this point Schley seemed too tired to care. "Well, Cook," was his only comment, "after what's happened today, I think we can give them a pretty good circus, anyway."

What followed had some suggestion about it of the Big Top, though it was not so funny for a moment or two. The mysterious ship was sighted in no time, and Schley ordered the *Brooklyn's* port guns, which hadn't had so much wear and tear, readied for action. Upon studying her through his glass, though, Captain Cook wasn't so sure. She couldn't be the *Pelayo*—not unless the current issue of *Jane's Fighting Ships* had erred seriously. The *Pelayo* had no turrets and this ship obviously did. Nevertheless the red-striped ensign hanging limply from her masthead in the deepening twilight seemed to identify her as an enemy warship of some variety, and Schley ordered the gunners to sight on her.

Just then a string of flags broke out on the stranger's fore-yard-arm and one of her searchlights was turned on them to make sure they would be seen. "This is an Austrian ship. Please do not fire." The *Resolute*, Schley and everybody else had confused the red-and-white flag of Franz Josef's navy with the crimson and gold colors of Spain. An English-speaking lieutenant from the intruder came aboard to explain that his captain merely wanted to make port at Santiago for the night, and wondered, since that seemed impossible, where he now ought to go. Schley had to smile as he read the lettering on the stern of the ship's launch. Twenty miles offshore, was his suggestion. It was no night for strangers to be nosing about, he mused, particularly if the American fleet got word of the Austrian's name. As a final surprise in a day that had had its share of them, she'd turned out to be another *Maria Theresa*.

✳✳✳

There now remained only the duty of getting some word through to Washington on the almost unbelievable success of the United States Navy. What should have been a mere formality turned into a proceeding with more than one questionable aspect, and would give the spark to enmities that would be a long time cooling. It was while finishing up his notes on the deck of the *Brooklyn* that George Graham saw the *Vixen* run up alongside the *New York*, and assuming that she was going to take dispatches to Siboney, which was the nearest cable station, he asked if he might catch a ride with her. Siboney was her destination, true enough; in fact Lieutenant Staunton, Sampson's flag lieutenant, was already aboard and sitting right next to him was Goode, Graham's colleague from the Associated Press, who had been at the admiral's side during the battle.

Staunton objected to waiting for Graham, suspecting that, if the latter got to the telegraph, he would undoubtedly give credit for the victory to Schley, but the correspondent had friends of his own and was nevertheless allowed to go. Considering all that had been won that day, it was not exactly a gleeful group, and the *Vixen* had barely got under way when a dispute broke out between Staunton and Lieutenant Commander Sharpe, her skipper. Sharpe, who had seen most of the action at close range, maintained, and rightly, that the *New York* was never for a moment in the fight or even within signal distance, and that the *Brooklyn* had borne the brunt of the whole thing, while Staunton argued that while the

New York had hardly fired a gun she had been "fairly near" to battle and it was therefore Admiral Sampson's victory.

The argument and the trip to the cable office was postponed when the *Vixen* happened to spot the unfortunate Austrian battleship and sped back to the fleet with the news, and it was not until about 9:30 that evening that Staunton and Goode again started for Siboney—this time on a torpedo boat—with Sampson's dispatch to the Navy Department. They arrived off the town at two o'clock on Independence Day morning, and to his surprise and annoyance, Staunton had no sooner stepped ashore than he bumped into Lieutenant Sears, Commodore Schley's own flag officer. The *Brooklyn's* investigation of the *Pelayo* had brought her close enough to Siboney for Schley to land Sears in the ship's steam cutter with his own account of things for Washington.

It was an unorthodox thing to do—all communications to the Secretary of the Navy were supposed to go through the senior officer present—but Schley was smarting under what he considered Sampson's unforgivable rebuff, and had decided that a sailor who'd done away with all his country's available enemies in one morning's work ought to be able to stretch standard operating procedure a bit. His personal cable to Secretary Long read:

> Spanish squadron came out of Santiago harbor this morning, July 3, at 9:30, and were all captured or destroyed in a running fight to the westward of about three and a half hours. Very few casualties in our fleet; Ellis, chief yeoman killed, and one man wounded on *Brooklyn*. Reports from the other ships not yet in. Commander-in-chief now superintending transfer of prisoners from *Cristóbal Colón* which surrendered to the *Brooklyn* and *Oregon* at 1:15 P.M. Victory complete. Details later. Several watertight compartments on the *Brooklyn* filled with water. Probably pierced or strained.[18]

It stuck to the facts in the straightforward manner characteristic of Navy communiqués and it made no mention of Schley's personal role in the action; however, Washington was never to pass judgment on it. When Staunton made the request, Sears had no choice but to hand it over to him to read, for as an admiral's aide, the latter outranked him when officially representing his

chief. It was no surprise when Staunton ruled his own dispatch
had top priority, and that once sent there would of course be no
need for Schley's to go at all. He then showed Sears a sheet of
Sampson's personal stationery bearing the admiral's own account
of the battle:

> The fleet under my command offers the nation as a Fourth of
> July present the whole of the Spanish fleet. It attempted to escape
> at 9:30 A.M. this morning. At 2 the last ship, the Cristóbal Colón,
> had run ashore 75 miles west of Santiago and hauled down her
> colors. The Infanta María Teresa, Oquendo and Viscaya were
> forced ashore, burned and blown up within 20 miles of Santiago.
> The Plutón and Furor were destroyed within 4 miles of the port.[19]

This announcement, particularly the first sentence of it, would
be the sore point of the controversy to follow. "The fleet under
my command" was of course purely technical and absolutely
correct, though in light of the circumstances, it would have been
politically expedient and perhaps a good deal fairer to say it
differently. As it turned out, the wording of the dispatch was not
Sampson's at all—it had been composed by Staunton and signed
as a matter of course by the admiral—but to the latter's credit he
never used that as a defense against those who were soon to level
their guns at him loaded with charges of braggadocio, envy, stealthy
opportunism and worse.

✳✳✳

Darkness dropped down over the Cuban coast with tropical
suddenness, giving a dramatic quality to the still-blazing wrecks
of Spain's West Indian squadron, which now plainly marked, like
the victory beacons of some pagan race of antiquity, the step-by-
step saga of the day's triumph. The Colón, the ship that was to
have been the U.S. Navy's first major prize since the War of 1812,
was slowly settling where she was, too. At Sampson's orders the
Oregon had attached a hawser to try to pull her off the beach, and
though Captain Cook had reported it to the admiral some time
before, it was only after she had been floated again that it was
realized her sea cocks were open and she was taking in water
steadily. She had a prize crew from the Oregon aboard (chosen

because Sampson had felt the battleship had more to do with her surrender than any other) and the only hope of salvage now lay in pushing the big vessel back up on the sandy shelf from which she had just been hauled.

The *New York* was called upon for the job and approached the after part of the Spanish cruiser slowly and warily, like some great sea animal sniffing at another member of its species. The American's sleek prow was muffled in bulky protective fenders which had been lowered over her ram, and there was a soft bump as Captain Chadwick, handling the 8,000-ton *New York* like a harbor tug, nosed into the *Colón*'s stern. Three times he backed off and repeated the shoving operation, and although the Spaniard was worked up into shallow water again, she could not be saved. She listed more and more and scarcely had the prize crew been taken off than she rolled over on her side, her masts flopping in the water and her screws in the air.

Most accounts of the time speak angrily and contemptuously of the "treachery" involved in not delivering the vessel into American hands, yet Spanish naval custom in such instances was set down very plainly in black and white. Spanish captains were directed to battle superior forces if necessary in a way that would be considered "honorable by the enemy" and, when no longer able to fight their ships in deep water, to run for the shore, continue to work from there and finally scuttle them as a last resort.[20] If the *Colón* had opened her sea cocks before she had hauled down her flag, and there is only questionable evidence that this was not the case, then her commander was merely exercising one of his prerogatives.

By the time Commodore Schley returned in the *Brooklyn* from his confrontation with the Austrian warship, it was after midnight. On the way back there came an anxious megaphone hail from where the *Indiana* lay hove to. "*Brooklyn* there, what's become of the *Cristóbal Colón?*" The answer, "She's ashore, forty miles to the west," brought a happy shout from the decks of the battleship. A little further on the *Massachusetts*, which had been cheated out of any share in the day's glory by coaling at Guantánamo, asked the same question and the men lining her rail hurrahed just as loudly at the reply. As the *Brooklyn* neared the *Iowa*, there came a similar hail, which the cruiser answered in the same manner, but there was no cheer in return; instead a call from the battleship's O.D. saying, "Admiral Cervera is on this ship." Captain Evans had forbidden any celebration out of respect to the captive commander in chief.

As soon as he could, Schley changed his uniform and was rowed to the *Iowa*, where the officer of the deck told him the admiral was below with the wounded Captain Eulate, who was also a prisoner there. Cervera had the little yacht *Gloucester* to thank for his safety. Leaving the chase after the *Colón* to the bigger ships, Captain Wainwright had spent the rest of the day ferrying medical supplies, biscuit and canned meat to survivors from the other beached Spanish cruisers. Several dozen seamen from the *Teresa* had been grouped by the water's edge next to the fire-blackened hulk, and when Lieutenant Norman came ashore in a lifeboat, the admiral stepped up to introduce himself and the members of his staff, which included his own son. All had swum to the beach in their underwear or in nothing at all, so when Norman brought the high-ranking prisoners out to the *Gloucester*, Wainwright had to scrounge what clothes he could from the ship's stores and the personal wardrobes of his officers and himself. Cervera was found a pair of blue trousers, a black alpaca coat, a civilian shirt and a white straw hat, and thus decent once more, was invited to lunch in the ship's little wardroom. The usual courtesies were soon dispensed with, and victor and vanquished nibbled in rather embarrassed silence until executive officer Lieutenant Huse thought to venture the gallant remark: "*Nous avons remporté la victoire, mais la gloire est à vous!*" *

"*C'est tres bien!*" murmured Cervera gratefully, and from then on the ice was thawed.

All that afternoon and evening the Spanish admiral had passed among the wounded, trying to cheer them up, and assisted as well in the burial of five seamen who had died since being brought on board. They were interred at sea with full naval honors under the

* "We have gained the victory, but the glory is yours."

battle flag of Spain and by their own priest, while the American ships stood off respectfully with colors at half mast. Many more had been killed, of course, and the full total would not be known for some time.[21] The circumstances of Captain Lazaga's death were still not cleared up, though the presence of a jeweled sword and a revolver in the *Oquendo*'s charred conning tower gave cause for speculation long afterward. Five of the cartridges in the cylinder had been discharged by heat and one bore the imprint of the hammer. The mortally wounded Captain Vilaamil, who commanded the two torpedo-boat destroyers, had died on the beach, and rather than abandon the body, some of his men tied it in a wicker chair which had been washed up by the waves and hid it in the rocks before they made off through the jungle for Santiago. Years later Vilaamil's remains were found and identified, and they were then taken to Spain and buried with military honors.

Schley found Cervera in the cabin of one of the *Iowa*'s officers, seated quietly and looking "somewhat dejected," though the Spaniard quickly stood up to receive him. The two men shook hands and Cervera immediately unburdened himself: "If we could have passed the *Brooklyn*, I believe we would have gotten away," he said. "My orders to concentrate our fire on the *Brooklyn* were carried out, but your ship has a charmed life, sir. My career is ended. I shall go back to Spain in disgrace." [22]

The admiral spoke in French, the international naval language, but Schley, whose sympathy was aroused by his adversary's state, put a hand on his shoulder and answered him kindly in flawless Castilian: Cervera had showed great bravery and his country would honor him as it should. From then the two men talked in Spanish, and the admiral's naturally good spirits gradually returned, helped by his relief that the bloody business was over and done with. It was quite evident that the expectation of the horror and the "hecatomb" that would result from the foray he must order had preyed on his mind for weeks, and when he spoke of it, his eyes filled with tears. Now that the tragedy had been played out in full, the burden fell away from him.

Before Schley left the battleship for the *Brooklyn*, Cervera asked his permission to frame a dispatch to Havana giving the details of the fight, and he may have taken some satisfaction in pricking the smug General Blanco's illusions:

> I went out with the ships at 9:30 and sustained a very hot battle with the enemy. The defense was brilliant, but it was not possible to fight against the hostile forces, which were three times as large as ours. The *María Teresa, Oquendo* and *Viscaya*, all with fire on board, ran ashore and were then blown up. The destroyers *Plutón* and *Furor* were sunk by shots from hostile guns. The *Colón*, the Americans say, surrendered after running aground. I estimate our losses at least 600 killed and wounded. The rest of the crew have been taken prisoner. Vilaamil was killed in the battle; also I believe Lazaga. Among the wounded are Concas and Eulate. The Americans have allowed the latter to retain his sword because of his brilliant conduct. I must say that the American sailors are treating us with all possible consideration. We have lost everything and I shall need funds.

Whether because of his "brilliant conduct" or because he was a personal acquaintance, through his New York visit, of some of his captors, Captain Eulate was indeed allowed to keep his sword. Shortly after Cervera was picked up, the captain had been hoisted onto the deck of the *Iowa* in a chair, covered with blood from three wounds and with a gory handkerchief wrapped around his bare head. He lifted himself to his feet, and the token of surrender was gracefully presented with a bow to Captain Evans, who just as gracefully declined it, accepting his prisoner's parole instead. As he hobbled to the door of Evans' cabin, he turned, raised his arm and saluted his fire-shrouded ship dramatically—"*Adios, Viscaya!*"—and just then the forward magazine of the Spanish cruiser, in an answering gesture of its own, exploded with stupendous effect. It was a totally Wagernian finale to everything.

★★★

✱✱✱✱✱✱✱✱

CHAPTER VII

Fallen Idols Leave Clear Horizons

Admiral Sampson had described it correctly; it was as much of a Fourth of July gift to the nation as anyone could have wished for. It left most people a little stunned and very jubilant, and General Shafter a little stunned and very perplexed. Cervera's defeat had eliminated the only strategic reason for wanting to take Santiago, yet there he was, all dressed up for battle and no place to go. It seemed absurd to send his infantry against the still-formidable Spanish defenses to secure an objective which was no longer of any military value. On the other hand he shrank from the idea of simply packing up and pulling out. The name Santiago would always be a reminder of what an unfinished job had cost him in men and effort. It would hurt the prestige of the Army and do nothing for his own reputation, which stood none too high right then anyway. The alternative wasn't a happy one, either. Could he really sit where he was, beset by the rains and by his myriad supply problems and starve the dons out before the fever, which was now making itself felt in the American ranks, could decimate his army? To make the decision more pressing, he learned that the enemy reinforcing column had finally arrived from Manzanillo to bolster the city's garrison.

Shafter turned to the Navy once more. Having won a crushing victory over the only seagoing force that Spain possessed in that end of the world, there seemed no reason why the fleet could not now risk a ship or two. Since the general had carried out his mission of forcing Cervera's fleet from the harbor for the Navy's benefit, could not his colleague reciprocate on the part of the

Army? On July 4, the day after the fight, Shafter sent Sampson Independence Day greetings by repeating his request in regard to what he felt was the latter's clear duty: "Now, if you will force your way into that harbor, the town will surrender without any further sacrifice of life. My present position has cost me a thousand men and I do not wish to lose any more." [1]

Sampson received the familiar demand calmly and with as little inclination to comply as ever, for the same reasons he had set down before—mines in the harbor and batteries in the hills—and he was, he let it be known, getting tired of repeating them.

Driven to equal measures of anger and desperation, Shafter threw his case before Washington via a series of telegrams. It was imperative that the Navy make an attempt to force their way in, he said in one; if he was expected to do anything else offensively, he would require no fewer than 15,000 men to do it, said another, and he needed them right away. His pleas went to Secretary of War Alger, who took them to the President, who called for a closed-door meeting between the Secretary and Captain Mahan (who had been summoned as the Navy's chief advocate) with himself—McKinley—as referee. Warm words passed over his head between the two services for some time, and finally in a summation that allowed him to keep his position on the fence, the President ruled that Sampson and Shafter ought to confer themselves to see who was going to do what.

Just about everybody was at odds with everybody else now; Shafter's telegrams had been published, which put the Navy in a bad light and made Sampson furious, and the general, disgusted himself with the response from Washington, now turned his attention to the Spaniards. He might have profited much from doing so earlier, for as was his custom, he had been maximizing his own problems and minimizing those of the enemy. Cervera's defeat, American verbal persistence in demanding the surrender of the Santiago garrison, and the fact that the latter was already down to its last ration of rice and *garbanzos* had in fact already convinced General José Toral (a replacement for General Linares who had been wounded in the lines) that capitulation was the only way out.

Still pouting over the Navy's lack of cooperation, Shafter was at first willing to let the Spaniards simply deliver up the town and take a walk out into the jungle, where they could have done no harm anyway, but this plan was immediately vetoed by a suddenly intransigent Washington, which had just now set its heart on unconditional surrender. Even that didn't sound too harsh to Toral, though, after Shafter made the generous promise that, if he surrendered, his army would be released and transported at American expense back to Spain. Would that include his entire command? Shafter was asked. The command turned out to embrace 11,500 men at Santiago, 7,000 men at Guantánamo, 3,000 more at San Luís, about twenty-five miles away, and 1,500 additional troops thirty miles away. The astonished Shafter agreed, "thunderstruck" that the Spaniard would of his own free will offer him 12,000 fighting men that were absolutely beyond his reach.

Shafter had been so quickly and so completely delivered from his predicament that he wasn't even bothered when the subsequent proceedings dragged out with an interminable presenting of credentials, negotiation and delay of one kind or another, while he and his men camped beyond the city walls in the rain. Considering the forces involved, the to-do did seem lengthy, but at last the final niceties of Old World diplomacy were satisfied, and on the morning of Sunday, July 17, two weeks after Admiral Cervera's sortie, General Toral watched the Spanish flag over Government House lowered for the last time, mounted his horse solemnly and rode out with his staff and an armed escort for the official surrender. It was a very brief ceremony. Between the lines he was met by the American generals with their own staffs and escorts, and the mounted contingents of officers drew up to face one another, silent and formal. Shafter rode up to Toral and offered him the sword of General Vara del Rey, the Spanish defender of El Caney. Accompanying troops on both sides then presented arms and the Spaniards marched back to the city, where they stacked their weapons at an arsenal which was found to contain eleven 6- and 8-inch howitzers, eighteen Maxim guns and 5.5 million rounds of ammunition. Riding in after them, the American generals passed through no fewer than four complete lines of defense, each marked by regular banks of barbed wire running every which way all across the road, and supported by rifle pits both flanking and enfilading the approaches.

At eleven o'clock in the morning, following a meeting with the civil governor, the archbishop and the foreign consuls, after which a polite lunch was served, the American officers trooped out to the city plaza where thousands of the Cuban populace were already on hand to watch the flag raising. The whole thing was planned to go off without a hitch, and would have, had not one of the correspondent faction felt the urge to immortalize himself at the expense of the moment. Seeing a battery of photographers aiming their cameras at the flagstaff on top of the palace, Silvester Scovel of Joseph Pulitzer's New York World climbed the roof in an attempt to appear in the forefront of the ensuing picture. After all, William Randolph Hearst had been at El Caney and had boarded the still-sizzling decks of the Viscaya in yachting cap and blue flannels to "capture" twenty survivors. The World couldn't be outdone. The reporter was quickly ordered down, first by the officer in charge and then by Shafter himself. He obeyed, but strode up to the general indignantly, shouting protests as only the hot-tempered Scovel could; one word led to another, the newsman swung a roundhouse right at the commander in chief, and it was only by the narrowest of margins that the conquering hero of the day missed having the kibosh put on by the working press at his own surrender ceremony.

The situation was saved in as timely a way as any film director might have willed, for just then the clock in the cathedral struck noon, the Stars and Stripes were raised, the sound of twenty-one guns crashed across the square magnificently from building to building and the band of the Sixth Cavalry struck up a traditional tribute to the Republic: "Hail Columbia, happy land. . . ." [2]

And with the exception of one of her sons who was speedily paraded off to the calabozo, there was no doubt that she was.

***

The bickering that had begun over the Sampson-Shafter disagreement about the respective duties of Army and Navy was still a sour note, however. Sampson had let Shafter know that he expected to be represented in any surrender negotiations, and though the general had agreed and duly informed the admiral of the enemy's capitulation, it had somehow been found impossible to do so until the very day of the ceremony. When the Navy's deputy arrived, the papers had already been signed—by the Army. Sampson seethed at this and promptly put a prize crew aboard the *Alvarado*, which was still in the bay and which had been claimed by the Army as the spoils of war, and sailed her off to Guantánamo.[3]

It was mean and petty on the part of both men. Things hadn't been helped when the harbor defenses were examined after the fall of the city and it was found that, with the exception of the guns from the *Reina Mercedes*, Santiago was defended almost wholly by bronze muzzle-loaders from the eighteenth century. One piece was dated 1668. Even the dreaded electrical mines were faulty; many could not be fired. It was an embarrassment added to Sampson's general frustration over having his battle won by a subordinate; Shafter on the other hand was envious of the Navy's success and smarting under the criticism that was beginning to be leveled at him, at his tactics, at his losses, at his seemingly inexcusable foot dragging that had invited the sickness now spreading through the American Army.

The public was even disillusioned with the Cubans. Continued contact with the patriot armies which had so captured fancies back home kept building on an initially unfavorable impression. They had been so heroic on the front pages of the papers before the war; at close hand too many of the rebels now seemed thieving, cruel and unreliable. The failure of García's men to prevent the arrival of the Spanish Manzanillo relief column was severely commented on, and in return it was found the Cubans bore no love for their saviors either. Word went around that, after they had rid themselves of Spain, they expected to find themselves at war with the *yanquis*, and not a few acted as though they might welcome the prospect. It was quite a comedown. General Young, one of Shafter's divisional commanders, spoke for many when he labeled the insurgents as a bunch of degenerates, absolutely devoid of honor or gratitude, and no more capable of self-government than the savages of Africa.⁴ People were finding out Mr. Kipling's burden could chafe as well as uplift!

Against this disquieting background of troubles on the island the Navy's image began to stand out ever more heroically. Sampson had done his best to perpetuate it by promptly appointing a board of survey to examine the wrecked Spanish cruisers and report on the effect upon them of the gunfire of "the fleet under his command." They went over the hulks carefully, cataloguing the damage, and found that the enemy ships showed visible evidence of 123 hits. The *Oquendo* had been punished the most severely, being struck 57 times, the *Teresa* and *Viscaya* were hit 29 times each and the *Colón* 8 times.

This was in striking contrast to the case on the American side, where the fleet had got off with even more minimal damage than had been realized. True, the *Brooklyn* had been hit by twenty projectiles of one kind or another, her smokestack punctured and her halyards cut, but nothing severe at all. In the *Texas* a shell had severed the hammock nettings and the forced-draft ducts, but that ship seemed to have suffered as much from her own broadsides as from those of the enemy: the firing of her 12-inch main battery had caused her deck frames to bulge severely. The *Iowa*'s starboard side was holed twice by shells; one entered the forward cofferdam and remained there without exploding at all after making a 16 x 7-inch hole, the other hit a little further aft and exploded on the berth deck, spraying fragments around. The *Oregon*, the *Indiana*, the *Vixen* and the little *Gloucester*, which had been closer to the enemy guns than any other vessel, were not hit at all.

Sampson was quick to attribute the significance of these findings to the "very manifest" gulf in marksmanship between the American and Spanish seamen which, he added, had not been created in a day. Constant drills and practice had obviously paid off, it was pointed out, and he praised his turret captains without stint. It had been reported to him that many of the Spanish gun sights were found after the battle to have been adjusted to a totally unrealistic range, as if the enemy gunners had been given a set of numbers by their officers when the ships came out of port and first opened fire, and in their excitement had forgotten to keep them corrected as the distances changed. It was obviously a matter of men freezing under pressure, and from it one could draw a comparison between the spirit which actuated the officers and men of the two nations. Despite Cervera's every preparation for a successful sortie, the United States Navy, Sampson boasted, was able to strike with a "perfect confidence which the Spaniards found it impossible to resist." [5]

***

All this was devoured eagerly by the public back home. When Admiral Sampson's ships were sighted off the Narrows on the morning of August 20, a fleet of steamers, yachts and tugs loaded almost to the gunwales with an excited populace put out to meet them. Through the upper bay and up the Hudson River the men-of-war passed in review to "deafening huzzas and applause"; whistles blew, bells rang, bands played, flags flew from every pole, and jetties, piers and windows all along the way were lined with ecstatic, cheering faces.

It was undiscriminating acclaim while it lasted, which wasn't long; with honors came promotion and with promotion the end of the idyllic mood. President McKinley saw fit to reward his Caribbean heroes by jumping Admiral Sampson eight numbers on the Navy list, and Commodore Schley six. Both men had thus been elevated to permanent rear-admiral status, but whereas Schley had outranked his colleague from the time he left Annapolis until the beginning of the war, he was now to be officially Sampson's junior. The name of the sailor who had defeated Cervera would remain just beneath that of the man who had been elsewhere on the day of battle.

Schley was able to take comfort in the fact that this obvious slight did not represent the majority judgment. When he arrived in Washington a few days later, he was met by an enthusiastic crowd which gave him a see-the-conquering-hero-comes welcome in the classical tradition. A corps of over a hundred bicyclists formed an escort on either side of his carriage as it was driven down Pennsylvania Avenue to the Shoreham Hotel. And if official naval opinion refused to coincide with this popular show, the press intimated it was only what might be expected. Caustic comment on the jealous inability to give honor where honor was due filled the editorial columns. In print Sampson emerged not only as a politician who had been promoted by influence over the head of a better man, but as an opportunist who had selfishly tried to deprive Schley of the credit for his victory (as was evidenced by that postbattle dispatch).

The issue served as a means by which the Democrats could brew political ferment, and in the bitterness of the hour each camp combed the record for every misjudgment and mistake on the part of the other's champion. Jealousies and hatreds long hidden came out into the open—anything was fair game if it would discredit the other side—and a split took place that would divide the Navy for years and would embitter the sweetness of what had been, after all, a stunning and inexpensive victory complete enough to satisfy the most rabid prewar jingo.

Sampson was deeply injured by all the charges and countercharges, and he was not the same man at all when he was given command of the Brooklyn Navy Yard after peace was signed. Schley was mollified on his own part when a presidential appointment was offered him to serve on the Puerto Rican Commission, and later to assume command of the Navy's South Atlantic station. With his absence from the country and a near-desperate directive of Secretary Long's prohibiting Navy personnel from discussing Sampson or Schley, the whole business might have died a natural death had not the academy at Annapolis introduced its classes to a new textbook—A History of the United States Navy, by E. S. Maclay, a government clerk in the Brooklyn Navy Yard. In it Maclay, obviously a Sampson man, described Schley's behavior at Santiago as disgraceful, "deliberately turning tail" in the face of the enemy and practicing "caitiff flight" as he did.[6]

On Schley's part resentment of Sampson had been fading, but seeing himself presented to naval posterity in such terms was a new twist of the knife. He demanded a court of inquiry to clear his name. It was convened in September of 1901 with Admiral

Dewey as president, and in the following weeks suffered the ordeal of listening to no fewer than 1,700 pages of testimony on Schley's and Sampson's activities off the Cuban coast. At the end of it all a recommendation was made that the Navy Department withdraw the offending book from the academy curriculum and dismiss the author, but Schley's victory was a Pyrrhic one, for in all other respects the court was to prove hard on him. The former commodore was censured for "vacillation and dilatoriness" in the hunt for Admiral Cervera, his official report on his coaling difficulties off Santiago was judged inaccurate and misleading, and he was charged with "lack of enterprise" for making only a feeble attempt to engage the *Cristóbal Colón* when she lay moored in the harbor entrance. It was terribly humiliating. Only the court president, the hero of Manila Bay, dissented, yet that disagreement was so decidedly put that it left no doubt as to the division of feeling in the case. In Dewey's opinion "Commodore Schley was the senior officer of our Squadron off Santiago when the Spanish Squadron attempted to escape on the morning of July 3, 1898. He was in absolute command and is entitled to the credit due such commanding officer for the glorious victory." [7]

Vilification on the part of the popular press was heaped on the court majority decision, and as a last measure, Schley appealed to Theodore (now President) Roosevelt for justice. To the final crushing of his cause, Roosevelt approved the board's findings and urged that the proceedings be ended, for the sake of the Navy's reputation.

When he heard an inquiry was to be held, Sampson was very disturbed and would have liked to testify, but his health would not permit it. He was very unwell, a condition due in large part to the obloquy to which he had been subjected. Had he been able to appear, it might have thrown some light on several aspects of the relationship between the two men that have remained cloudy. Under all the turmoil and mudslinging his own laurels had withered perceptibly, and the general public had soon tired of the business anyway; searching for fresh heroes was part of the new spirit of the times. He retired in May, 1902, and when he died two months later in Washington, D.C., he was already fading in the memory of a nation that was eager to let the recent past lie and look to an exciting and intriguing future.

Schley had left the Navy the year before and lived until 1911, when he was felled from a stroke suffered on a New York street. The retirement of the quasi-hero of Santiago Bay was equally quiet and uneventful; he had his friends, time passed quickly for the still-erect, bearded sailor who seemed toward the end so much a relic of the nineteenth century, and only those closest to him knew how much the years were embittered by the failure of the Navy to sustain him in his hour of triumph and of need.

In the way that people will sometimes embrace former enemies, the popularity of the defeated Pascual Cervera came to equal that of any of the national champions on the winning side. When he was brought to Portsmouth, New Hampshire, to visit the prison camp where his crews were being held, the old grandee was received most cordially and gained so much in local esteem that a suggestion was made to buy him a house in Florida. The grateful Cervera had to beg off, for duty called him back to Spain to stand trial with all his captains before the supreme naval and military court of the realm. Americans no less than Spaniards were pleased when all were honorably absolved from guilt for the Santiago defeat, and many in this country continued to follow the career of the man they once feared would burn their seaports as he was appointed in turn vice admiral, chief of staff of the Spanish Navy, and at last, in 1903, life senator. He died six years later, in 1909, at home, in bed, surrounded by love and respect, a happier man than either of his conquerors.

***

Aftermath
****

Every war and every battle in it has its lessons to teach—tactical, material, moral, psychological—even if they are no more than reiterations of old ones that never become obsolete. The land fighting around Santiago—the clashes at Las Guásimas, El Caney and San Juan Hill—had no great innovations to suggest; relatively small numbers of men fought in terrain particularly unsuitable for maneuver; the weapons that dominated the battlefield were the rifle and, to a lesser extent, the field gun, the same basic arms that had won the day at Gettysburg and, if one wants to go back further, at Waterloo as well. The power of the long-range, high-velocity rifle as well as the rapidly developing machine gun had already given the advantage to the defense (the success of the Gatlings offensively really only proves the point), but this was not fully realized as yet. It would take Kitchener's destruction of the Mahdi's tribesmen at Omdurman in September of 1898, the marksmanship of the Boer farmers a year or so later, and finally the bloodbath battles of the frontiers in 1914 to demonstrate convincingly the power of rapid-fire small arms against infantry.

Other aspects had remained just on the far side of the threshold of change. In Cuba all transport was still horse- and mule-drawn—the internal-combustion engine was only about to make an appearance; medical facilities had not advanced much since the Civil War, and the suggestion of air power, in the form of the clumsy observation balloon, may have foretold a revolution to come, but did little at San Juan but provide a diversion for the man from the motion-picture company and a hot afternoon to those troops whose position was pinpointed by the presence of the big gasbag to the enemy.

If we can draw a conclusion from the Santiago land campaigns, it has to be that luck and providence do play a part in war. Under ordinary circumstances it is definitely unwise to assume, in the event one makes a mistake, that the enemy will make an even bigger blunder to compensate for it; that, when one is outnumbered, in poor position and saddled with uneven generalship, the foe will fail to make tell his preponderance in strength, his domination of the field, and his experience with the terrain, climate and local methods of combat. Yet a look at these little battles gives the impression that someone, somewhere, was looking out for the fledgling American military expedition.

To begin with, had the Spanish Army shown any kind of initiative at all, it might have turned the Daiquirí landing into a bloody disaster. Lieutenant General Linares commanded more than 36,000 troops in the province of Santiago. There were 9,500 in and about the city and the harbor, and between there and Siboney. A quarter of these were within a radius of twenty-five miles. 8,300 more were further to the north at Holguín, 6,000 were at Guantánamo and another 8,700 were eighty-five miles west at Manzanillo. About 12,000 of these could and should have been concentrated in an emergency and within a few hours at any point near Santiago, Siboney or Daiquirí. Had Linares chosen to leave only a thin line of defense against García's largely ineffective Cubans and align his troops in the blockhouses that ringed the Daiquirí beach (Shafter's general destination had, incredibly enough, been published in the newspapers even before he left Tampa), he would have had every chance of halting the American invasion at the water's edge. The naval bombardment did nothing to knock out the forts, and if Shafter were to face the volume of fire on the beaches that he later ran up against in the approaches to Santiago, he would have been driven back into the sea, or at least been forced to pay a far greater price than a few drowned horses.

Failing this, the Spanish general still had a chance to make the most of his position at Las Guásimas, and there are strong arguments that he should have fought the decisive battle of the war there. From their trenches at the crest of the 250-foot ridge the Spanish troops commanded terrain that stretched all the way back to the beach. They could not be bypassed without leaving the American supply base at Siboney defenseless. Linares could have drawn up his army there with no risk at all to Santiago, and might have protected the city more effectively than he ultimately did, at the same time guarding his own supply lines and the road over which additional troops could and should have been rushed from Guantánamo, forty-two miles away.

Finally, he blundered yet a third time in the defense of San Juan Hill and El Caney where he again employed but a small portion of the men available to him in the Santiago district—less than 6 percent, in fact, of the 29,000 under his immediate command. The truth is that the battles of July 1, which were the major encounter between the United States and Spain in Cuba, were fought by less than 1 percent of the 196,000 Spanish troops on the island! It was inexcusable and, as it turned out, fatal. The crucial ten days between June 20—when the American expedition arrived off the mouth of Santiago harbor—and July 1, gave the Spanish commander plenty of time to draw on the forty-five companies of fighting men which could have reached the battlefield within four hours. Had he done so, he would have had, by noon of the day of battle, 6,300 defenders on San Juan and Kettle Hills instead of the 521 who were actually there. Other things being equal, the Americans could not have made any headway, and Shafter would have had no choice but to assume a defensive posture and wait for reinforcements. At that point the outcome would have depended on a race between supply and the progress of the fevers in the area. Needless to say, it might have been much in question.

The American Army should have been grateful for those three missed opportunities, for the events of July 1 uncovered no genius of Napoleonic stamp within its ranks either. Attributing to Shafter a "criminal incompetence" unmatched since classical times may have been an exaggeration; nevertheless the general's illness and his absence from the battlefield can in no way excuse the tactical errors he made, which were serious and could have been

very costly had the Spaniards taken advantage of them. His first
mistake was to fight the battles of San Juan and El Caney simultaneously; by dividing his army he gave the enemy the opportunity
of massing his force against either segment, when there was no
real reason to attack El Caney in strength at all.[1] A successful
assault on the San Juan heights would have succeeded in isolating
the town from Santiago, and its garrison would have been compelled to surrender anyway; the American Army could have made
do by holding a possible flank attack in check with five or six hundred men and a couple of field guns. Shafter, in following a battle
plan in which all his divisions were to combine before making the
main attack, forced the success of the operation to depend on a
questionable factor—the actual strength of the Spanish El Caney
position—which might or might not turn out as he expected. He,
too, wound up shorthanded, and was compelled to fight the battle
of San Juan Hill with 8,400 men instead of the 15,000 he had
intended to have available.

While the Army had fought no textbook campaign, it had been
"blooded" against a foreign foe, and with the help of the afore-
mentioned God of Battles had acquitted itself satisfactorily. The
fighting men, with the exception of the panicky Seventy-first New
York (and they were militia), had stood up well and those at
home had a right to be proud of them. The nation did learn at
the same time that its supply facilities were wretched and its field
hospital arrangements primitive, that many of the weapons with
which it had armed the American soldier were a quarter of a
century out of date, and that it had clothed him suitably enough
for the plains of the North Platte in November but for nowhere
much more temperate. American leadership was inconsistent, too,
the dash of Wheeler and Roosevelt being dampened effectively by
a commander in chief who seemed unable to sustain either the
physical or mental pace. Shafter labored under disadvantages, true
—he lacked the respect of many of his subordinates and he had a
bad press—but this was to some extent his own fault. From the
vantage point of hindsight his actions and personality in particular
might be said to be suggestive of the inarticulate, unimaginative
generalship of the First World War. He emerges as a sort of

prototype of "Papa" Joffre or Field Marshal Haig, though with a considerably lower panic threshold. Where a real or imagined impasse would merely spur these later military models to call for fresh drafts and more shells, they tended to make Shafter lose his self-possession altogether. One can't help wondering what use he might have found for a million men and a fleet of taxicabs. Perhaps he fought the right war after all.

On the naval side some more interesting conclusions can be drawn. Warship development held such a high priority and nineteenth-century actions at sea were so scarce that, when one did take place, marine experts and politicians alike gathered like football coaches at a rival team's game film, hashing over what happened and what might have happened in order to update their own fleet tactics and future construction.

The totality of the Santiago victory astonished everybody, including the Americans and most Spaniards. Of course Spain's fleet was weak in comparison with her Army, and for this reason a big portion of the blame for its defeat must lie with the commander in chief in Cuba, Captain General Blanco, who demanded too much from his sailors and almost nothing from his 200,000 soldiers.

When Madrid received news of Dewey's victory at Manila Bay, the Spanish government's first reaction was a defensive one—to augment naval strength in home waters. The Minister of Marine therefore sent two dispatches to Cervera, who was then at Martinique, giving him the option of returning to Spain if he thought he could do nothing where he was, and telling him of the arrival in Martinique of a collier sent to refuel the squadron. The messages came too late—Cervera had already sailed for Curaçao—however they did reach the ears of General Blanco, who wired the Admiralty in a state of indignation. Recalling Cervera, he protested, would invite panic and lose him the support of all the loyalist elements in Cuba, and though the arguments he used were not very pertinent, the general was persuasive enough to make the government think better of its decision to recall the fleet.

Had Cervera stayed at Martinique one day longer, or had Blanco not interfered, the admiral would have been on his way back to

Spain, a withdrawal that would certainly have changed the course of the war. Santiago and its immediate vicinity would have become strategically unimportant, the fighting would most likely have centered around Havana instead, where the Spaniards had greater troop strength and a much more sophisticated defense system. It assuredly would have been more bloody. It's difficult to understand just what Blanco expected the ships to do in Santiago, anyway. At anchor they were certainly unable to prevent the landing of American troops on the island, and couldn't, in fact, even pose the threat of a "fleet in being."

The admiral himself, however, must bear much of the blame for his being bottled up in port. With the exception of the short period when Schley, unaware of his presence, had first arrived off Santiago harbor, there was not a single hour between May 23 and the evening of the 28th, when Schley returned to take up permanent position, that he could not have escaped scot-free. His original orders required him to stay in West Indian waters, but gave him the latitude to enter any harbor he wished, and fight or decline battle as he deemed best. Once he had coaled, he might have left Santiago for San Juan, which was his original first choice of an operational base, anyway. Or he might have gone to Havana itself, for if his informants were correct as to Sampson's and Schley's whereabouts, the capital city would be free of large enemy ships, its blockade maintained in all likelihood by monitors and unarmored vessels.

As it developed, Spanish intelligence was faulty; Sampson was not off the south coast of Cuba as Cervera was told, but was instead patrolling in the San Nicolas Channel east of Havana in expectation of Cervera's possible appearance. This was even better. Sampson had with him in the channel the *New York*, the *Indiana* and three clumsy monitors. The speedy *Oregon* only joined him on the 28th, after her dash around the Horn, and had Cervera sailed for Havana on the morning of the 24th, he would have covered the 640 miles quickly enough to arrive there two whole days before the *Oregon* appeared. Until that time the only armored ship of Sampson's force faster than his own sluggish *Viscaya* would be the *New York*. If she had pursued, he might have turned on her with his four cruisers, and with any luck at all could have slipped by the slower American vessels, driven off the unarmored blockading ships at Havana and gained the shelter of the city's powerful batteries. Schley, of course, dawdling at Cienfuegos and outside Santiago, wouldn't have been on the scene at all. Cervera lacked neither courage nor a realistic grasp of the strategic situation, but the continual tendency to underestimate his enemy's difficulties and exaggerate his own, which kept him on the defensive when he had at least two other options, does point out his lack of boldness and enterprise. It cost him the chance to evade one of the American squadrons and bring his entire force against the other, which had always been his only hope of success in a meeting of the fleets at sea. Did he really consider how many strategical and tactical gifts he was to offer the Americans at Santiago—the opportunity of falling on his ships one by one when he was finally forced to come forth and do battle, and the possibility of the enemy practically winding up the campaign before the greater part of the armies had the chance to fire a shot?

Of course once the American land-sea trap was set, the Spaniard was forced to try to break out, and on this point opinions diverge on whether he went about it the right way when he did. Herbert L. Sargent, in his fine analytical study of the campaign, thought Cervera's arguments for making the sortie in the daytime instead of night were conclusive. The admiral had felt it would be difficult to negotiate the long narrow channel in the dark, with the glare of American searchlights in the pilots' eyes, without running some ship or other aground. If that had happened, it would of course have jammed the passage and prevented the escape of vessels coming behind. Sampson's blockading ring tightened close inshore at night, and the leading Spanish ships would have been in great danger of being sunk in the channel before getting clear to the open sea; even if they had made it to the harbor mouth, each vessel emerging would have been pounded in turn by the concentrated fire of heavy guns at short and fatal range.[2]

On the other hand there was a strong argument that the Spaniards could and should have attempted to make their escape in some kind of scattered formation. The wreck of the *Merrimac* didn't constitute that much of an obstruction and the patrol boats, according to Admiral Sampson were lying from one to two miles from Morro Castle (depending on weather and visibility), were too far away to light up the channel really effectively. There was no reason, either, why the shore batteries could not have opened fire on them to keep them there. One observer, Commander Jacobsen of the German Navy, though that two large Spanish merchant vessels in Santiago harbor ought to have been used as shields, that is, taken out ahead of the warships to draw the American fire. Guided by lights masked from the sea and marking the channel, the six big cruisers, totally darkened, would then have followed one another out in predetermined order and at top speed. Once at sea they would have steered different courses with orders not to fight unless compelled to do so. On the other hand, if Cervera was determined to make his try in the daytime, he ought to have gone all out, heading his ships straight at the enemy, using guns, torpedoes and finally rams in a bold, close-formation attack. A charge *à outrance* was the only chance in such a case of inflicting telling damage on superior forces.

To anyone accustomed to swapping pieces in a chess game in order to clear the board, either one of these might seem to be a more effective way of making a fight of it. A night sortie and torpedo attack in particular would certainly have damaged, perhaps sunk some of the American ships and would have made victory a lot more costly for Sampson. It's possible, too, that some of the Spaniards might have got away in the dark and confusion; night fighting in 1898—as it was to be for many years after—remained prehistoric at best. Perhaps Cervera's real belief, in spite of his pessimistic protestations to the contrary, was that the supposedly superior speed of his ships would tell if they weren't forced to remain together. Some might escape, even in daylight, and with less loss of life than an all-for-nothing night engagement would exact. To the old sailor "sons of Spain," not pawns, were still involved.

Had the American fleet not been so much more powerful altogether, through Admiral Sampson's concentration at Santiago of the entire battleship and cruiser strength of the U.S. Navy; had

Schley not had such an enormous tactical advantage due to the confinement of the narrow harbor channel which enabled him to concentrate on each Spanish ship in turn a collective and overwhelming fire; had American gunnery not been so much more effective on the ship-to-ship level, and the infliction of punishment so terribly one-sided; and finally had the U.S. forces, at sea as well as on land, not been motivated by such an aggressive spirit and by the policy of pursuing the offensive at every opportunity—things might have been different.

In a broad sense this underlying confidence had been a deciding factor and Commander Jacobsen sums it up rather well:

> According to the "Revista General de Marina," August, 1898, the Admiral [Cervera] was entirely convinced of the impossibility of defeating the enemy or of reaching another Cuban harbor, even if he should succeed in steaming straight through the hostile fleet. It is to this feeling of helplessness and impotence as against the American naval forces more than to anything else that I attribute the defeat . . . from the very moment that this feeling . . . took possession of the Spaniards . . . their fate, psychologically speaking, was sealed.[3]

✷✷✷

Psychologically speaking, too, the U.S. Navy was elated by the way the ships and men had come through the clutch, especially their "superb and deadly" gunnery, which the press was quick to join Sampson in attributing to incessant training and work at the tow targets. If the fleet had fired off more than 9,400 rounds to get its 123 hits, if only two of its 12-inch shells had struck home during the engagement, and *all* of the forty-seven 13-inch projectiles which it fired had missed, few seemed concerned about it in the warm glow of success.

There were some, however, who looked at that percentage with a critical eye, and the enlightenment of one far-seeing lieutenant, and his subsequent efforts to make others see things as he saw them did much to make a decisive swath through the self-congratulatory fog. William S. Sims's sensitivity to what foreign powers thought of the potential of big naval guns would finally convince America's own top brass what really efficient shooting could mean, though it would take some doing. Sims was no unknown; during the war he had set up an ingenious spy network in Europe while serving as naval attaché in Paris, and his rank (he was forty-three years of age) was a good example of how long merit had to wait for its reward back at the turn of the century. Now, in 1901, while assigned to the staff of the commander, Asiatic Fleet, he had learned that British ships on the China station were racking up phenomenal target scores due to the efforts of one of their own gunnery officers—Commander Percy Scott. The Royal Navy was abandoning "spot aim" and was experimenting with "continuous" aim techniques, whereby the target was kept in the sights regardless of the pitch and roll of the firing ship. It all had to do with a device which was something like a penny-arcade, electric-eye shooting gallery and which enabled gun crews to aim and practice "dry" firing. The Englishman called it a dotter.

Why, Sims asked, could not some of these new innovations be adopted by us? They, or something like them, had better be, before we fought anyone else. He pointed out that at Santiago not one of the enemy cruisers had been damaged in a vital part of her hull or machinery, nor had the armor belts in any of them been pierced. They had been destroyed by fires caused by hits from our secondary weapons, but in the future we might be facing battleships, and it would be the big guns that would tell the tale. They had to be made more accurate.

Sims sent off reports to Washington which eventually totaled 11,000 pages, and which both exhausted and impressed Navy planners. The White House rewarded this single-minded persistence by making him inspector of target practice, the best thing that could have been done. In the months to follow, Sims, aided by his assistant, the brilliant Ridley McLean, modernized gunsights, developed and improved standard drill, and insisted on daily practice in the turrets. The almost instantaneous results showed how bad things had been in the first place. Before long the 13-inch rifles of the new battleship *Alabama* could be loaded and fired in thirty-eight seconds, an operation that had taken five minutes before the war. After three months the ships using Sims's system were achieving a creditable 40 percent hits. By 1907 this figure had been upped to 77.6 percent, and two years later the percentage of misses was down to what the percentage of hits had been in 1901.[4]

Sims wasn't entitled to all the credit; he had appeared at the right time to build on the groundwork laid by other officers, notably the imaginative Lieutenant Bradley Fiske, whose experimental innovations might have accomplished the same thing earlier had the Navy been ready for them. Fiske had envisioned director firing as far back as 1890, and the following year had designed a telescopic sight which was given a trial but which only drew the comment from Fighting Bob Evans that it would be "of no value aboard ship." In 1894 he developed a range finder which was brushed aside in the same offhanded way by superiors who simply were not interested in change. In every effort at technological reform Fiske was later proved right, and nearly every time he was thwarted by higher powers. After the war had opened a few eyes at the top levels, Fiske and another lonesome voice, Albert L. Key, came into their own and were to remain constructive and valued critics of the system from within, championing the role of the United States as a pace setter in ship construction, communication, fire control and over-all naval organization.

The American public was proud to bursting of the new Navy, and Washington was inspired, too; so much so that Congress now authorized enough big ships to build a whole new fleet. In prewar days an appropriation of three battleships and twenty-nine smaller vessels had been considered extravagant; now in March, 1899, three more battleships and three armored cruisers were voted with no difficulty at all, and the following congressional session provided for two more capital ships and three more of the cruisers. Facilities weren't neglected either; in the ten years after the war $110 million would be spent on East Coast shipyards alone.

When Theodore Roosevelt entered the White House in 1901, the U.S. Navy was ranked fifth in the world, and before he left it was number two. A general board of the Navy had been created to form and carry out policy, and to make plans for future cooperation with the Army, and Fiske's efforts had produced a permanent special board as well to keep abreast of technical advances. These began to accelerate at an arms-race quickstep, particularly after the revolutionary all-big-gun *Dreadnought* was introduced by the British in 1905. Ships took on more armor, grew bigger engines and boilers and added tonnage almost geometrically. Battleships designed in 1906 were double the displacement of those of 1890, and by 1909 they were 25 percent bigger still. By then all "dreadnoughts" were equipped with the new Marconi wireless and the first warships powered by oil were in operation. Already a tiny, 54-foot-long American craft powered by a primitive 45-horsepower engine had been nine years in commission. If ever anything suggested the epithet "pigboat," she was it, but as the first completely successful submarine, she would typify the era of multidimensional technology that heralded the great days of world naval power lying ahead.

✳✳✳

Mahan had been right, of course; the big Navy would be needed to expand and police new spheres of interest commensurate with the ambitions of a global power, and now that a taste of success had whetted even isolationist appetites, most would agree he was right about the colonies, too. Powerful jingo elements had never averted their eyes from what they considered the nation's primary duty of acquiring territory—challenging Spain was merely a means to an end—and machinery for the purpose was put into action from the time hostilities began. The last shots fired at the *Cristóbal Colón* ended the serious fighting between the Spaniards and ourselves, but two other campaigns, half a world apart from one another, were still to be won. They had little to do with subduing Spanish military power, which was subdued already, and much to do with gaining for the United States what were now felt to be the well-deserved spoils of war.

The foray into the Philippine Islands, though it was eventually to net us a rich and loyal possession, was from the beginning marked by confusion of motives, an embarrassing lack of communication, and what must surely be one of the weirdest relationships between enemies and allies in American history. The Teller amendment to the declaration of war, disclaiming any United

States intention to exercise control over Cuban affairs, was a squelch to imperialist designs on that island; however there was no such fly in the ointment of Spain's Pacific colonies. Here was balm aplenty to soothe the acquisitive itch. In fact even before confirmation of Dewey's victory at Manila Bay reached Washington, it was decided to send an army of occupation to the Philippines, and as in the case of Cuba, it was thought the task of vanquishing them would be made easier by the fact that an insurrection against Spanish rule was in ferment there also.

Contact was made through Far Eastern consular channels with Filipino leader General Emilio Aguinaldo, who was persuaded that his men and the American military might work in concert to expel the colonial power for the benefit of both. Dewey had eliminated the only Spanish naval threat in the Pacific, but he had no intention and no means either of annexing anything himself, or even of occupying Manila. The land fighting was to be left to the insurgents until an American expeditionary force could be mounted and sent out from home, and home was a long way off.

Its extreme remoteness and the fact that the Hong Kong cable had been cut kept that whole part of the world under a cloud of speculation, and it was with some surprise that Washington learned Dewey had not "captured" the Philippines, but instead was merely blockading and would need 5,000 well-equipped men to take and keep possession. Well enough, if it took a brigade or two to win us a Pacific empire, the hero of Manila Bay would have them. On May 25, 1898, a fleet of transports carrying the first Army expeditionary force to leave the Western Hemisphere sailed for Luzon, 7,000 miles away. Sheer distance made it anybody's guess what they might find there—taking control of a capital city or perhaps an attempt to occupy the whole of the archipelago might be in the offing—at this point it was best to play it by ear.

On June 18, while the ships were still two weeks out at sea, General Aguinaldo issued a declaration of independence for the islands, stressing the fact that his definition of "independence" meant the complete freedom of the Philippine peoples. Suspicious of the motives of Western powers, Aguinaldo was not altogether happy over the landing of American troops, whose first contingent came ashore on July 1, at the moment when Shafter and his men were prepared for their assault on San Juan Hill. The American General Anderson, however, did his best to keep relations with the insurgent chief on a cordial level, knowing that a second Army expedition was due soon, and with more force at his disposal he might not have to be so diplomatic.

Back home the imaginations of Washington and the public at large were already picturing a Far Eastern suzerainty upon which the sun would never set. Imperial enthusiasm was given further impetus when Dewey outbluffed the belligerent gamesmanship of a German naval squadron which had been skulking about, looking for a means to secure a cheap territorial prize in the confusion, and cartoons showing the Kaiser wading ashore to a palm-fringed island to be confronted by "No Trespassing" signs and a scowling Uncle Sam were applauded vigorously.

By the end of July nearly 11,000 men had been landed, and as the Spanish garrison seemed on the verge of surrender (for Spain herself was by now about to sue for peace), the invaders found themselves in the peculiar bind of having to deal with a very half-hearted enemy in the teeth of the growing hostility and distrust of Aguinaldo and his Filipinos. The Spaniards were willing to give up the capital, Manila, but neither they nor General Anderson wished delivery to be made into the hands of the insurgents. Consequently, a bizarre "mock battle" was arranged, whereby the Navy would make an ineffectual bombardment in the general direction of the city, and the Army would then pour in and quickly hoist the American flag. The little plan was enacted, with the now understanding and almost friendly Spaniards entering into the unofficial conspiracy to withhold the capital from the Filipino patriots—our allies—until U.S. forces could take charge. There was noisy firing from the insurgents, of course, and from others who had not got the word, but Manila turned out to be a very cheap prize. Five men were killed and thirty-five wounded, which brought the total cost of the campaign against Spain in the Philippines to all of eighteen dead and 108 wounded. The articles of surrender were drawn up and dated August 14, two days after the conflict with Spain itself had come to an official end.

No such complications were to mark the Army's conquest of Puerto Rico, which turned out to be the most bloodless venture of the war. Purely from the military standpoint, the island had occupied an important place in the minds of the strategic planners, at least as long as it was felt the port of San Juan might provide a refuge for Cervera's squadron. That threat over and done with, it then became the logical choice among the expansionists for an American colony in the Antilles, taking its place along with the Philippines as fair compensation for the extensive intervention in Cuba.

General Miles, for one, had never been able to get the attractive Puerto Rican prize out of his mind—the reader will remember his original recommendation that the main American Army be put ashore on the island, and the fact that the Santiago campaign had only been born out of his own suggestion to detour the force on its way there. Now, disgruntled over Shafter's appointment as commander in chief and what appeared to him as his own relative eclipse, he pressed for a follow-up landing in Puerto Rico by troops under his command. The island *was* attractive, the venture appealed to more than Miles, so it was duly authorized, and because it was believed the campaign would not be a very tough proposition, the best of the American volunteer regiments were to be allowed to show what they could do.

Their departure was delayed—it was thought better to wait and see how Shafter's attack on Santiago would turn out—but finally on July 18, the day after General Linares' surrender and the same day the Spanish government took the first step through its Paris ambassador to begin peace talks, Miles got permission to sail. Leaving Guantánamo with 3,000 volunteers, he landed at Guanica on July 25, virtually unopposed and to the enthusiastic *"vivas"* of the *puertorriqueños*. Local skirmishing—a few shots here and there —was all the trouble he had, and Miles struck out from his headquarters in Ponce, advancing in four columns over a modern macadam road which cut through the central mountains and led down the length of the island toward San Juan. It was not a battle against the Spaniards any longer—they were fleeing satisfactorily— but against time: to establish a *fait accompli* occupation of the island before an unfavorable turn in the peace negotiations now in progress could deprive Miles' armies of the territory they already controlled. On August 12 an armistice was signed, and word reached the American Army the next morning just in time to halt the artillery as it was about to open fire on the town of Coamo. Miles had won his own particular battle—Spain had accepted our terms, and the cession of Puerto Rico to the United States had been among them.

The imperialists had won theirs, too. A number of smaller Spanish islands in the West Indies were to pass into American hands, as well as the strategic outpost of Guam in the Pacific. It was almost wholly a real-estate transaction—under the terms of the peace treaty signed the following December, all claims for indemnity on either side, national or private, were formally relinquished—however some money did change hands. During the final weeks of the parleying Spanish delegates had fought against having to submit to American demands for the entire Philippine Island group, and in order that the commissioners might return to Madrid with some semblance of having driven a bargain, it was agreed to pay Spain $20 million in compensation. It salved Old World honor and American consciences to some extent; no one could now accuse the United States of having made a forcible annexation of the Philippines by conquest, and for this McKinley, at least, if not the expansionists, was thankful.

With a few scratches of the pen the latter had acquired a Pacific empire of sorts, or, looking at it more realistically, the right to fight for one. The ensuing struggle against the Philippine insurgents—a dirty, guerrilla-type conflict with which nations in our own time have become all too familiar—an operation which was to drag on for several years and which was to cost as much in life and effort as the whole of the campaign of 1898, was a sad sequel to this first venture into hemispheric colonialism.

It only continued to emphasize the fact that the Navy was the big winner in the Spanish war. With two astonishing victories to its credit, the fleet was able to keep the particulars of its short-comings in the family, so to speak; the public didn't really care. On the other hand, everyone had become used to jumping on the Army's neck, a situation which certain postwar disclosures did nothing to relieve. The sickness which decimated the troops in the final weeks before peace, the pitifully inadequate hospital facilities for the wounded outside Santiago, the supply fiasco, the black powder, the infamous "embalmed beef" all demanded some sort of explanation. It was obvious that the military had been guilty of serious logistical deficiencies, and the War Department and Secretary Alger in particular were taking the blame for them. McKinley at first tried to shield Alger as best he could, realizing that the attacks on his appointee implied criticism of his own direction of things, but when even deeper scandal and more def-amations were generated during the hearings of a commission which made an official investigation of the war, the President accepted the Secretary's resignation and replaced him with a vir-tual political unknown.

Elihu Root had enjoyed a long and distinguished law career, and his protestations when approached that his talents lay almost entirely in this field were met with the explanation that the main task of the War Department now lay in the administrative and legal problems of governing the new territories acquired from Spain. On this count he was persuaded to take the job, but his exposure to the Philippine business was like an immediate and sobering cold-water bath. With her most important "colony" al-ready in open rebellion, it was obvious that along with the law books the United States was going to need a fighting force, and if all he heard was true, it had better be a stronger one—in the field and organizationally—than had been put ashore in Cuba. Like the Navy, the U.S. Army was now going to have to reflect broadening American responsibilities in international politics in general.

Root believed that, unless the nation became embroiled in something foolishly, the regular Army of the United States might never have to fight a war without allies, and therefore he didn't see any reason to adopt the continental mass-conscript idea. What America needed was quality, not a "Russian steamroller." This, along with the capacity to expand quickly if and emergency made it necessary, and, above all, the ability to plan effectively. As things stood, there was no single body whose job it was to form policy and make decisions, and one of the first things needed was to provide an "upper story" to the headless *corpus* of the American military, which up till then had been submitting to the authority of the Secretary of War, the commanding general and all the chiefs of the various bureaus, with their insularity, their jealousies and their almost complete inability to agree on anything.

His concentration on these problems led Root to an intensive study of foreign military organization, particularly the experienced machines of the continent. Though he may have rejected the huge-standing-army principle, he realized the leading European powers had developed something necessary for the efficient making of war on either a large or small scale. That something was the concept of the general staff. America needed this kind of "brain"; any army did that expected to do something beside fight Moros in Luzon. As he envisioned it, such a body would be headed by a Chief of Staff and would completely take over the planning function, exploring all possible contingencies that might arise during present or future conflicts, and making certain that men and material would be available at the right time and place.

From the start he ran into such opposition from the old staff bureaus, who were jealous of their authority, and from those who accused him of trying to introduce European—particularly German —style militarism into the United States, that he was forced to content himself for the time being with the creation of a War College Board for the advancement of Army education and the study of military policy. In February, 1902, however, he was able to get a general-staff bill introduced, and though it was damned as perseveringly as ever by the bureaus, their very opposition only exposed the weakness of the existing organization. After a year of debate—in February, 1903—Congress voted to establish a general-staff corps the following August.

From then on the path was easier. The War College Board gave way to the Army War College, and before the year (1903) was over, Root also had been able to set up a Joint Army and Navy

Board to pursue formal cooperation and planning between the two services. It was a step forward that would, had it been made earlier, have done much to eliminate the self-defeating narrow-mindedness and animosities of the late war.

The Army reserve also came in for renovation. With the passing of the Dick Act in January, 1903, the militia could look forward to better training and being more closely allied with the regular Army. Henceforward the National Guard companies and regiments were to be known as Organized Militia, and as such would be issued arms and equipment without charge by the government. To maintain their status all units had to hold a prescribed number of drills and make one summer training encampment every year, where they would be put through their paces by regular Army officers. The new directive may have meant the end of the old Guard's tendencies toward segregation and social snobbery, but at the same time it would do much to eliminate the contempt in which the militiamen had once been held as soldiers. Now the President would be able to call up the Guard before asking for other volunteers, and when Congress specified that the units could be enrolled into federal service "either within or without the territory of the United States," the Organized Militia became a reserve for all wars—foreign and domestic.

Root's most successful program, and one that was not so well publicized outside the Army itself, introduced an improved military school system. Beginning in November, 1901, every Army post of any size was to provide facilities for officer instruction in a prescribed course that taught both theory and practical application. Men who showed special promise would be sent on to the advanced classes, which by 1910 had evolved into the Army School of the Line, the Signal School, the Field Engineer School and the Field Service and Correspondence School for medical officers— all at Fort Leavenworth; the Mounted School at Fort Riley, the Coast Artillery School at Fort Monroe, and the Engineer and Medical Schools, both in Washington. The Staff College at Leavenworth and the Army War College in the capital stood at the "graduate" level of the system.

Other postwar changes that reflected the new thinking were

the numerical expansion of the Army and the updating of its equipment, areas in which Root was a motive power, too. Colonial responsibilities, he was finally able to convince Capitol Hill, required not only new dreadnoughts but a permanent military beef up and improvement as well. Congress responded by increasing the authorized regular Army strength to 3,820 officers and 85,000 men. A serious weapons-development program was launched, producing a new 3-inch field gun, which used smokeless powder, fired high explosive and shrapnel and was equipped with optical sights and a recoilless carriage. Subsequent improvements were to put the gun virtually on a par with the famous French "75" of the First World War. Even more long lasting was the official adoption of the Model 1903 Springfield rifle, a strong and accurate weapon which served as the standard shoulder arm for nearly forty years. The United States was starting to think like a winner. Without really knowing it she had turned down the path that would lead sooner than most would have dreamed to the arena of continental and global war, to the time when she would send a well-led and superbly equipped mass land force to support the greatest navy ever assembled against an Axis of the most determined, and skilled of Old World foes.

As for now she had only offered a mercy death to poor senile Spain, and though the world took due note of it, some time would pass before the realization would dawn elsewhere that the doing had been such a watershed in American affairs. This is understandable, for in a strict military sense the campaign in the Caribbean and the war itself was not in any way decisive, aside from being the deciding influence on which way the United States would move in the ensuing years.

In our own country its effects were much more immediate. It seemed beyond doubting now that the prewar "spread-eaglist" voices had been right—America had earned a place on the world stage. She had been tested in her ability to carry off the role and the nation had been astonished at how cheap the audition had been. From the time a state of war had existed till the last shot was fired 2,926 men had died—most of those from sickness—and 1,645 had been wounded.[5] Even the more economy-minded were willing to concede that the dollar cost—$321,833,000 [6]—was a buyer's market when one was dealing in empires. Rockefeller or Morgan could have footed the bill with no more inconvenience than a bookkeeping notation. It wasn't so much the new square miles of territory—compared to the vast African dominions of the European powers, they made no great splash on the map—but the prizes were nevertheless rich and colorful and the subject peoples exotic enough to satisfy the most romantic of the imperialists.

What meant a good deal more was that the country had gained bases that would guard the hemisphere and protect the Isthmian canal about to be dug, and on the other side of the world, won long-strided steppingstones which spanned the earth's greatest body of water, of paramount importance to the naval power America had every intention of becoming. In the Caribbean there would be a station at San Juan, and the Navy base at Guantánamo Bay, which would be leased in perpetuity from Cuba in 1903, would become the strongest outpost in the West Indies. The Stars and Stripes now flew over three of the best harbors in the Pacific— Pearl, in the recently annexed Hawaiian Islands, a vital mid-ocean bastion soon to become the heaquarters of the Pacific fleet; Guam, further west, with its fine, protected Apra harbor anchorage; and finally, Manila Bay, which included the facilities at Cavite and the forts at Corregidor, a stronghold destined to command the north-south shipping lanes from Japan to the East Indies.

The fact that there was a rival on the scene did not take Europe completely by surprise, and understandably, since most of the world's promising territory had been spoken for, it was another late-comer to the imperial concept who felt the threat most keenly. For some years afterward it was believed in this country that Kaiser Wilhelm's Germany had sought a European concert against the United States during the Spanish war. The German press had been openly critical, and then there was that squadron at Manila that had harassed Admiral Dewey. It was true the Kaiser had worried lest a Spanish defeat jeopardize the monarchical system on the continent and that an American victory would interfere with Germany's own plans in the Pacific. He had in fact sounded out the chancelleries of Europe on the question of intervention, and the pope as well, but he didn't care to have Germany take the first step, and when nobody else seemed willing to either, the idea was dropped.

Great Britain on the other hand was conspicuous by her friendly attitude toward American ambitions, and thus the scale was balanced. The Venezuelan troubles of 1895 had apparently been forgotten, and Whitehall was so cool to the Kaiser's intervention feelers that the Foreign Office was never officially approached. Colonial Secretary Joseph Chamberlain had gone so far as to suggest an Anglo-American alliance in May, 1898, and the Salisbury government was congenial on the whole, deciding that support of the American Philippine acquisition was a good way to see Wilhelm's imperial plans frustrated.

Considering her newly recognized potential, the vocal urgings of her fire-eaters and the disinclination of the rest of the world to place any real obstacles in her way, the United States showed a good deal of restraint in subsequent years in the matter of exercising the prerogatives of an expansionist power. One could hardly accuse her of being colonial-minded at all. We must remember that the belligerent "big-stickishness" of the Lodges, the Hearsts and the Roosevelts, which seemed so prevalent and which was to carry Teddy straight to the White House, was vociferous but not universal. If they had been unsuccessful in preventing it, the war in turn had done little to change the attitudes of the anti-imperialist factions, which remained active and which boasted some very celebrated and influential names. Ex-Presidents Benjamin Harrison and Grover Cleveland, presidential-aspirant William Jennings Bryan, educators Charles W. Eliot and William James, Carl Schurz, Charles Francis Adams, Smauel Gompers, Andrew Carnegie, Mark Twain and many more were all strongly against what they considered the demeaning of the American heritage through a slavering land-grabbing policy, and though they could hardly hope to turn back the clock, they were enough to give the more boisterous imperialists pause.

America in effect was to remain more of a "power in being" for some years, split by a half-isolationist, half world-view dichotomy: one side doctrinaire and intransigent about traditional warnings on foreign entanglements; another, self-styled as more aggressive and prideful, equally determined that nothing important should pass in world affairs without United States say-so. The pride, the growing awareness of power, the stimulus toward exercising her strength in the way that was best for America and what she felt were civilized ideals would be a slow-growing process, but it had been awakened by the sound of the guns of Manila Bay and Santiago, and purified, it was felt, by the blood of her youth before San Juan Hill.

Once stirred, these emotions never slept again, and the world took note of this, too. An equal seat at the Hague peace conference, where Captain Mahan had a prestigious voice he never would have enjoyed two years before, the revised Clayton-Bulwer treaty, guaranteeing an exclusive right to regulate and manage the new Isthmian canal, and through it the east-west commerce of this hemisphere, the first concerted overseas military venture, when the nation joined the great powers in sending a force to help quell the Boxer rebellion, and finally the reluctant but seemingly inevitable entry into two world-wide conflicts was merely a culmination of all that had taken place up to and during the "splendid little war" of 1898. Americans had marched to it with light hearts, with Old Glory high in the breeze and the band playing "The Girl I Left Behind Me." How many back then felt the winds of change that rippled the flag, or realized it was the old life they had left behind them and that things would never really be the same again?

✱✱✱

The Fleets at Santiago

Ship	Commanding Officer	Displacement (tons)	Speed (knots)	Armament

AMERICAN

Battleships (First Class)

Ship	Commanding Officer	Displacement (tons)	Speed (knots)	Armament
Iowa	Capt. Robley D. Evans	11,340	16.5	Four 12-inch, eight 8-inch, six 4-inch r.f., twenty 6-pdr. r.f., six 1-pdr. r.f., four Gatlings.
Indiana	Capt. Henry C. Taylor	10,288	15.5	Four 13-inch, eight 8-inch, four 6-inch, twenty 6-pdr. r.f., six 1-pdr. r.f., four Gatlings.
Massachusetts	Capt. F. J. Higginson	10,288	15.5	Four 13-inch, eight 8-inch, four 6-inch, twenty 6-pdr. r.f., six 1-pdr. r.f., four Gatlings.
Oregon	Capt. Charles F. Clark	10,288	15.5	Four 13-inch, eight 8-inch, four 6-inch, twenty 6-pdr. r.f., six 1-pdr. r.f., four Gatlings.

Battleships (Second Class)

Ship	Commanding Officer	Displacement (tons)	Speed (knots)	Armament
Texas	Capt. John W. Philip	6,315	17	Two 12-inch, six 6-inch, 12 6-pdr. r.f., four 1-pdr. revolving cannon, two Gatlings.

Armored Cruisers

Brooklyn	Capt. Francis A. Cook	9,200	21	Eight 8-inch, twelve 5-inch r.f., twelve 6-pdr. r.f., four 1-pdr. r.f., four Gatlings.
New York	Capt. French E. Chadwick	8,200	21	Six 8-inch, twelve 4-inch r.f., eight 6-pdr. r.f., four 1-pdr. r.f., four Gatlings.

Armed Yachts

Glou-cester	Lcdr. Richard Wain-wright	786	17	Four 6-pdr. r.f., four 3-pdr. r.f., two Colt machine guns.
Vixen	Lt. A. Sharp, Jr.	800	16	Four 6-pdr. r.f., four 1-pdr. r.f.

SPANISH

Armored Cruisers

*Infanta María Teresa**	Capt. Victor Concas y Palau	7,000	20.2	Two 11-inch, ten 5.5-inch, eight 2.2-inch r.f., eight 1.4-inch r.f., two machine guns.
*Almirante Oquen-do**	Capt. Juan Lazaga	7,000	20	Two 11-inch, ten 5.5-inch, two 2.7-inch r.f., eight 2.2-inch r.f., eight 1.4-inch r.f., two machine guns
*Viscaya**	Capt. Juan Antonio Eulate	7,000	20	Two 11-inch, ten 5.5-inch, two 2.7-inch, eight 2.2-inch r.f., eight 1.4-inch r.f., two machine guns.
*Cristóbal Colón**	Capt. Emiliano Díaz y Moreu	6,840	20	Two 10-inch,† ten 6-inch, six 4.7-inch r.f., ten 2.2-inch r.f., ten 1.4-inch r.f., two machine guns.

Torpedo Boat Destroyers

Plutón	Cdr. Pedro Vasquez	400	30	Two 14-pdr., two 6-pdr. r.f., two 1-pdr. r.f., two 14-inch torpedo tubes.
*Furor**	Cdr. Diego Carlier	370	28	Two 14-pdr., two 6-pdr. r.f., two 1-pdr. r.f., two 14-inch torpedo tubes.

* Sunk or beached.
† Guns not mounted.

****

Steaming Distances

From	To	Statute Miles
Cape Verde	Martinique	2,400
Martinique	Curaçao	576
Curaçao	Santiago	723
Curaçao	San Juan	555
Curaçao	Cienfuegos	1,036
Havana	Cienfuegos	570
Havana	Cienfuegos	560
Havana (by Windward Passage)	Santiago	736
Havana	San Juan	1,133
Key West	Cienfuegos	570
Tampa	Daiquirí	950
Santiago	Guantánamo	43
San Francisco	Manila	6,900

APPENDIX C

✸✸✸✸✸✸✸✸

V Army Corps

Major General W. R. Shafter, Commanding

1ST DIVISION—*Brigadier General J. F. Kent*
    1st Brigade—*Brigadier General H. S. Hawkins*
        Sixth U.S. Infantry
        Sixteenth U.S. Infantry
        Seventy-first New York Volunteer Infantry
    2nd Brigade—*Brigadier General E. P. Pearson*
        Second U.S. Infantry
        Tenth U.S. Infantry
        Twenty-first U.S. Infantry
    3rd Brigade—*Colonel C. A. Wikoff*
        Ninth U.S. Infantry
        Thirteenth U.S. Infantry
        Twenty-fourth U.S. Infantry

2ND DIVISION—*Brigadier General H. W. Lawton*
    1st Brigade— *Brigadier General A. R. Chaffee*
        Seventh U.S. Infantry
        Twelfth U.S. Infantry
        Seventeenth U.S. Infantry
    2nd Brigade—*Brigadier General William Ludlow*
        Eighth U.S. Infantry
        Twenty-second U.S. Infantry
        Second Massachusetts Volunteer Infantry
    3rd Brigade—*Colonel Evan Miles*
        First U.S. Infantry
        Fourth U.S. Infantry
        Twenty-fifth U.S. Infantry

INDEPENDENT BRIGADE—*Brigadier General J. C. Bates*
> Third U.S. Infantry
> Twentieth U.S. Infantry

CAVALRY DIVISION—*Major General Joseph P. Wheeler*
> 1st Brigade—*Brigadier General S. S. Sumner*
>> Third U.S. Cavalry
>> Sixth U.S. Cavalry
>> Ninth U.S. Cavalry
> 2nd Brigade—*Brigadier General S. B. M. Young; Colonel Leonard Wood*
>> First U.S. Cavalry
>> Tenth U.S. Cavalry
>> First U.S. Volunteer Cavalry

ARTILLERY CORPS—*Major J. W. Dillenback*
> First U.S. Artillery
> Second U.S. Artillery

ENGINEER CORPS—*Lieutenant Colonel G. M. Derby*

SIGNAL CORPS DETACHMENT—*Lieutenant Colonel Frank Greene*

APPENDIX D

****

The *Maine* Inquiries

It would be wrong to assume that the inflammatory state of public and press opinion at the time was prejudicial to the fairness with which the American *Maine* inquiry was carried out. Because of the mystery surrounding the destruction of the battleship and the disfavor into which the Spanish-American War fell in more recent years, later generations somehow inferred that facts were hidden, distorted, or ignored in the desire to convert what was actually a tragic accident into an excuse for a fight with Spain. This is untrue. It was no kangaroo court and Sampson no hanging judge; on the contrary the board seemed to bend over backward to be thorough and satisfy itself fully on each point of the examination, and the questions which remain unanswered deal not with a lack of evidence of foul play, but rather the lack of motive for its being instigated by the Spanish government.

The court was most intent on proving or disproving that the catastrophe was due to internal causes, and until divers could be sent down to the wreck and their findings analyzed, Sampson and his colleagues confined themselves to examining evidence which might establish this point. The whole case, of course, rested upon it. Everyone agreed that there had been two separate explosions and some time was spent questioning the crew and various eyewitnesses on the nature of the first one. What did it sound like? Was it a "sharp report" as one of the witnesses had maintained, or was it a "muffled explosion, more felt than heard" as another had described it? Did it raise the ship out of the water at all and, if so, what part of the ship? These were important details, and as might be expected, testimony was conflicting. Everybody remembered the second or overwhelming blast; the first was less clear in their minds.

With no preponderance of evidence that a mine or torpedo had been involved, the court proceeded under the assumption that the first explosion was an internal one. A great deal of testimony, from Captain Sigsbee on down to the lowest fireman, was heard, and one by one the possible causes were disposed of. The bunkers adjacent to the magazines had all been inspected on the morning of the disaster, and Sigsbee had insisted that the heat-sensitive thermostats were in good working order. There were no high explosives in or near the magazines which had blown; torpedo warheads and all detonators and primers were stored aft; the powder in the magazines had been the relatively stable brown prismatic type. There were no steam pipes in the *Maine*'s forward magazine, lights were shielded in special boxes and no instances of exposed wiring had been noted. No men were working near the ammunition that night, nor was there any loose powder lying about, and soft shoes, which would not strike sparks on the deck, were always worn. The only boilers in use at the time were the after pair, far from the blast. They were in good condition and operating at low pressure. All naphtha, alcohol, whiskies and inflammable surgeon's stores were stowed aft, beneath the wardroom deck, and oily cotton waste, which was sometimes known to ignite if left to itself, was kept in metal cans and was not allowed to accumulate. The supposition that a criminal lunatic among the crew had engineered the whole thing was highly improbable; the normal cheek-to-jowl atmosphere of a warship would make it virtually impossible to hide a mental quirk of this kind. Spanish claims that American discipline was lax and American sailors psychologically irresponsible weren't taken seriously by anybody.

The reports of the divers—that some powerful force had driven the ship's keel up from below and punched in her armor and plating as well on the port side—pointed to a very different cause. They also found, as everyone expected they would, the vessel's starboard plates blown outward. and since it had been established that there were two separate explosions—the first one to port—this seemed to indicate the initial shock was an external one and the second was her exploding magazines. A crater of the sort that might be caused by a mine was found in the harbor bed, too (the bottom was soft mud and it was hard to be certain), and though it was not at the point where the keel plates were thrust upward this wasn't considered important; if the blast had caused the *Maine* to shift at her mooring, as was certainly the case, the hole wouldn't line up anyway.

Commander George A. Converse, a torpedo and mine expert called upon for his professional opinion, claimed that an internal magazine explosion would not have lifted the ship out of the water in the way some witnesses described, nor would it have produced the inverted-V distortion of her keel; a big charge, placed near the ship's bottom, would have done both. This settled things for the court. In their final decision Sampson and the other members ruled that such a mine, exploding the *Maine*'s magazines, had caused the ship's destruction (private opinions were that it was an electrical device set off from the shore) but beyond that the court would not attempt to fix the blame. The verdict was reached, as it had to be, by a process of elimination confirmed by certain indications in the wreck and certain probabilities. It was unfortunate that no summing up of the evidence was published, and that the four-man body felt it unnecessary or unwise to list the reasons for its decision; it would have been better were the latter clearly stated.

The Spanish court of inquiry met simultaneously, and a spirited legal, or at least verbal, confrontation might have been expected had it been allowed to send down its own divers to look the wreck over. As it was the Spaniards were forced to base their case almost wholly on the lack of observed phenomena which might be expected in the case of an underwater explosion. The absence of a visible geyser, of any shock transmitted beneath the surface to other nearby ships, of any bodies of dead fish, were all held up as evidence that there was no mine, no torpedo, nothing but an accident or carelessness on the part of the American crew. The findings were recorded as follows:

(1) On the night of Feb. 15 last an explosion occurred in the forward magazines of the *Maine,* causing the destruction of that portion of the vessel and resulting in her sinking at her anchorage.

(2) It is known by the ship's plans that these magaiznes contained other explosives than powder and shells of various kinds.

(3) The same plans show that the said magazines were surrounded on the starboard side by bunkers containing coal, and those who witnessed the explosion are agreed in saying that it was due to a purely accidental cause.

The absence of all circumstances which necessarily acompany the explosion of a torpedo [mine] having been proved by witnesses and experts, it can only be honestly asserted that the catastrophe was due to internal causes.

The U.S. Navy's case was far from airtight, but it is hard to work up much sympathy for the Spanish arguments, and no suspicion that the Sampson court was guilty of a great injustice is roused by these perfunctory and somewhat arrogantly stated points. They contradict the American evidence in one area—the ship's plans—that would be relatively easy to clear up, and the unanimity of the witnesses regarding the "purely accidental" cause seems a little silly in its suggestion that those questioned were in a position to say one way or another.

Nevertheless, responsible Americans still made every attempt to be fair. A Senate Foreign Relations Committee hearing held some time later recorded testimony by Admiral Irwin that a mine set at a depth of fifteen feet or more might hardly cause a bubble on the surface, much less a geyser, that a British bark berthed nearby *had* felt a shock, serious enough to make her skipper think he'd been rammed, and finally that the admiral himself had once participated in a four-week exercise on Mobile Bay involving mines and torpedoes and had not seen one dead fish!

Even that didn't end the controversy, which continued to simmer in the atmosphere of other unsavory revelations about the war. When the wreck was raised and exposed to view in November, 1911, a second court of inquiry under Rear Admiral Charles E. Vreeland met to reinvestigate what happened on that February night. Any passions that might have influenced the judgments of 1898 had long since cooled; Spain was our friend and there was every desire to set the record straight if it needed setting. Yet no new evidence was uncovered; the court ruled once again that the first blast had been outside the ship's hull, but decided that it had taken place further aft than had been thought. "The board finds that the injuries to the bottom of the *Maine* . . . were caused by the explosion of a low form of explosive exterior to the ship. . . ."

And there the matter stands, though expecting it to rest may still be asking too much.

***

APPENDIX E

****

Guantánamo Bay—
Then and Now

After the war the principles of Mahan, and among them the concept of a series of steppingstone stations scattered about the globe to provide means for refueling and maintenance of naval vessels, became one of the foundations for American policy. When a postwar treaty was signed with the new Republic of Cuba, it was therefore decided to negotiate for one or more potential base sites on the island in order to support America's new role as a major Caribbean power. Two locations were settled upon, the most important being Guantánamo Bay, which had seen the first landing on Cuban soil by United States Marines; and on December 10, 1903, the terms of a lease signed between President Theodore Roosevelt and President Estrada Palma of Cuba gave the United States control of 19,621 acres of land and the right to the surrounding water areas to be used as a "coaling and naval station" in return for the annual payment of $2,000 in gold.

Though it possessed great potential, with one of the largest and finest harbors in the western hemisphere, it was not until the First World War that much effort was made to expand the station; then its importance grew steadily. Fuel-oil facilities to replace the old coal piles, water-storage tanks, quarters for personnel and other buildings were constructed, and during the 1920's and 1930's the base could easily accommodate and service the ships that were then being sent to the area for winter training.

With the outbreak of World War II and the subsequent massing of enemy U-boats in the Caribbean, the strategic importance of Guantánamo Bay was fully recognized. Gitmo, as it came to be called, served not only as an important antisubmarine-warfare center and convoy-assembly point, but as the principal training base for the U.S. Atlantic Fleet, a distinction which it maintained during the postwar years. Present facilities are valued at between $80 and $90 million, and the more than 1,400 buildings include large and modern housing units for personnel and dependents, machine shops, a supply depot, fuel and ammunition storage, two airfields—one for jets and a smaller strip for propeller planes—and an extensive recreational complex for visiting ships' crews and the 3,000 officers and enlisted men who now man the base.

Guantánamo Bay began to make the headlines with the rise to power of Fidel Castro, who chafed at this "imperialist" bastion on the island and who saw it as a means whereby he might pose threats to the American military and gather support from his own countrymen against the *yanqui* presence. The base was and is too strong and can be too easily reinforced to succumb to any direct attack by Cuba; as a further safeguard many of the 3,600 Cubans employed there—workers who had been continually subject to propagandistic and other more direct pressures from their government, and who represented a possible sabotage threat—were replaced with Jamaicans and other Caribbean nationals.

Early in 1964 Premier Castro attempted to put the squeeze on Guantánamo in retaliation for the imprisonment by Florida authorities of thirty-six Cuban fishermen who were charged with violation of the Territorial Waters Act. On February 6 of that year its water supply, which was obtained from a pumping station four miles outside of the base limits, was cut off, and the U.S. Navy promptly moved in water tankers to help provide the 2.5 million gallons which are used daily. After our own retaliatory discharge of a number of the Cuban workers (whose wages funneled more than $7 million into the local economy), the crisis subsided and the water was again made available.

The Navy immediately took measures to correct what might have remained an embarrassing weakness, and the erection of a desalination plant, along with many more storage facilities, has now made the base independent of outside water supplies. By the terms of the original treaty and those of another which was signed in 1934, Cuba retains "ultimate sovereignty" over the territory, but American jurisdiction and control continues indefinitely unless we abandon the base or agree with the Cuban government to alter the treaty terms. The latter cannot be revised or abrogated by Cuba alone.

Guantánamo remains vital to United States hemispheric defense as a training center, a logistical base and staging point for aircraft en route to Central and South America, and, as guardian of an important door to the Caribbean, a key link in the Panama Canal defense chain. Perhaps its greatest importance today has to do with American prestige. Whatever happens at Guantánamo will have an effect on the touchy Canal Zone question, where U.S. rights are guaranteed by a similar treaty, and in fact on our entire position in Latin America. In a narrower but no less important sense it has the distinction of being a lone "voice of America" in a hostile climate; as things stand, it represents the only means by which the passage of information and ideas between the American and Cuban peoples can take place. For these reasons it is certain that any decision to pull out of Guantánamo will be the U.S. government's and nobody else's. Washington's firmness during the 1962 missile crisis demonstrated its intention not to tolerate any direct Cuban or indirect Soviet threat to the continental United States. Present policies dictate that any intimidation of the sixty-six-year-old Gitmo be met the same way.

✶✶✶

Notes
****

CHAPTER I   An Idea Whose Time Has Come

1. Julius W. Pratt, *Expansionists of 1898* (Baltimore: The Johns Hopkins Press, 1936), p. 9.
2. Walter Millis, *The Martial Spirit* (Cambridge: The Riverside Press, 1931), p. 33.
3. Henry Cabot Lodge, "Our Blundering Foreign Policy," *Forum* (March, 1895).
4. Millis, *op. cit.*, p. 29.
5. George Bronson Rea, *Facts and Fakes About Cuba* (New York: G. Munro's Sons, 1897), p. 236.
6. Spanish sources estimated the number of insurgents in Santiago province at 5,000 and in the whole of Cuba at 15,000. Spain's own troop and garrison strength in the island at this time was well over 100,000. In considering the appropriateness of a "search and destroy" policy we must of course remember that the disparity in mobility and firepower between a "regular" army of 1898 and a group of roving guerrilla bands was not nearly so marked as it is in our present day of ultra-sophisticated weaponry. Current American military involvements of course come to mind, but because of the fact that Cuba was and had been a Spanish colony, with her affairs at least indirectly administered from Madrid, her revolt can be more aptly compared to the Malayan insurrection against British rule in the 1950's than to the situation in Vietnam.
7. John Edward Weems, *The Fate of the "Maine"* (New York: Henry Holt and Company, 1958), p. 53.
8. *Ibid.*, p. 92.
9. *Ibid.*, p. 97.
10. Millis, *op. cit.*, p. 139.
11. *Ibid.*, p. 142.
12. *Ibid.*, p. 143.

CHAPTER II   The Game in Progress: The Queen's Knight Gambit Accepted

   1. Walter Millis, *The Martial Spirit*, p. 160.
   2. William Allen White, "When Johnny Went Marching Out," *McClure's Magazine* (June, 1898).
   3. The increasing size and power of ordnance had been a major characteristic of the gestatory period of post–Civil War naval progress, and as such became a telling influence on battleship construction. For some three hundred years—from the time warships had been seriously armed with cannon—down to the 1850's when steam came into common use, vessels had been rated according to the number of guns they carried. Capital ships had two or three gun decks extending almost from stem to stern, the cannon firing through ports pierced in the sides, with the size of weapons being virtually uniform.

   Great changes were just ahead, however. The development of rifling and the exploding shell—also products of the fifties—soon convinced defensive experts that it was not feasible to sheathe a vessel with armor along the whole of her length, since the weight created too much of a burden for the marine engines of the day. Protective plating, therefore, began to be concentrated where it would safeguard a ship's motive power and other vitals, and since the larger, more potent guns enabled a vessel to carry fewer of them, it was found they, too, could be grouped somewhere amidships where the men working them could be protected in an "armored citadel."

   The broadside system continued to prevail for a while, but having fewer guns demanded that they be employed more efficiently. This meant giving each a wider traverse of fire, and so newer ships placed their armament on the center line or at points on the beam. In the seventies and eighties the barbette system enjoyed great favor. It provided for the main batteries to be mounted on revolving platforms within heavy fixed cylinders of armor extending down within the ship to the lowest protective deck, with the guns designed to fire over the parapet of the cylinder. The major weakness of the barbette was the lack of protection on the top and to some extent on the sides, and it was only a question of time before the problem was solved by the hooded barbette or completely enclosed armored mounting. This was simply a reintroduction of the turret principle that had first been employed by the ironclad *Monitor* in her fight with the Confederate *Virginia* off Hampton Roads in 1862, and which had been used on and off in the interim, especially by smaller craft.

   By 1898 the completely armored, revolving gun housing was an established feature on all the most modern battleships, as designers experimented with different mountings and turret combinations—

placing them amidships, between the funnels, on the beam—in an attempt to gain the greatest scope and effectiveness of fire without interfering with the upper works topside or the propellant machinery below. Space was a major consideration, for as a ship's guns got bigger —12-inch, 13.5-inch, 14-, 15-, 16-, and finally, as in the case of Japan's World War II superdreadnoughts, 18-inch—the turret, and particularly the substructure which extended several decks down, grew correspondingly extensive, with its complex loading and handling machinery, magazines and personnel all needing room to operate. It was solved successfully, however, the builders always pursuing a "mobile fortress" concept, and by the first decade of the twentieth century the ship-of-the-line, whose elegant spread of canvas could once belie her deadly qualities, had become in all essential respects a thick shell of hardened steel wrapped round combinations of guns and boilers, the two pre-eminent factors in the search for ever-greater power and performance at sea.

4. At the gunnery practice of the German Navy efforts had been made to improve accuracy by a more modern method, that of firing salvos in an attempt to straddle the target—that is, allow for the fact that some shots would fall over, some short or wide, just so long as the target was somewhere in the center of the pattern. If an enemy ship could be so bracketed, it was assumed that a certain number of hits would be made. The experiment was ahead of its day, however, and was not as yet practical. Because of the limits of visual spotting, actions were expected to be fought within the ranges of a battleship's secondary guns, which would complicate things greatly, the spotter confusing the splashes of the larger and smaller guns.

5. This concept was soon to be as outdated as nearly everything else in the rapidly changing naval sphere. By the time of the battle of Jutland (1916) Admiral Beatty was to consider the ideal fighting range of the 12-inch gun then in use as 16,000 yards, and in 1941 the British battle cruiser *Hood* and the German battleship *Bismarck* opened fire at 25,000 yards—over twelve nautical miles.

6. George E. Graham, *Schley and Santiago* (Chicago: W. B. Conkey Company, 1902), pp. 62–63.

7. Rear Admiral F. E. Chadwick, *The Relations of the United States and Spain: The Spanish-American War*, Vol. I (New York: Charles Scribner's Sons, 1911), pp. 40–44.

8. Even these erred on the conservative side. After the war Spanish authorities informed historian Herbert H. Sargent that at the time there were 196,000 Spanish troops in Cuba—more than 130,000 regulars and 40,000 irregulars and volunteers—with an additional 9,000 in Puerto Rico.

9. Herbert H. Sargent, *The Campaign of Santiago de Cuba*, Vol. I (Chicago: A. C. McClurg and Company, 1907), p. 64.

10. Poultney Bigelow, *Harper's Weekly* (May 28, 1898).

11. Charles Belmont Davis, *Adventures and Letters of Richard Harding Davis* (New York: Charles Scribner's Sons, 1918), p. 244.

12. There is a general impression that Dewey and the Spaniards fought this action with big ships; however the protected cruiser was thought of as the "eye" of the fleet, not the fist, and was certainly never designed to operate in the line of battle. It was a relatively small class of vessel ranging up to 5,000 tons, armed with 6-inch guns and generally having an armored deck but no plating on the side. These ships did employ watertight compartmentation, though, had peripheral coal bunkers to absorb shell hits, and in some cases their hulls were packed with cocoa fiber or cornstalk pith which would swell and prevent the entrance of water (!). Not exactly what one would send out to a latter-day Trafalgar.

13. As a warship the monitor in general proved a headache in the open sea, an element for which it was totally unsuited. Patterned in effect after their Civil War namesakes, these vessels retained the "cheesebox on a raft" characteristics as long as they were employed, which in the case of the British Navy was up to the time of World War II. Mounting one or two castoff battleship guns on a light hull, they could prove valuable provided they were used in the purpose for which they were designed—harbor defense or as gun platforms for bombardment. They rolled terribly, their low freeboard keeping their decks under water in any seaway, and they had a reserve buoyancy of only 20 percent (making them liable to foundering if they took on as little as a fifth of their weight in water). For these reasons they were virtually useless in a fleet action.

14. Charles H. Brown, *The Correspondents' War* (New York: Charles Scribner's Sons, 1967), p. 255.

15. Millis, *op. cit.*, p. 231.

16. *Ibid.*, p. 234.

17. *Ibid.*, p. 234.

CHAPTER III   Courage and Confusion

1. Rear Admiral F. E. Chadwick, *Relations of the United States and Spain: The Spanish-American War*, Vol. II, pp. 12–13.

2. Walter Millis, *The Martial Spirit*, p. 246.

3. Frank Freidel, *The Splendid Little War* (Boston, Toronto: Little, Brown and Company, 1958), p. 66.

4. Chadwick, *op. cit.*, pp. 19–20.

5. Richard Harding Davis, *The Cuban and Porto Rican Campaigns* (New York: Charles Scribner's Sons, 1898), pp. 90–91.

6. Stephen Crane, "War Memories," *Wounds in the Rain* (London: Methuen and Company, 1900).

CHAPTER IV   The Battle That Fought Itself

1. Frank Freidel, *The Splendid Little War*, p. 113.

2. *Ibid.*, p. 143.

3. To these we must add General García's insurgents, even though their effectiveness seemed to be questionable. "About 1,500 Cubans . . . were posted on a hill above the village. Like Thessalian or Epirot peasants, they fired at long range against stone walls and entrenchments and did not advance. They reveled in the plentiful supply of ammunition and about the middle of the day they sent to General Chaffee for more. But General Chaffee was unsympathetic." (John Black Atkins, *The War in Cuba*, p. 114).

4. Herbert S. Stone and Company, *The Events of the War as Described by Eyewitnesses* (Chicago and New York: 1899), p. 122.

5. *Ibid.*, p. 123.

6. Richard Harding Davis, *The Cuban and Porto Rican Campaigns*, pp. 218–220.

7. Freidel, *op. cit.*, p. 143.

8. *Ibid.*, p. 139.

9. *Ibid.*, p. 140.

CHAPTER V   Signal "250"

1. The reader may wonder why the guns of the fleet could not be used against the city and its defenses. The centrally located cathedral of Santiago was 7,200 yards from the sea, and every part of the town itself was within range of the 13-, 12- and 8-inch naval guns offshore. Had Sampson been informed soon enough, they probably could have been used against San Juan Hill (four nautical miles away) as well, perhaps eliminating the necessity for an infantry attack at all. It indicated, as Rear Admiral Chadwick later wrote, a sad "want of correlation between the Army and Navy."

2. Herbert H. Sargent, *The Campaign of Santiago de Cuba*, Vol. II, pp. 194–195.

3. Frank Freidel, *The Splendid Little War*, p. 186.

4. Sargent, *op. cit.*, p. 208.

5. Colonel A. C. M. Azoy, *Signal 250!* (New York: David McKay Company, Inc., 1964), p. 151.

6. Freidel, *op. cit.*, p. 194.

7. George Graham, *Schley and Santiago*, p. 290.

8. Captain John W. Philip, "The Story of the Captains," *The Century Magazine* (May, 1899), pp. 90–91.

9. In a communication to the Naval Committee of the United States on February 18, 1899, Schley said that he turned the *Brooklyn* away because he didn't want to blanket the fire of the other vessels in the fleet. This is in contrast to the statement he made just after the battle, which indicated that he made the maneuver to avoid being rammed. The point was explored at some length during the postwar court of inquiry, and unfortunately for Schley, neither of his explanations seemed to stand up too well in the cold light of analysis.

10. Captain Robley D. Evans, "The Story of the Captains," *The Century Magazine* (May, 1899).

11. Captain Henry C. Taylor, "The Story of the Captains," *The Century Magazine* (May, 1899).

12. Philip, *op. cit.*, pp. 90–91.

CHAPTER VI   "Tell Your Bullies They're Doing Great Work!"

1. Lieutenant Commander Richard Wainwright, "The Story of the Captains," *The Century Magazine* (May, 1899).

2. Lieutenant José Müller y Tejeiro, *The Battles and Capitulation of Santiago de Cuba* (Washington: U.S. Government Printing Office, 1899), p. 106.

3. *Ibid.*, p. 107.

4. Rear Admiral Pascual Cervera y Topete, *The Spanish-American War* (Washington: U.S. Government Printing Office, 1899), p. 123.

5. *Ibid.*, p. 124.

6. Murat Halstead, *Official History of the War with Spain* (New Haven: Butler and Alger, 1899), p. 514.

7. George Graham, *Schley and Santiago*, p. 426.

8. Lieutenant Edward W. Eberle, "The Story of the Captains," *The Century Magazine* (May, 1899).

9. W. A. Goode, *With Sampson Through the War* (New York: Doubleday and McClure Co., 1898), p. 202.

10. Graham, *op. cit.*, pp. 313–314.

11. The account is interesting from the *Oregon's* point of view; however, the lieutenant's claim as to the "awful effect" of the battleship's big guns has to be attributed to overenthusiasm. The official report of the board of survey sent by Sampson to examine the wrecked enemy cruisers indicated no shells of a larger caliber than 8-inch struck the *Viscaya* at all. She was horribly cut up by the *Oregon's* secondary batteries, however, and had taken in so much water from the explosion in her bow that Captain Eulate was forced to abandon all ideas of ramming Schley and remove his ship from the fight.

12. Cervera y Topete, *op. cit.*, p. 130.
13. Frank Freidel, *The Splendid Little War*, p. 24.
14. *Ibid.*, p. 220.
15. Goode, *op. cit.*, p. 204.
16. Graham, *op. cit.*, p. 368.
17. According to Goode, who was with Sampson at the time, the hail was reported to the commander in chief as "Commodore Schley claims the honor of the capture of the *Cristóbal Colón*," and Sampson, who at that moment had "no thought of division of spoils and honors," merely went ahead soliciting casualty figures from the other ships. If it was not a deliberate attempt to humiliate Schley, at least that was the effect it had.
18. Colonel A. C. M. Azoy, *Signal 250!*, p. 192.
19. *Ibid.*, p. 193.
20. "If possible you will run your ship aground on own or hostile coast rather than surrender, if there is no immediate risk of the crew perishing in the shipwreck; and even after running aground it will be your duty to defend the ship and finally burn it, if there is no other way of preventing the enemy from taking possession of it." (*General Ordinances of the Spanish Navy*, Part 3, Chap. I, Article 153.)
21. Spanish casualties in the engagement were 323 killed, 151 wounded and 1,813 made prisoner.
22. Graham, *op. cit.*, p. 440.

CHAPTER VII   Fallen Idols Leave Clear Horizons

1. Walter Millis, *The Martial Spirit*, p. 322.
2. The topping on the whole incident was the reaction of the other correspondents present. Through some rare insight into the gravity of the occasion, all voluntarily avoided any mention of the fracas in their news stories, a collective act which must surely be the most striking example of self-denial in the experience of turn-of-the-century journalism!
3. He was unable to do the same with the cruiser *Reina Mercedes*, for she was in no position just then to be taken anywhere, though the *Reina* was eventually to become one of the United States' most notable and long-cherished prizes of war. The day after Cervera's defeat the Spaniards attempted to sink her as a blockship in Santiago harbor, but she came under the fire of the American fleet and went down instead outside of the channel mouth. She was raised by the U.S. Navy in March of 1899, towed to Norfolk, Virginia, for repairs and, when seaworthy once more, was taken to Newport, Rhode Island, as a station ship and later, in 1912, to the U.S. Naval Academy at Annapolis to serve in the same capacity.

During the next twenty-eight years she was used as a signal and harbor-control station, as a brig for erring midshipman who were sent to her for confinement to quarters, and as a barracks ship for the stewards who manned the mess hall at the academy. After 1940 she was refurbished to provide accommodations for the naval-station commander and his family (the only ship in the U.S. Navy with such facilities for dependents) as well as a certain number of bachelor officers and chief petty officers.

In 1957 the Spanish ambassador to the United States, Conde de Areilza, made an informal request for the return of the *Reina* to Spain, or at least for removal from her mooring in the Severn, where her presence was a continual reminder to successive generations of American midshipmen of Spain's defeat and humiliation years before. When it was decided to act on the matter, it was found that the years had not been kind to the old cruiser's hull, and the Navy felt she would never make it—even being towed—across the Atlantic. She was decommissioned in November, 1957, and subsequently sunk at sea instead, a solution that seemed to satisfy all parties.

4. Millis, *op. cit.*, p. 362.
5. W. A. Goode, *With Sampson Through the War*, p. 228.
6. Colonel A. C. M. Azoy, *Signal 250!*, p. 197.
7. *Ibid.*, pp. 197–198.

AFTERMATH

1. In justice to Shafter it must be said that it was originally Lawton's idea to attack El Caney. "I caused it to be carefully reconnoitered ...and determined it was an important position which was necessary to be occupied." (Lawton, *Investigation of the Conduct of the War with Spain*, Vol. IV, p. 901.)
2. Herbert H. Sargent, *The Campaign of Santiago de Cuba*, Vol. II, pp. 222–223.
3. *Ibid.*, p. 229.
4. Lieutenant Commander Brayton Harris, *The Age of the Battleship: 1890–1922* (New York: Franklin Watts, Inc., 1965), pp. 124–125.
5. Rear Admiral F. E. Chadwick, *Relations of the United States and Spain: The Spanish-American War*, Appendix D, pp. 482–485.
6. Sargent, *op. cit.*, Appendix X, p. 229.

Selected Bibliography
****

Books

ALGER, RUSSELL A., *The Spanish-American War*. New York and London: Harper and Bros., 1911.

ATKINS, JOHN B., *The War in Cuba*. London: Smith, Eller and Co., 1899.

AZOY, COLONEL A. C. M., *Charge!* New York: David McKay Co., 1960.

———— *Signal 250! The Sea Fight Off Santiago*. New York: David McKay Co., 1964.

BROWN, CHARLES H., *The Correspondents' War*. New York: Charles Scribner's Sons, 1967.

CERVERA Y TOPETE, REAR ADMIRAL PASCUAL, *The Spanish-American War*. Washington: U.S. Government Printing Office, 1899.

CHADWICK, REAR ADMIRAL FRENCH E., *Relations of the United States and Spain: The Spanish-American War*. New York: Charles Scribner's Sons, 1911.

CONCAS Y PALAU, CAPTAIN VICTOR, *The Squadron of Admiral Cervera*. Washington: U.S. Government Printing Office, 1899.

DAVIS, RICHARD HARDING, *The Cuban and Porto Rican Campaigns*. New York: Charles Scribner's Sons, 1898.

The Events of the War as Described by Eyewitnesses. Chicago and New York: Herbert S. Stone and Co., 1899.

FREIDEL, FRANK, *The Splendid Little War*. Boston, Toronto: Little, Brown and Co., 1958.

GOODE, W. A., *With Sampson Through the War*. New York: Doubleday and McClure Co., 1899.

GRAHAM, GEORGE E., *Schley and Santiago*. Chicago: W. B. Conkey Co., 1902.

HALSTEAD, MURAT, *Official History of the War with Spain*. New Haven: Butler and Alger, 1899.

HARRIS, LIEUTENANT COLONEL BRAYTON, *The Age of the Battleship: 1890–1922*. New York: Franklin Watts, Inc., 1965.

JACOBSEN, COMMANDER HERMANN, *Sketches from the Spanish-*

American War. Washington: U.S. Government Printing Office, 1899.

KENNAN, GEORGE, *Campaigning in Cuba.* New York: The Century Co., 1899.

MAHAN, CAPTAIN ALFRED THAYER, *The Influence of Seapower upon History.* Boston: Little, Brown and Co., 1950.

MILEY, LIEUTENANT J. D., *In Cuba with Shafter.* New York: Charles Scribner's Sons, 1899.

MILLIS, WALTER, *The Martial Spirit.* Cambridge: The Riverside Press, 1931.

MITCHELL, DONALD W., *The History of the Modern American Navy.* New York: A. A. Knopf, 1946.

MORISON, ELTING E., *Admiral Sims and the Modern American Navy.* Cambridge: The Riverside Press, 1942.

MÚLLER Y TEJEIRO, LIEUTENANT JOSÉ, *Battles and Capitulation of Santiago de Cuba.* Washington: U.S. Government Printing Office, 1899.

O'GARA, GORDON C., *Theodore Roosevelt and the Rise of the Modern Navy.* Princeton: Princeton University Press, 1943.

POST, CHARLES J., *The Little War of Private Post.* Boston: Little, Brown and Co., 1960.

ROOSEVELT, THEODORE, *The Rough Riders.* New York: Charles Scribner's Sons, 1924.

SARGENT, HERBERT H., *The Campaign of Santiago de Cuba.* Chicago: A. C. McClurg and Co., 1907.

SPEARS, JOHN R., *The History of the Navy from Its Origin to the Present Day.* New York: Charles Scribner's Sons, 1899.

WEEMS, JOHN EDWARD, *The Fate of the Maine.* New York: Henry Holt and Co., 1958.

WEIGLEY, RUSSELL, *The History of the U.S. Army.* New York: Macmillan and Co., 1967.

WILSON, HERBERT W., *The Downfall of Spain.* London: Low, Marston and Co., Ltd., 1900.

Periodicals

BALDWIN, HANSON W., "Guantanamo: Ours or Castro's?" *The Saturday Evening Post,* September 24, 1960.

BIGELOW, POULTNEY, *Harper's Weekly,* May 28, 1898.

CHRISTY, HOWARD CHANDLER, "An Artist at El Poso," *Scribner's Magazine,* September, 1898.

CLARK, CAPTAIN CHARLES E., "The Story of the Captains," *The Century Magazine,* May, 1899.

COOK, CAPTAIN FRANCIS A., "The Story of the Captains," *The Century Magazine,* May, 1899.

Davis, Richard Harding, "The Battle of San Juan," *Scribner's Magazine*, October, 1898.

Eberle, Lieutenant Edward W., "The Story of the Captains," *The Century Magazine*, May, 1899.

Henderson, W. J., "A Warship Community," *Scribner's Magazine*, September, 1898.

Hobson, Lieutenant Richmond P., "The Sinking of the Merrimac," *The Century Magazine*, December, 1898; January, February, 1899.

Lee, Captain Arthur H., "The Regulars at El Caney," *Scribner's Magazine*, October, 1898.

Lodge, Henry Cabot, "Our Blundering Foreign Policy," *Forum*, March, 1895.

Marshall, Edward, "A Wounded Correspondent's Recollections of Guásimas," *Scribner's Magazine*, September, 1898.

Philip, Captain J. W., "The Story of the Captains," *The Century Magazine*, May, 1899.

Sigsbee, Captain Charles D., "Personal Narrative of the *Maine*," *The Century Magazine*, November, December, 1898; January, 1899.

Wainwright, Lieutenant Commander Richard, "The Story of the Captains," *The Century Magazine*, May, 1899.

White, William Allen, "When Johnny Went Marching Out," *McClure's Magazine*, June, 1898.

✱✱✱

Index
*****

BATTLE OF SANTIA

0   1   2   3   4   5
NAUTICAL MILES

SIERRA

MAESTRA MOUNTAIN

Rincon de Sevilla

Acerraderos

VISCAYA

NEW YORK

IOWA

INDIANA

OQ

HARVAR

COLON

OREGON

TEXAS
VIXEN

BROOKLYN

N

19°50

76°10

C A R I B B E A N

76°10